Purchasing Fundamentals for Today's Buyer

Purchasing Fundamentals for Today's Buyer

HARRY HOUGH

PRENTICE HALL

Library of Congress Cataloging-in-Publication Data

Hough, Harry E.
    Purchasing fundamentals for today's buyer / Harry E. Hough.
        p.   cm.
    Includes index.
    ISBN 0-13-246356-3 (cloth)
    1. Industrial procurement.   I. Title.
    HD39.5.H684   1998
    658.7'2—dc21

                                                                98-47965
                                                                CIP

Acquisitions Editor: *Susan McDermott*
Production Editor: *Jacqueline Roulette*
Formatting/Interior Design: *Robyn Beckerman*

ISBN 0-13-246356-3

9 780132 463560

90000

Printed in the United States of America
    10 9 8 7 6 5 4 3 2 1

ATTENTION: CORPORATIONS AND SCHOOLS
Prentice Hall books are available at quantity discounts with bulk purchase for educational, business, or sales promotional use. For information, please write to: Prentice Hall Special Sales, 240 Frisch Court, Paramus, New Jersey 07652. Please supply: title of book, ISBN, quantity, how the book will be used, date needed.

PRENTICE HALL
Paramus, NJ 07652

On the World Wide Web at http://www.phdirect.com

Prentice Hall International (UK) Limited, *London*
Prentice Hall of Australia Pty. Limited, *Sydney*
Prentice Hall Canada, Inc., *Toronto*
Prentice Hall Hispanoamericana, S.A., *Mexico*
Prentice Hall of India Private Limited, *New Delhi*
Prentice Hall of Japan, Inc., *Tokyo*
Simon & Schuster Asia Pte., Ltd., *Singapore*
Editora Prentice Hall do Brasil, Ltda., *Rio de Janeiro*

Preface

Purpose and Scope

There are several ways people become buyers for business. They may start employment as clerks, expeditors, secretaries, or in various other positions unrelated to purchasing. Then they may be promoted to an assistant buyer's position, be given the title of Junior Buyer or even Buyer. Another way is to be hired directly from college into the purchasing function. In either case, rarely do the individuals so selected have any formal training in purchasing.

Many company managers who hire buying help have had little purchasing experience or, if they have been buying for their companies, learned the purchasing process on the job. They often don't know what knowledge is required to do a good purchasing job and how costly that lack of knowledge can be.

New purchasing employees seldom receive any formal instruction. New buyers learn by observation. They learn by watching how other buyers do the job or how salespeople react, or fail to react, to what they do. Obviously, this is a poor way to learn if the new employee copies less-than-satisfactory methods. And even when sales people may know better purchasing methods and could be helpful, it is not always in their interest to enlighten the new buyer.

v

When smart buyers and those who become purchasing managers realize that what they have observed or tried yields less-than-optimum results, they look for better ways to conduct business. Sometimes it takes years for them to find more successful methods. Meanwhile, thousands of dollars have been wasted. Seldom do they develop the most efficient and profitable ways to purchase. The purpose of this book is to provide a quick and easy way to learn well-recognized purchasing techniques that have proven successful for all types of businesses. While even the most seasoned purchasing professional may benefit from its contents, it is primarily aimed at the new and inexperienced buyer. As the title indicates, it is intended to offer the fundamentals of purchasing. However, some of the material provides insights into "state of the art" methods yet to be adopted by all major organizations.

This book will be particularly helpful to the small- and medium-sized companies that have not yet developed a modern purchasing function. It provides the essential information needed to upgrade purchasing operations. Likewise, entrepreneurs and new businesses will find information and techniques needed to establish a purchasing function that contributes to profits rather than eroding earnings and restricting the growth of the organization.

The information contained herein reflects what has been written elsewhere about purchasing and related topics. The information has been verified by thirty years of personal business experience as a buyer, purchasing executive, and consultant to both large and small companies. It has been broadened by discussions with hundreds of purchasing professionals attending seminars and formal college courses throughout the U.S.

Nevertheless, the reader should not assume that he or she knows everything that is necessary after completing this book. Some of what is included reflects the opinion of the writer. There are other viewpoints. Furthermore, new methods are always being tried. Some may prove better than what is considered the best today. One of the goals of purchasing is to help keep the organization profitable. To do so, purchasing professionals must stay informed about the latest developments in the field. It is a never-ending task. But before worrying about what is new, the buyer must learn what is today. This book's main purpose is to provide that information.

Acknowledgements

Writing a book in your spare time when you are under everyday pressure from normal business problems is often difficult. You try to produce a quality work on schedule but are constantly interrupted because of the need to handle the requirements of business, home, and family. Unless you have an unusual personality, you can become morose and irritable because you are not living up to the standards that you set for yourself. At least I became annoyed with myself for procrastinating or being diverted by other interests.

My wife, Lynne, and my daughter, Caroline Sieben, put up with my sullenness and did everything they could to encourage me to finish the work. They did this without harsh criticism for my tardiness. They supported my efforts by helping to edit the manuscript and by taking on other duties that I would have handled if I had not been occupied with writing. I thank them for their understanding and help.

Thanks also to the publisher, Prentice Hall, for giving me the opportunity to prepare this work, and particularly to Susan McDermott, my contact editor at PH. She has been patient and kind in her encouragement.

The information that is contained in the following chapters was obtained in part from thirty-four years of purchasing experience. I learned some of it by trial and error. Mistakes, some small and some not so small, taught lessons that I will never forget. I hope this book will help others to avoid the problems I had to overcome. Other information contained here was learned from various writers on law, negotiating techniques, and purchasing methods. I hope readers of this volume will expand their purchasing knowledge by reading some of these authors. A list of them is included in the bibliography.

Harry E. Hough
Aurora, Illinois

About the Author

Harry E. Hough studied mechanical engineering at Drexel University and holds a BA degree in Economics from the University of Pennsylvania. He received an MBA from the University of Chicago Executive Program. Early in his career, Hough became Senior Purchase Analyst at Ford Motor Company after being an industrial engineer in the Ford Division offices and previously holding various other positions at the plant level in that organization.

Later he was Director of Purchasing and Materials Management for the AIM Companies, Vice President of Purchasing for North American Car, and Director of Worldwide Purchasing for the Ekco Housewares Company. He has given seminars throughout the U.S. and has taught at several colleges in the Detroit and Chicago areas.

Dr. Hough is founder of the American Purchasing Society, the first organization to have a certification program for purchasing professionals. He is co-author of the *Handbook of Buying and Purchasing Management* and author of *Purchasing for Manufacturing*. He now spends his time writing for APS and consulting for members of the Society. He can be contacted by e-mail at **propurch@aol.com** or through the American Purchasing Society's web site at **www.american-purchasing.com**.

Contents

Chapter 3
Different Types of Organizations and Buying Systems   *31*

Chapter 4

Keeping Transactions Legal   *53*

Chapter 7

Using the Computer for Better Purchasing   *123*

Chapter 8

Purchasing Management Concerns   *141*

Buyer Specialization • Authorization for Purchases • Degree of
Automation • Easier Credit Approval • Amount of Purchase
Control • Control of Procurement Cards • Large Companies
Shop • More Thorough Analysis of Supplier Capabilities •
Increased Negotiations on a Regular Basis • Team Approaches •
Auditing Purchasing Activities • Value Analysis • Internal
Specialized Advice • Increased International Sourcing

Chapter 9

Buying the Quality Needed   *163*

Methods of Cost Minimization   *186*

Chapter 11

Business Functions Related to Buying   *203*

Bibliography   223

Appendices

Glossary   375

Index   395

Chapter 1

Introduction to Purchasing for Business

Salaries of Purchasing Occupations

Most successful business people agree that purchasing products and services at the right price is important for the success of a business. Experienced executives in large corporations, managers in medium-sized companies, and entrepreneurs realize that making a profit is more difficult if you pay too much for material. Nevertheless, there is a wide discrepancy between their stated belief and how they support the efforts of their own buyers and purchasing managers. On the high end of the scale, a large corporation may employ hundreds of professional buyers and dozens of purchasing managers with salaries that match those of any other business function. A top purchasing executive with a major corporation can earn up to $200,000 per year or more. A nationwide survey of firms of all sizes, conducted by the American Purchasing Society in 1997, revealed that the average annual base salary of those with the title of Buyer was $31,000. The average for Purchasing Manager was $48,800*. These average salary levels are deceptively low because they include salaries reported by a large number of very small organizations as well as those of young and inexperienced employees (see Exhibit 1-1).

---

* "American Purchasing Society's Annual Report of Purchasing Salaries and Employment Trends—1997" Copyright 1997, American Purchasing Society, Inc.

3

Exhibit 1-1.
1997 Salaries Rounded to Thousands of Dollars

Titles	Average	Median	Min	Max
Buyer	31	30	20	54
Buyer/Planner	34	33	23	50
Purchasing Agent	38	36	20	87
Senior Buyer	42	41	18	71
Purchasing Manager	49	49	23	83
Materials Manager	45	46	24	64
Director of Purchasing	63	59	25	133
Vice President	87	95	40	125
All Titles	47	43	17	190

Reprinted with permission from the "American Purchasing Society's Annual Report of Purchasing and Employment Trends—1997." Copyright 1997, American Purchasing Society, Inc.

On the other end of the scale, some executives have advocated major cuts in the purchasing staff or have even suggested eliminating the purchasing department altogether. This could be because of poor experience with certain purchasing personnel or because of pressure to reduce costs. It seems apparent that this is a misguided effort to reduce expenses. Someone in the organization must place orders for the material needed to conduct the business. Someone must deal with suppliers when that service cannot be performed by purchasing department personnel. Elimination of the purchasing department simply transfers the duties of that department from professionals, or at least employees dedicated to making economic purchases, to other employees whose jobs, interests, and objectives are primarily elsewhere. Several hundred years ago Adam Smith, the father of the economics profession, clearly showed the advantages of the division of labor where by dividing duties, output is multiplied many times.

Most businesses fall between the extremes of having either many buyers with high salaries or no professional purchasing personnel whatsoever. Often the person handling purchasing in very small companies may also be responsible for another business function as well. For example, a small company may have an office manager who does the accounting and the buying for the organization. As the company grows a full-time person is assigned to this function. However, unless its importance is sufficiently appreciated, the person selected may not have enough knowledge or experience function properly. It may seem more economical to hire someone who requires only half the salary of another person who has more experience and more knowledge of professional purchasing techniques. It is easy for the manager to think, "How hard is it to call and place an order for goods?"

Of course it is difficult to do just that, but that is misleading. The enormous extra expense and numerous problems when an order is placed improperly can reduce or entirely eliminate a company's profit. At worst, poor purchasing practices can force a company into bankruptcy or at least significantly contribute to the failure of the business. When costs rise as a result of purchasing incompetence, the company must either raise the price of its products or be satisfied with less profit. Raising the price may make the company uncompetitive in the marketplace and result in reduced sales volume.

Purchases made with care and skill can enable a company to sell its product at a lower price and still make a profit. When the price the company charges is lowered, sales increase and consequently as long as marginal cost is lower than the additional revenue, total profits also increase.

Today, more organizations of every size and in every type of business realize the importance of purchasing. In the salary survey mentioned earlier, 19% of the respondents indicated they planned to hire additional help for the purchasing function.

Well-informed executives realize that savings from purchasing activities, in the form of reduced cost, go directly into profits with little if any reduction for associated expenses. Compare this with the profits generated from efforts to increase sales. An organization can add sales people, increase advertising efforts, and spend money for travel to meet with potential customers. All of these expenses plus the cost of the material sold must be deducted from the gained revenue before any additional profit is realized.

Similarities and Differences in Buying Techniques

Years ago, before I taught a class of 40 hospital purchasing agents, my experience had been entirely with manufacturing companies. I had assumed that most buying methods would apply to all organizations and was surprised when the students claimed that they had unique and different problems. For example, they said that each surgeon acted like a "prima donna," wanted special treatment, and demanded a different brand of suture. This prevented the buyers from ordering in volume thereby obtaining a large price discount. The irony was that I had experienced the exact phenomenon in manufacturing companies. Each machinist demanded a different brand of end mill, a cutting tool used in metalworking. Each was certain that any other brand would not cut properly or would break or not last as long. Each machinist was given a number of brands to test. The ones that each machinist originally preferred always did better. The others would break. We were sure that the breakage was not deliberate, but unconsciously the tools they liked were used differently from the ones they didn't like. Both the surgeons and the machinists exhibited one of the many universal problems about human nature that professional purchasing people must overcome. To solve the problem with the machinists, we had each of them test different brands, but marked them so they could not tell which brand was which. We then standardized on the one that performed best but made sure that no brand name was revealed.

There are many examples of common problems that buyers have in all types of organizations. Therefore, it is not surprising that most purchasing policies and procedures can be easily adapted to any type or size of organization. In part, for this reason, most books on the subject have not indicated any need for special techniques in different types of organizations. It is also because, in the past, professional purchasing has made its largest advances in manufacturing companies and, in particular, in large manufacturing companies.

But in practice and partly of necessity buying is handled differently in various types of firms. The size of the firm makes a difference. Retail companies buy differently than manufacturing firms. Entrepreneurs and small firms differ as well. The profit contribution from purchasing activities differs not only by the size of the firms but by the type of products purchased and the industry involved. This book will try to point out many of those differences. Let us look first at size.

How the Size of the Organization Affects Purchasing Methods

PURCHASING IN LARGE ORGANIZATIONS

Large firms can have a specialist who buys one category of products. This allows the buyer to become thoroughly familiar with that particular category. Such firms can afford purchasing staff personnel to handle administrative matters or analyze purchasing activities. Some large firms even have a separate company division that does nothing other than buy or manage material for the organization. Some have an individual assigned to handle personnel matters for the purchasing function alone. Others have a person within the purchasing function assigned to training purchasing personnel only.

Not all large companies divide the responsibilities in this fashion. A major factor is the organizational structure. If it is highly decentralized, purchasing may be delegated to local people at a branch office or plant. If the plant is small there may only be one person who handles all purchasing-related aspects for hundreds of different products used by the plant. Sometimes the plant manager does some of the buying or the plant buyer may also handle another non-purchasing function. With so little time to devote to many items, special techniques and efficient methods must be used to keep costs within reasonable bounds.

Even when large corporations are decentralized, they often have a central purchasing staff function that performs certain duties for which a local operation does not have time. In a modified centralized organization, the central staff may even buy certain items to be used throughout the organization or at many locations.

Large organizations purchase large quantities and that almost always means lower unit prices. Because they buy so much, they wield significant power over the supplier, especially one who relies too much on too few customers. Suppliers have been known to go out of business because they lost one or two major customers accounting for most of their business. On the other hand, a larger company usually requires more people to approve purchases or make changes. Generally speaking, the larger the company, the slower decisions are made and things get done.

Large firms with a large purchasing organization generally have well-defined purchasing policies and procedures. They often have different levels of buyers with different titles and different degrees of purchasing authority. The lowest level buyer may have the title of Junior Buyer, followed by Buyer with more authority, and then Senior Buyer who has still greater authority. When a purchase is beyond one's authority level, measured by the dollar-value of the order, each must obtain approval from the next higher level or the first supervisory level. The title of Purchasing Manager, Commodity Manager, or Purchasing Supervisor guides the activities of the buyers. In large companies, many purchasing managers may report to a Director of Purchasing. There may even be several Directors of Purchasing for the various divisions of the company, and they may represent the highest level position, or depending on the company, may report to a Vice-President of Purchasing. Buyers are not permitted to deviate from company policies and procedures. Legal departments often predetermine acceptable terms and conditions. Some companies always require formal contracts; some only for purchases for certain types of goods; some only for purchases above a certain dollar amount and then those agreements must be reviewed by legal counsel. Often standard terms on the back of purchase order forms are approved by company lawyers and may not be changed without approval. Buyers for a large well-known company probably get very few questions about the company's credit standing. Salespeople rarely ask them for financial statements or even obtain references.

Large companies usually require a college degree for anyone to qualify for a buyer job. Some large companies prefer an advanced degree. Most favor a degree in business, although some prefer a degree in engineering or law. Those with a combination of degrees have a real advantage. Once in a while a person with no college education is selected, usually someone who has had extensive experience with a technical product.

PURCHASING IN MEDIUM-SIZED ORGANIZATIONS

A typical medium-sized company has a few Buyers and a single Purchasing Manager to do all of the purchasing activity. Although many have a Director of Purchasing, frequently the person with the title of Purchasing Manager may be the top level for the function. Whatever the title, that person usually has little or no non-buying staff to help do purchasing research, analyze suppliers, predict cost changes, or gather data. Anything related to purchasing activities must be done either by the manager or the buyers. The manager of the department usually buys or handles transactions for one or several classes of items that account for most of the dollars spent. The remaining categories are divided among the buyers. Typically, the purchases of maintenance, repair, and operating supplies (MRO) are assigned to one person, capital equipment purchases to another, and certain products or product categories to other buyers.

There are usually fewer forms, fewer written policies and procedures, and fewer restrictions on the authority of the buyers and the manager. Of course there are many exceptions depending on the philosophy or management style of top management.

Obtaining good payment terms is less easy than it is with a large corporation, but if the company has existed for many years and its name is well recognized, normal business terms are usually available. Once in a while, a supplier will ask that a credit application form be filled out or references be given, but few ask for this if the firm is listed on any of the stock exchanges.

Most medium-sized companies also require purchasing managers and buyers to have a college degree; those without a sufficient degree but with sufficient experience, however, are given more consideration and do obtain purchasing positions if they sell themselves and look hard enough.

PURCHASING IN SMALL COMPANIES

Smaller companies may have only one person with the title of Purchasing Agent or Purchasing Manager who does all the buying, with perhaps an assistant to do the clerical work. Many such companies have few if any written policy and procedure manuals. There are few forms and the ones that are frequently used lack detail. For example, they may lack standard terms and conditions, or if they do have some, they are often out of date. The terms may fail to mention the Uniform Commercial Code or other important stipulations that protect the company from legal problems.

Those in a one- or two-person department must shop, negotiate, and provide paperwork for MRO, capital equipment, and any other purchased materials. Certain material may need to be obtained by personnel outside of the purchasing function because of the workload of the assigned purchasing people. This may also occur due to a lack of confidence in the ability of the purchasing people, or a belief that they lack certain product knowledge. For example, the President may purchase a major commodity, or the Plant Manager may negotiate for the purchase of steel or some other material. In those cases the purchasing person may be asked to fill out the paperwork (purchase order). Often the delegated purchasing agent may not even know that products are being obtained outside of the purchasing function. It is not unusual to encounter problems with purchasing done in this fashion; the official purchasing agent may even be blamed for not preventing unauthorized purchases or for not bringing the problem to the attention of senior management.

It is more difficult in a small company to initially obtain credit or obtain normal business payment terms with a new supplier. Credit application forms and/or references are often required. Late payment by the buying company may result in less satisfactory terms such as full or partial payment in advance or C.O.D. (Cash on Delivery).

Smaller companies require less education when hiring someone for a purchasing position, but they also expect to pay less salary. A college degree, technical training or experience is required if the products are of a technical nature. This is not necessarily true if company engineers are heavily involved in the purchasing decision or deal directly with the suppliers. In such cases, purchasing personnel act more like order placement clerks rather than professional buyers.

How New Businesses and Entrepreneurs Buy

Companies that are either just starting out or that consist of only a few people may not have any formal purchasing department at all. The President or owner of the company may do all or most of the purchasing. Sometimes, he or she will only buy what constitutes the most significant expenditure while low value purchases may be delegated to a secretary or assistant. Many companies allow the maintenance supervisor to make most of the purchases.

New and one- or two-person companies may not even use purchase order forms. All goods and services are obtained via the telephone or oral order placement. Good payment terms are difficult to obtain, and to secure credit personal charge cards are used for office supplies and other equipment. This permits the owner to improve cash flow, and provides better record of the purchase. It is also easier to stop payment and return goods than it would be if cash were used. However, not all companies accept credit cards; particularly those organizations that sell products exclusively to businesses. Such companies may require payment in advance or immediate payment upon delivery.

The successful new businessperson or entrepreneur is particularly concerned about cash flow. Consequently, a purchase may be made from a supplier that has a higher price, but will be more lenient with credit terms.

Some More Words About Titles

On the surface it seems to matter little if a person has the official title of Buyer, Purchasing Agent, Purchasing Manager, or other designation. One buyer may be an engineer; another may be the company's controller. What possible difference does it make as long as the purchase is made appropriately? However, in certain situations, an impressive title can add status and can affect negotiating success. Like it or not, a title helps define areas and limits of authority.

The application for membership in the American Purchasing Society has a line for title and nearly everybody who applies fills in that line. But once in a while someone will simply write the word "purchasing" in that space. Occasionally someone at an APS seminar will not have a calling card and will claim no title even though he or she does the buying for the organization. No problem for the Society or for participation at the seminar, but it would be an embarrassment if the same person were negotiating with a Japanese supplier. The Japanese take pride in their business cards and the titles that they exhibit. They present the cards in a special way holding the edges with both hands and bowing slightly. They expect others to do the same and they will pay close attention to the card you give.

The omission of a title and business card usually results from using a junior person to handle purchasing for a young or very small firm. However, as the company grows the absence of these seemingly insignificant symbols reflects poorly on a company's professionalism and seriousness about conducting business.

One other point about titles. There is confusion about the title of Purchasing Agent. The words have two meanings: one use is a title, and the other designates a person who is given the authority to buy for the organization. More about this in Chapter 4.

Summary

Although purchasing operations have not always been given the support that they deserve, more and more companies now realize the importance of good buying practices and the value of well-qualified buyers. Purchasing salary levels at major corporations are comparable to those of other business occupations and, in some cases, even higher.

Books and seminars about purchasing and negotiating techniques explain how the large- and medium-sized organizations make purchases and recommend methods used by the best of them. But in practice, smaller companies, of necessity, use different and simpler procedures. The following chapters are certainly going to cover the best practices of the larger companies, but in addition, we will explain different methods that may be more economically used depending on the size, the type, and the business of the organization.

Chapter 2

Establishing Proper Purchasing Objectives

This chapter will provide you with an essential element in purchasing success. It discusses the importance of objectives for better results from purchasing operations. It also discusses how to plan to achieve those objectives. It covers leadtimes, specifications, and time and cost value of money when measuring purchasing performance.

The Importance of Objectives

To use the overworked simile, without objectives in life, we are like a ship without a rudder. We drift along with the wind or currents and there is a good chance we are not going to end up where we would like to be. With objectives we are able to plot a course and achieve better results. Purchasing activities are significantly improved by having goals.

Setting proper objectives in business can appear to be deceptively easy. For example, if you ask a somewhat naive businessperson what his or her objectives are, the reply might be simply to make money. Someone else might say to get rich. Such objectives are useless to provide the basis for making plans. Similarly, a buyer might say the objectives are to buy at the lowest price. Another buyer might indicate that the objective is to obtain goods on time. Still another might say to obtain quality products.

Of course there is an element of truth in all of these but they are too general and simplistic to be meaningful. They fail to define the terms used. What is meant by "on time"? What do "quality products" mean? Most important, such objectives probably make unwarranted assumptions and leave out key information about purchasing goals. Let us look at each of these insufficient objectives and see how we can improve upon them.

The Difference Between Price and Cost

The naive buyer who says the objective is to buy at the lowest price will eventually receive inferior goods. Probably the product will be so poor that it will not be usable and the buyer will either try to return it or get the company's money back. That is not always possible, but even if credit can be obtained, much time and effort will have been wasted in correcting the situation. It soon becomes apparent to the intelligent buyer that price cannot be the sole consideration.

If our naive buyer is lucky, the purchased goods may be exactly what is desired, but the supplier may not ship them to arrive when the company needs them. Therefore, the company's workforce may have to be used for other purposes while waiting for the needed goods. Some people may need to be sent home because no work is available. The company may be unable to fill a customer's requirement on schedule and consequently the customer cancels the order.

What would constitute an "on-time" shipment? Is within a week of the scheduled date sufficient? Will arrival at any time on the specified date be acceptable or is delivery required in the morning or in the afternoon? Is the leadtime given by the supplier the measure of punctuality or is it the time specified on the purchase order? Has the scheduled delivery date been accepted by the seller or is the delivery date simply the buyer's wishful thinking?

A different supplier had a higher price but could have delivered the same quality goods on time. As you see, price is not the only factor and not necessarily the most important factor to consider. Price is a component of cost. So is quality. So is the ability to obtain the goods on time.

Purchasing is or should be primarily concerned about product cost, but cost is not the same as price. It is a combination of many factors.

Planning to Eliminate Stock Shortages and Obtain Material When Needed

As we have discussed, one important cost factor is obtaining delivery of products at the time and date you stipulate. This is a cost factor in several different ways. You can usually get earlier delivery if you pay more or if you use certain suppliers who charge more because they specialize in providing early delivery. Other suppliers have two different prices, either for normal or fast delivery time.

Once in a while even companies that plan well and use normal sourcing have an emergency caused by errors or failures in equipment. In those cases they may require quick delivery from their suppliers. If the company is a good customer and faster delivery is possible without undue cost, the supplier will usually accommodate the customer without adding charges.

If the product cannot be obtained without incurring significant additional cost from overtime pay or disruption of schedules, the supplier will ask to be reimbursed for the added cost. In practice, suppliers don't usually offer to work overtime. They simply say they can't make the requested delivery. It is usually up to the buyer to initiate the request and offer to pay for the overtime cost.

This scenario assumes that in most cases the buyer is allowing sufficient time to make deliveries under normal working conditions. If the buyer habitually wants delivery in less time than is normally needed, the supplier who accepts those orders may routinely charge that buyer more even though no reason for the higher charge is ever stated or the supplier may simply accept the orders and ship the material so that it arrives later than scheduled. In either case the cost is greater to the buyer. The added cost may be apparent in higher prices or hidden in the form of inefficiencies in receiving, stockkeeping, and rescheduling of production because of late shipments.

Companies try to get around habitually late shipments by carrying higher inventory, doing excessive follow-up, and ordering material from many sources of supply. Those methods work to a limited extent because the material is available when needed, but the added cost of higher inventory and inefficiencies is a clear indication that this is not the best solution.

Keeping inventory as low as possible means keeping no more stock than is needed within a very short time. Many manufacturing businesses today use a system called "Just In Time", or JIT for short. It means the purchased material only arrives as it is needed, neither earlier nor later than when it is to be used. But any type of business tries to minimize inventory levels without running out of stock. For example, a retail business will probably lose sales if it does not have products when the customer wants them. And it can be disastrous for a hospital to run short of supplies.

On the other hand, all types of businesses suffer if there is too much inventory on hand. Excess material takes up costly warehouse space. Stock deteriorates or spoils over time. Some items become obsolete.

Too much follow-up means wasted time, and time is money. It is a clear indication that something is wrong if it is necessary to telephone a supplier over and over again to find out the status of an order. Either insufficient time was allowed in placing the order or the supplier is not capable of filling the requirements and a different supplier should have been selected.

Establishing Leadtimes

The time required to receive needed goods is referred to as "leadtime." Production control personnel and schedulers sometimes give purchasing leadtime to obtain the material by estimating the amount of time it will take a supplier to either manufacture the goods or pull them out of stock and ship them. Salespeople sometimes use a similar method when they tell buyers how long it will take to "deliver" the goods (see Exhibit 2-1). However, those leadtimes do not consider various component times that

Exhibit 2-1.
Sample Leadtime Report

(Note: Length of leadtimes are not actual. Do not use for planning purposes.)

LEADTIME REPORT
Average Leadtime in Days as of March 1992

Item or Category	Shop for New Item	Place Order	P.O Delivered	Supplier Sched.	Shipping Time	Total for Shelf or Repeat Items	Make Tooling	Manu-facturing	Total for New Item
Abrasives	15	2	2	2	3	9	10	10	44
Bearings	15	2	2	2	10	16	9	12	52
Castings	25	2	3	3	5	13	25	14	77
Chemicals	12	2	2	2	5	11	—	23	46
Corrugated	6	2	2	2	2	8	11	2	27
Forgings	28	2	3	3	5	13	31	3	75
Mill Supplies	3	1	1	1	1	4	—	5	12
Nickel	15	2	2	3	5	12	—	3	30
Paper Towels	1	1	1	1	1	4	—	3	8
Plastic Resin	15	2	2	5	3	12	—	3	30
Rubber Mats	10	2	2	2	3	9	—	15	49
Screws, Custom	7	2	2	2	2	8	10	10	35
Screws, Standard	3	2	2	1	1	6	—	—	9
Stationery	3	2	1	1	1	5	—	—	8

are required between the time the requestor asks for the goods and the time that they are available for use. A more realistic schedule includes time for the buyer to receive the request and begin action. It includes the time for placing the order and perhaps some more for some amount of negotiating. While repeat orders may require little or no time to negotiate, new items may require more for shopping, negotiating, and writing a proper purchase order or agreement. These time components may be referred to as the buying company's internal leadtime which may be as little as a few hours or as long as several weeks, depending on the type of product being purchased and the structure and administrative procedures of that particular company. For example, some companies require certain managers or accounting functions to check available budgets and approve expenditures before any purchases can be made.

External leadtimes are the time components required by the supplier and by the selected carrier to transport the goods from the seller's location to the buyer's location. Moreover, additional internal leadtime at the buyer may be required by the receiving operation for inspection of the goods by quality control personnel, and for internal delivery of the goods to the requestor.

Ensuring Prompt Delivery

To obtain prompt delivery, the buyer must initially stress the importance of meeting schedules before the order is placed and make sure the seller understands when delivery is required. Legally, the buyer can protect the company's interest by including a clause in the purchase order or in the written contract that says, "Time is of the Essence." Rather than give a required delivery date in terms of days, weeks, or months, it is better to request material or completion of a service by a specific date. Make sure it is in writing and agreed upon by the seller.

Be aware that salespeople are anxious to obtain the business and are prone to make promises that may not be possible for their organizations to keep. Make sure that the selling company agrees to the requested date. Make your request clear and forceful in writing and obtain a signed acknowledgment by someone who is authorized to make a commitment for the selling organization. Not all salespeople are authorized. It is best to ask them if you have any reason to doubt their authority; often they are not so authorized.

Specific leadtime objectives could be to reduce average leadtime by only one day. This could be done by using more efficient suppliers, by getting the requestors to plan better, or by improving communications to the suppliers about your requirements. By the way, a useful method of obtaining sufficient leadtime from the requestors is to issue a periodic report showing the time required to obtain different types of goods. See the sample report. (Exhibit 2-1, on page 19.)

If reducing average leadtime is a good objective, even better ones relate to reducing component Leadtimes. For example, the buyer may investigate the possibility of reducing inbound transportation time by comparing the various modes of transportation and checking shipments from different carriers.

Another leadtime objective might involve reducing the time required to get the order from the buyer to the seller. Since some suppliers will not begin work on an order until they receive a written confirmation of an order, the buyer may be able get most suppliers to agree to accept FAX orders in place of orders received by regular mail.

A frequently used purchasing objective is to reduce internal processing time to place an order. If handwritten paper requisitions are used, it will speed up the ordering process by notifying the purchasing department through a local area computer network. Converting manually typed purchase orders to computer-generated orders will reduce order-processing time, as will using standard forms and standard clauses.

Obtaining or Preparing Proper Specifications

No single factor affects successful purchasing efforts as much as good specifications. Even when buying as a consumer, you are more likely to get a better product when you know exactly what you want. When the product or service requirements are clearly spelled out you are better able to negotiate. You can shop and compare various suppliers' ability to match your requirements.

Good specifications include enough detail to make it easy for the buyer and supplier to understand what is desired by the requestor, but not so much detail that it limits the ability to shop and negotiate with multiple sources.

Take this somewhat exaggerated example. Suppose you receive a request for a writing instrument with no other description. You don't know if the requestor wants a pen, a pencil, or something entirely different. A better description would be for a writing pen. If the request were for just a "pen," it could also mean a pen for animals.

The request for a writing pen is better, but you still don't know if the requestor wants a ball point, a felt tip, or a fountain pen. You don't know if the requestor wants blue ink or black. You don't know if a fine point or a medium point is preferred.

Conversely if the requestor asked for an Ajax ball point with black ink and medium tip, you might not want to shop for a Cross, a Shaefer, or a Bic. Thus your ability to negotiate and get the best product for the purpose intended is extremely restricted.

Many suppliers are all too aware of the importance of getting their brand name or their unique product specifications incorporated on to engineering drawings. If they can accomplish this by influencing engineers or indirectly through advertising, they know the buyer will often have little choice but to purchase the goods from them. Consequently, the buyer will have little negotiating ability and will likely pay a higher price for the product.

ESTABLISHING PROPER SPECIFICATIONS IS A TEAM EFFORT

A part of the buyer's job is to work with engineers and requestors to help them supply good specifications. He or she needs to keep design engineers and requestors informed about alternative products and specifications that are available and also needs sometimes to inform, or teach if you prefer, what details are required. A proper description of a product may include color, length, width, height, weight, hardness, chemistry, or a multitude of other specifications. Sometimes drawings are a must.

It is difficult to change specifications once they are established, particularly in larger organizations, because the development process is often time-consuming and costly. However, if a product is to be purchased, often over an extended time, it is beneficial to change specifications to keep up with technology, and to the availability of a better product or a better supplier with a slightly different product. The responsibility to influence the change may rest in part or totally with the buyer.

Buying the Right Item for the Job

An organization can buy a high quality product at a bargain price without having proper specifications. How can this be in view of what was previously said? Consider this example. Assume a company has a dozen traveling salespeople for janitorial supplies that need automobiles that are supplied by the company for business use. The salespeople may want to drive a Lexus, a Mercedes-Benz or some other luxury vehicle. They may give strong arguments justifying their need for high priced cars. They may indicate that a luxury car gives them the image that they need to sell their product. Perhaps it can be shown that the type of vehicles they want have better quality, require less repairs, and last much longer. Furthermore, the sales manager has a brother who is a car dealer and can obtain the cars at dealer cost. With these facts, certainly a specification can be established that makes it mandatory for the buyer to purchase these high price vehicles. But the specifications are not really considering all the factors. Good and proper specifications are those that equate the product to be purchased for its suitability for the job intended. Surely most salespeople for janitorial supplies do not require a luxury automobiles to make sales calls.

One of the responsibilities of purchasing people is to advise and recommend suitable products. In order to determine costs, buyers need to consider the length of time that purchased products will be needed and how long they will last so that they can recommend proper specifications.

Authority to Establish Specifications

Specifications can be produced by various sources. They can come from the users of the desired product. They can come from marketing or from an engineering department that designs the product needed or at least provides the description of the product. In some organizations personnel within the purchasing department have sole authority to establish the specification for purchased products. However, this is unusual except for buyers in retail organizations that purchase merchandise for resale.

Buyers usually have limited authority to establish specifications. A buyer's role is generally to recommend products or to obtain product information from suppliers and pass it along to engineers, marketing people or other departments in need of the product. When purchasing has the responsibility to establish product specifications but lacks the technical knowledge to evaluate various products fairly, there are several ways to indirectly evaluate products or obtain assistance. One way is to compare generic specifications that have been written by an independent organization or other industry-related organizations like Underwriters Laboratories, the Copper Development Association, the American Standards Association, the American Society for Testing and Materials, and the National Electric Manufacturers Association. Most product categories commonly purchased have some industry organization that establishes standards to help the buyer adequately specify what is desirable.

Another way to obtain assistance is to simply ask suppliers what parameters need to be given in order to define the product you want. It is best to obtain such information from more than one supplier to make certain that no single supplier is including or excluding a requirement that might prejudice your purchase.

A request for a quote or for product information from many suppliers will often produce brochures or catalogs with enough detailed description to help make a specification. Make sure, however, not to establish a specification that excludes products that may be more economical. For example, a supplier may show that his machine has an MTBF (mean time before failure) of 120,000 units. A competitor may show her machine to have an MTBF of 75,000 units. This information is very helpful but must not be used without thought. Obviously the machine that lasts for 120,000 units before break-down would seem to be more durable than the other. However, the less durable machine may cost only half the price of the more durable one. A good specification should not exclude products that will satisfy the need.

Problem Specifications and How to Avoid Them

There are several types of problem specifications that prevent buyers from obtaining the best product for the job. The previous example demonstrates excessive specifications. Other such examples of excessive specifications include a product with a fixed dimension that is unique to one supplier and has nothing to do with its functionality. Unless there is good reason to require this or any other unique specification of the product, then the buyer's ability to buy economically and wisely is restricted.

A common mistake is for engineers or others to include tolerances that are not needed. If the requirement indicates that the product must be to so many thousandths of an inch where only hundredths of an inch would suffice, then the requirement is excessive and is probably costing the company much unneeded expense.

Brand names are usually another example of excessive specifications. They are used because they are believed to be associated with a desired level of quality or because the specifier is willing to accept that brand as a standard for the product. The specifier is unable to list all the criteria for the product either because of lack of time or because of lack of technical knowledge. However, over time manufacturers often change the standards for a particular brand. Using a brand name excludes all competition and in most cases results in a higher cost. Some companies get around this problem by requiring engineers or other specifiers to state that equivalent products are acceptable. The specification then reads "brand X or equivalent." Although this gives the buyer a bit more latitude, arguments often develop over whether something is or is not equivalent. Few products are exactly equivalent.

Insufficient specifications often create problems because they result in inferior quality or in products that do not fit the purpose intended. It is often left to the buyer to discover excessive or inadequate specifications.

The buyer should then inform specifiers and convince them of the advantages of revising the requirement. This is not always easy to do because it may be necessary to make new drawings or get agreement for the revision from a number of people within the organization. Nevertheless, this is a key role for the buyer who must use every persuasive power to get the changes made if they are justified.

It is easier to help establish proper specifications in the beginning than it is to get them changed later. The buyer should become involved with suppliers, engineers, marketers, or any other requestors to help provide the criteria for product selection. This involvement should be done early in the planning for products so that good communications are established and minimum time is wasted.

Evaluating Time and the Cost of Money

It takes time to earn money, either personally or for a company. Making money requires an investment of time so this becomes an important factor when planning and conducting purchasing activities. Time must be measured for the labor needed to plan, shop, negotiate, and do the necessary work required for a proper purchasing transaction. It should be considered when comparing the durability of products so that a correct cost can be assigned to the various alternatives. Let us look at a few examples.

Example 1

A buyer at the plant for a major corporation was responsible for making all purchases for maintenance, repair, and operating supplies. He received many requisitions from foremen and other supervisors throughout the plant. Most were for small quantities of items of small value. Many were for purchases that were made frequently in the past and were expected to be made many times in the future. He would receive requests to obtain a dozen light bulbs, or a dozen screws, or a dozen rolls of paper towels, and myriad other requests of a similar type. Each time the buyer received one of these requests he would call four or five suppliers to obtain a price from each. He was very proud of his ability to pick the one with the lowest price. However, he never measured the time it took to shop for the lowest price on every item and every repeat order. Because he spent so much time shopping for these low-valued transactions, he never had time to negotiate long-term agreements. Not only was his price much higher than it might have been if he had established an agreement with one or two suppliers, but his total costs were much greater because he was wasting valuable time unnecessarily repeating work for similar transactions.

Example 2

Another buyer believed he could obtain the proper paint for a manufacturing plant at $3 per gallon less than any competitive product. However, he failed to consider the cost of applying the paint or how long the paint would last after it was applied. Subsequently he attended a seminar and discovered the error of his ways. When he calculated the cost based on his new knowledge he discovered that he should have purchased another product, priced at $5 per gallon more than what he paid, because of the ease of application and its durability. The cost of the higher priced paint over a five-year period turned out to be less. He then felt fortunate in getting another chance to prove his worth because he received a new requisition for paint for the general office. Based on his new knowledge, he purchased the higher priced paint. Unfortunately, he did not determine how long management expected to remain in those offices. The intention was to fix the place up so that it could be sold because the company wanted to move to new offices within eighteen months. In this case the lower priced product would have been more economical.

These examples illustrate the need for information. To make a wise decision the buyer must have all the facts. It is not necessary to know everything all the time, but you should know labor rates, interest rates that the organization must pay, and the short- or long-range plans involving the use of a requested product to be purchased. The requestor is not usually aware that the buyer needs such information and may resent being asked for it as simply slowing down the buying process or needlessly complicating the transaction. Many times requestors cannot supply certain information, such as the appropriate interest rate. It is up to the buyer to explain the need for the information or to seek out the proper individuals to obtain it. For example, interest rates are normally available from the controller or financial manager.

Obtaining all the necessary information doesn't automatically produce the right buying decision. It often must be used in calculations to obtain the correct answer. It may be necessary to apply present value formulas to determine if it is wise to make a certain purchase or what terms are or are not acceptable.

Planning and Setting Objectives Properly

There are various degrees of planning. Many companies set aside specific dates each year to make plans for the next twelve months. But plans may be extensive or brief. They may involve every aspect of an operation or simply be concerned with making a particular purchase. The important thing to remember is that it is better to plan than to rush into a negotiation or make an impulsive purchase. Take a few minutes to think about what you are doing before you do it. Think about the pros and cons of taking each action. Following are some of the subjects that buyers should usually plan to a greater or lesser extent:

- Scheduling time for shopping and negotiating
- Scheduling time for investigating suppliers
- Determining negotiating strategy and tactics
- Listing both acceptable and unacceptable terms and conditions
- Determining cost objectives
- Determining quantity to order and the reorder point
- Determining number of suppliers to use
- Setting priorities for shopping and negotiating

Setting objectives gives direction to your efforts. Proper objectives should be quantified and specific whenever possible. Don't just say you want to reduce average leadtime. It is more meaningful to say you want to reduce average leadtime on widgets from ten days to seven days. This helps you make plans to accomplish your objective since it is very important to have a target completion date for each objective. This will provide motivation to get the job done and let you know your progress before it is too late. If half the time has passed since you set the objective and nothing has been done, you know you will have to get busy or you will miss the date and fail to achieve your objective. Following are some typical objectives that apply to purchasing activities:

- Reduce the number of late shipments per week by 22% by September 20th.

- Reduce the number of active suppliers from 1500 to 575 by the end of the year.

- Reduce the number of out-of-stock items by 75% by June 15th.

- Read three books on purchasing or materials management by December 30th.

- Attend an American Purchasing Society seminar this year.

- Obtain a 17% cost reduction in corrugated cartons by February 15th.

- Work with other departments to set up a value analysis team by March 3rd to meet each month for a cost reduction program.

- Shop and negotiate systems contracts for electrical supplies by October 9th.

- Apply for certification from the American Purchasing Society and take the examination by January 15.

Summary

This chapter has covered the importance of having objectives and the types of objectives that concern purchasing. It pointed out that buyers must understand the difference between price and cost. It also touched upon the importance of minimizing inventory while making sure enough material is available to meet requirements. A related objective is to reduce leadtime, both internal and external. Internal leadtime consists of time for administrative matters, shopping and negotiating. External leadtime includes the time for the supplier to produce and process the order and for the carrier to deliver the product.

Planning is an essential part of the purchasing process. Buyers must plan or help with planning to reduce shortages and should plan before negotiating with suppliers.

Proper specifications are essential for good buying practices and include an adequate description of the product to meet the needs of the organization without excessive costs. Purchasing interacts with all departments and most purchases involve a team effort. If information about products is not available within the organization there are many outside sources and services available to provide assistance.

Purchasing objectives involve the time value of money and buyers need to take this cost into consideration when establishing objectives, making purchasing decisions, and measuring results.

Chapter 3

Different Types of Organizations and Buying Systems

Advantages and Disadvantages of Different Organizational Structures

There are at least several reasons why it is important for the buyer to understand the different types of buying systems that are used in business today. Buyers for business may be owners, executives, or managers of any business function. They may have any title or any primary responsibility other than buying. In other words, purchasing may be their sole duty. Or it may only be a small part of their responsibility. The preferred purchasing system depends on the job the buyer is filling as well as the size and structure of the organization. The amount of responsibility and authority that the buyer exercises is a function of the system. The way the buyer conducts each transaction and the administrative requirements of the job are related to the organization's policies, procedures, and culture.

A new buyer who fails to understand the business environment of the organization can quickly exceed the limits of his or her authority and convey an unfavorable impression right at the beginning of his or her purchasing career. Without understanding the organization's operating style, the new buyer may be just as likely to underestimate his or her authority and responsibility. Such misunderstandings can result in job performance far below the expected level.

Understanding the structure and operating style of an organization is also important for another reason. It helps the buyer interpret political forces and pressures that affect purchasing activities. It may even help the buyer prevent legal problems for the organization and protect the buyer from personal legal repercussions, which will be discussed in Chapter 4. The following material is divided into four sections. The first discusses the various organization types, sizes, and structures. This is followed by a discussion of the forms used by most formal purchasing activities. The third section goes through the normal buying process. The final portion of this chapter covers traditional written documentation of purchasing transactions and the record retention usually required.

Comparing Organization Types, Sizes, and Structures

FORMAL AND INFORMAL PURCHASING FOR BUSINESS

Large-and medium-sized companies have employees with the title of Buyer, Purchasing Manager, and often Purchasing Director. Although many small companies use similar titles, most have no formal purchasing department. Most of these organizations have fifty or fewer employees. Many have only a few people that handle every aspect of the business. Thousands more are new companies and have little organizational structure and many undefined areas of responsibility, particularly for purchasing activities. Other business enterprises are one-person companies.

Nevertheless, all business organizations need to make purchases. Someone must do the buying. Whether it is done well or properly is another question. The intention here is not to disparage how many of these companies operate their purchasing activities. It is simply to describe how business operates and suggest possible ways of improving the results. Both experienced purchasers and new buyers can make their jobs easier in the long run if they follow well-established good purchasing methods and procedures.

The organization of companies, whether small, medium or large, falls into three categories referred to as centralized, decentralized, or a modification or a combination of centralized and decentralized structures. In the centralized organization everything is controlled from one central location and one person makes the rules and decisions. Conversely, in the decentralized organization, decisions are delegated to other departments or employees at other locations. There are a variety of ways to delegate authority under a modified system. Some companies keep purchasing decisions that involve certain products for central control, and delegate buying authority for other products to local employees at the branch or plant level. Others delegate buying for relatively small value items to local people, but keep authority for large expenditures. Still others base the delegation upon their broad categories of usage. The three areas most frequently defined are: capital equipment; raw material or items used in production; and MRO or maintenance, repair, and operating supplies. Sometimes a fourth category may be defined as items for resale.

All of this may seem unimportant to the new buyer, but it is key in understanding the limits of authority, the ease or difficulty in making purchases, and the place that purchasing activities have in the organization's hierarchy. That place affects salary levels and opportunities for advancement within the organization. For example, if purchasing is highly regarded as a key business function, it may be an area that offers a natural stepping stone to a general management position at a plant, division, or corporate level. If it is considered a service function only or a necessary evil merely representing necessary costs and expenses, then it can be a dead end for any career advancement opportunities and more vulnerable to layoffs than other areas. Salary levels are affected by the same philosophies.

In general, most small and new companies have informal systems that tend to be decentralized in nature. People from different areas within the company either do their own buying or buy for their areas of responsibility. Even when there is a named purchasing department, it may only act in a clerical function for foremen, section supervisors, or department managers from other areas.

Informal purchasing is carried out by someone recognizing a need for a product or service and either personally contacting suppliers or delegating someone to do so. Some negotiating may be done with the selected supplier before the order is placed. Finally, the supplier is asked to ship the goods or perform the service with little or no written documentation of the order. In some cases, documentation of the transaction, in the form of a letter or purchase order, is given to the supplier either as the order is placed or sent after the order has been placed. There are no computer files of purchasing transactions or activities. There are few copies of any written documents that can be easily retrieved.

Orders of this type are generally considered legal contracts, but can be difficult if not impossible to enforce. People conducting business in this informal way are sometimes aware of the deficiency of the method and the potential problems but also see its advantages. Let's look at the pros and cons.

By definition, small companies have few employees and cannot afford to hire specialists for every business function. The number of purchasing transactions do not warrant a full time person, or at least so it is believed. General managers does not want to establish systems and procedures that create needless paperwork that is time-consuming and nonproductive. They feel that any cost reductions achieved by more formal methods will not justify the added expense; furthermore the risk of added cost resulting from poor documentation is considered to be small. These managers of small and growing companies want fast action. If they want a product or service to achieve some goal, they do not want to wait for extensive shopping, negotiating, analysis of bids, investigations of suppliers' capabilities, and writing of carefully worded formal agreements or purchase orders.

Although sales people from thousands of organizations accept oral orders, many companies have a sales policy not to accept an order without a purchase order or a formal contract. Those companies that have been burnt by not having something in writing are particularly wary. State laws called the Uniform Commercial Code require that contracts for "goods" of $500 or more must be in writing to be enforceable. In spite of that, distributors and other types of companies will accept orders over the telephone if you have established credit or give acceptable credit references. Nevertheless, the dollar amount of purchases may be limited without a signed agreement. If the buyer fails to negotiate all terms and make sure that the writing is as agreed, the supplier will submit a writing that reflects terms and conditions in favor of the seller.

Various characteristics and symbols indicate that an organization is a serious and legitimate business venture. For example: an organization name that includes the word company or incorporated; a printed letterhead or calling card with the name of the company, the individual and the person's title; invoice forms, company checks, and purchase order forms.

If a dispute later develops about an order placed with a supplier, it is very difficult to rely on memory about what was said or agreed upon without written documentation. In the course of business, disputes will always occur sooner or later. Shipments may be delayed an inordinate amount of time. The goods may not be what were requested. The quality may be less than satisfactory. Some managers assume they can simply withhold payment if the material or service does not turn out as they would like, an erroneous and naive belief. Courts have ruled time and again in favor of the seller that goods or services must be paid for even though the goods were not what were expected if the buyer cannot show that the goods were different than agreed upon in the contract. In addition, defects in material may not be discovered or failure of the supplier to honor a warranty may not be encountered until the goods have been paid for.

Obviously there are advantages and disadvantages in having an informal buying system. So which is better? It really depends on many factors. An entrepreneur starting out doesn't have a purchase order designed or printed (although stock forms are available from every office supply store). A new company with only a couple of people has to accomplish many things in the beginning including the purchase of office furniture and equipment. That might have to come before any formal purchasing department is established.

It also depends on the type of business. Manufacturing companies usually buy a lot more than service companies. If a company is going to spend large amounts on material and issue many orders almost daily, then it is to their advantage to use more traditional and formal purchasing methods as quickly as possible. If the company is offering a professional service, such as accounting or consulting, very little will be purchased either in terms of dollars or in terms of the number of orders issued. It may be best to give formalization of purchasing low priority until other aspects of the business are under control. Nevertheless, every organization, whether it deals with a product or a service is well advised to eventually establish a clearly-defined and systematic purchasing operation.

Problems Created by Company Growth

The informal system may work satisfactorily for the new or small company. However, problems develop as the company grows, and the quicker the growth the more likely it is that the company will ignore those problems until considerable damage has occurred. Management of organizations that are growing quickly may not be likely to tamper with a system that is proving successful. If it seems that there is little or no damage being done by an informal purchasing operation, why change it? Management may not be aware of disadvantageous long-term legal commitments, or excessive prices that reduce profits, or quality problems that may not show up immediately. What is worse, they may not see that there are buried internal purchasing administrative costs that are not documented because purchasing activities are disbursed among many departments and individuals.

When companies become too large and still maintain an informal purchasing operation it becomes increasingly difficult to establish a strong professional purchasing operation. Those that have been doing the buying under an informal or decentralized system resist changing or relinquishing buying authority. Such resistance is not always apparent even to a strong general manager. Products purchased by a newly established buying department may seem to be of lower quality or less suitable than those purchased through the informal or decentralized system. There may be more late shipments, and certain items purchased by the new group may turn out to be higher priced than they were when the informal group made the purchases. Little credence is given to the fact that the economy has changed or that the specifications may have changed. It takes a smart and persuasive purchasing manager and well-qualified buyers to overcome these obstacles.

Forms Used in Most Formal Purchasing Activities

Only a few printed forms are used in purchasing by businesses of all types: the requisition, the request for bid, the purchase order, the purchase order revision, the price history and the release form. These forms, when used, were always "hard copies" of paper documents until fairly recently. Now, more and more companies are doing away with "hard copies" of some of these forms in favor of computer-generated forms. The data is then stored in the computer and may be transmitted directly from requestors to buyers and from buyers to suppliers. Some firms supplement the computer-generated forms with "hard copies" or still send formal paper purchase order forms to the suppliers. See Chapter 7 for a further discussion of purchasing activities with the computer and associated communications.

REQUISITION FORMS

There may be one or more types of requisition forms in any organization. Usually the end users prepare the available forms and send them to the purchasing operation for further handling. Among these may be the normal or simple requisition, the traveler, or a bill of material. The normal requisition may be a single or multi-part form (see Exhibit 3-1). Various styles of generic stock requisition forms are available at stationery supply stores. They have spaces or boxes for insertion of the quantity required, a description of the product needed, the date needed, and a space for the name of the requestor along with his or her signature authorizing the purchase. There may also be other spaces, sometimes shaded, both for the name and address of a recommended or selected supplier and for payment and delivery terms. The shading is to distinguish between what the requestor fills in and what the buyer inserts. Requestors sometimes provide the name of a supplier to let the buyer know where the product may be obtained. They may have even told the supplier they have the order, but they could be overstepping their authority if the company policy indicates that only purchasing has the authority to place orders. The original copy of the form is usually sent to purchasing. Additional copies may be for the requestor's records, for follow-up or for various other people within the organization for control purposes.

Exhibit 3-1.
Sample Purchase Requisition Form

Number _____

Company Name
PURCHASE REQUISITION

Requisition Date _____

TO THE PURCHASING DEPARTMENT   DELIVER TO:

Please order the items requested below (All boxes in italics are to be filled in by purchasing department only).

Requestor's known supplier(s), if any: Buyer's selected supplier(s):

1. _____   1. _____

2. _____   2. _____

3. _____   3. _____

☐ This is a one time purchase only.   ☐ Items may be purchased continually.

Delivery Date Requested:	Promised by Supplier:	Payment Terms:
F.O.B.	P.O. Date:	Shipping Point:	Ship Via:

Item	Order Quantity	Expected Annual Usage	Unit of Measure	Description	Price	Extension
					Total	

☐ Check if items are for resale or production.

Requested by: _____

Approved by: _____

APSREQ898

The illustrated sample requisition form in this chapter is typical of what many companies use. A full-sized reprintable hard copy or computer disk containing this form, that may be customized for individual needs, is available from the American Purchasing Society.

The traveler is the second type of requisition. The form is printed on heavy card stock for durability and continuous use. Spaces on the form are for the name and description of the product, names and addresses of the suppliers that may be used, terms that apply to those suppliers, bid information, and usage and ordering history. The history shows the dates orders were placed, the quantity that was ordered, and the purchase order numbers. Its purpose is to save paperwork and the buyer's time. It eliminates the need to look up the purchase history such as the prices previously paid, the quantity ordered or the name of the supplier. The quantity ordered gives a good indication of usage over time and helps in negotiating high volume purchases and long-term agreements. The requestor keeps the traveler card until material is needed. It is then sent to the buyer. The buyer immediately has enough information already on the card to place the order. Then the buyer inserts the updated purchase information and the form is returned to the user to keep until the user needs it again. Travelers were originally designed and used for MRO items (maintenance, repair, and operating suppliers) because the system is easy and well-suited for low-cost items that are purchased over and over, but do not require elaborate records, planning, and analysis.

Computer networks can carry the same information as the traveler; both users and buyers can access and store the information that used to be on the hard copy. Using the computer eliminates one of the problems associated with travelers. No record is kept or available when the hard copy is being sent from one person to another. Once in a while the traveler gets misplaced. However, if a computer system is not installed and the operation is relatively small, the traveler method is still a very good way to handle some purchasing needs.

Bills of material constitute the third type of document sometimes used to notify the buyer to purchase goods. Manufacturing companies usually use these to show what material is needed to make a finished product. The listed items may include sub-assemblies or material produced in-house as well as material that must be purchased from outside sources. Some companies prepare a separate list for purchasing only so the buyer does not have to look through more paper work than he or she needs to. Other organizations simply code the items so the buyer will know which items need to be purchased from other companies. Hard copies of bills of material seldom show much more than the quantity needed and a very brief description of the item needed. For example, the description may only amount to a part number. It is then up to the buyer to look up the other required information such as who the suppliers are, what was previously paid, the detailed specifications of the item, or any other information required to make an intelligent purchase.

REQUESTS FOR BIDS

Requests for Bids, often referred to as Requests for Quotes or RFQ's, are used to obtain information about prices or specifications from suppliers. Information needed prior to making a purchase may be obtained simply by making a telephone call, but time saved may be deceptive. Often several calls are needed to reach the person who can supply the information and then they have to gather what you want and call you back. A letter has the advantage of providing a document that may be reread by the supplier; it prevents the omission of some information and later can be referenced. The buyer who is requesting bids from three or more sources would have to repeat or copy the same requested information. This is obviously inefficient. Thus the advantages of a standard RFQ form.

The typical RFQ form provides spaces to insert the supplier's name and address, a description of the product or service you want, and the time the bids must be submitted. Well designed RFQ forms can accommodate three, four, or five suppliers. The number of copies of the form depends on how many suppliers can be inserted in the space provided on the original or top copy. The top copy is kept by the buyer and clearly indicates all the information showing each supplier's name and address. However, each of the copies shows only the name of one supplier, the one to whom it will be sent.The form is designed so that the spaces for the other suppliers are blank. It is not a good idea to tell suppliers whom you are asking to bid. They know who is most competitive and who is not and may tailor their bids accordingly.

PURCHASE ORDER: THE MOST IMPORTANT DOCUMENT

Most public and private organizations use purchase orders to document purchase transactions. There are two major reasons why their use is advantageous for all but the smallest firms. They provide legal protection for the buying organization and they help control administrative matters. They also make purchasing management easier.

Most firms continue to use a hard form, that is, a paper document, although the number of firms converting to electronic forms is increasing every day. The move to electronic forms speeds up transmission of the information and improves clerical efficiency. The purchasing operation has been a paper-intensive function and new ways to minimize the amount of paperwork are welcome.

Traditionally a purchase order form may be a simple one-part piece of paper or a multi-part snap-out form with eight or more copies either separated by carbon sheets or using NCR paper (no carbon required). At a minimum the form contains a heading with the name, address, and telephone number of the buying organization and areas or boxes designated for the insertion of the date of the agreement (see Exhibit 3-2). It must contain the name and address of the supplier, the description of the product being purchased, the quantity, payment terms, and the location where the buyer will take ownership. It should contain the price, the destination for delivery and the scheduled delivery date. There is a space for the buyer's signature authorizing the purchase. The illustrated purchase order in this chapter is typical. As indicated for the requisition, a full-size reprintable hard copy or computer disk containing a P.O. form that may be customized for individual needs is available from the American Purchasing Society.

Copies of the paper form are for the supplier and the buyer. Depending on the buying organization's structure and procedures other copies may be for the accounting department, quality control, and receiving (see Exhibit 3-3). Sometimes a copy is even given to users of the goods, although this is not recommended.

Each well-designed purchase order includes a preprinted consecutive number. Terms and conditions preferable to the buyer are included. Such clauses may be on both the front and reverse side of the form. A column

Exhibit 3-2.
Sample Purchase Order Form

PURCHASE ORDER   P.O. Number _____

Page ____ of ____

(Company Logo if Desired)

Company Name
Street, City, State Zip
Telephone (   ) xxx-xxxx FAX (   ) xxx-xxxx
www.xxxxxxxxxx.xxx

SUPPLIER: Code _____   SHIP TO:

Please furnish items requested below subject to the conditions shown on this form. Ship to the buyer's address at the top unless otherwise stated herein.

| Delivery Requested : | Terms: | F.O.B. | | P.O. Date: |
| Date Promised: | Shipping Point: | | Ship Via: | |

Item	Quantity	Unit of Measure	Description	Price	Extension
				Total	

☐ If box checked items are for resale and exempt from sales tax.   TAX NUMBER: _____

This order expressly limits acceptance to the terms of the order and any additional or different terms proposed by the seller are rejected unless expressly assented to in writing by the buyer. Time is of the essence with this order. If unable to ship as scheduled, advise the buyer immediately to obtain approval of any revised ship date. Any payment discount terms provided herein, shall date from the scheduled delivery date, the date the goods are physically received, or the date of invoice, whichever is later.

Buyer: _____

Approved by: _____

APSPO798

Exhibit 3-3.
Typical Purchase Order Form Flow

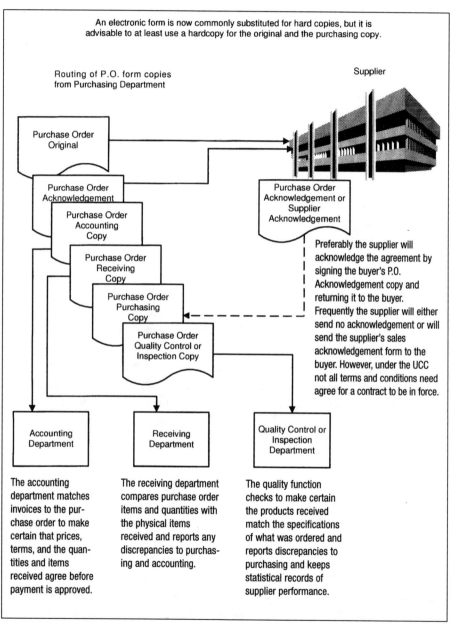

An electronic form is now commonly substituted for hard copies, but it is advisable to at least use a hardcopy for the original and the purchasing copy.

Routing of P.O. form copies from Purchasing Department

Supplier

Purchase Order Original

Purchase Order Acknowledgement

Purchase Order Accounting Copy

Purchase Order Receiving Copy

Purchase Order Purchasing Copy

Purchase Order Quality Control or Inspection Copy

Purchase Order Acknowledgement or Supplier Acknowledgement

Preferably the supplier will acknowledge the agreement by signing the buyer's P.O. Acknowledgement copy and returning it to the buyer. Frequently the supplier will either send no acknowledgement or will send the supplier's sales acknowledgement form to the buyer. However, under the UCC not all terms and conditions need agree for a contract to be in force.

Accounting Department

Receiving Department

Quality Control or Inspection Department

The accounting department matches invoices to the purchase order to make certain that prices, terms, and the quantities and items received agree before payment is approved.

The receiving department compares purchase order items and quantities with the physical items received and reports any discrepancies to purchasing and accounting.

The quality function checks to make certain the products received match the specifications of what was ordered and reports discrepancies to purchasing and keeps statistical records of supplier performance.

is provided to specify units of measure for each item described on the order and a space is allowed at the bottom of the price column for the total value of the order.

PURCHASE ORDER REVISION FORM

Buyers need to revise the orders they place with suppliers. The number of revisions depends on the type of company and how much planning is done by both users and the purchasing operation. Revisions to orders are necessary when a quantity is changed or when the specification is changed. For example, a user may decide to buy blue ink instead of black. Often the time the product is needed is changed, although such a request does not always require paper documentation if the change is minor and the supplier's word has proven to be reliable. Nevertheless, to make changes to any agreement legally enforceable, it is wise to put them in writing.

Many organizations use the normal purchase order form for any revisions rather than a separate one. Forms can be expensive and it is time-consuming to design. When the original purchase order form is used, the word "Revision" is usually typed on the form and there is a clear reference to the original order number. However, the added cost of a separate form is offset by the saving in the time of preparation. When a P.O. form is used in place of a P.O. Revision form, all description, terms and conditions must agree with the original except for any changes needed. P.O. Revision forms reference the original order and indicate all parts of the agreement will remain except for the indicated changes.

RELEASE FORM

Certain types of buying agreements are for multiple shipments over an extended period of time. Some of these agreements do not specify on the purchase order form what quantity to ship at any one time or the dates that shipments should be made. Such long-term agreements are made to obtain a lower price or other favorable aspects of the purchase such as to insure a steady supply. Rather than issue a purchase order when material is needed, the buyer or sometimes a person from other departments issues a form called a release. The release form references the P.O. number and specifies only the quantity and date to ship. No other terms or conditions are included. The price is not a factor because that was previously agreed and documented on the purchase order form.

PRICE HISTORY FORM

Even if you know proper purchasing procedures you are somewhat at a disadvantage when buying a product you never bought before for a new company. There is no price history to check to determine if a new price is reasonable. Companies that fail to maintain price histories of the products they buy have the same disadvantage. Without such information the only way to evaluate a supplier's price is to obtain competitive bids or estimate the labor and material cost of every component of an item. It is not always practical to do so because of time constraints or the complexity of the product.

Price history information may be in various forms. It may be on handwritten cards or in a computer database. Essential information includes a description of the product including a part number, if applicable, the quantity purchased, the date purchased, and the name of the supplier.

OTHER PAPER FORMS

There are various other customized paper forms used by some purchasing operations depending on their unique procedures. Two printed items that may be classified as forms are the "Welcome to Purchasing" brochure and the "Guide for Requestors." The former informs suppliers of the organization's purchasing policies and procedures. The "Guide for Requestors" is given to those employees who request the purchase of goods and services to help all concerned communicate properly. These items will be discussed in detail in Chapter 5.

Other forms also of particular importance to purchasing are either initiated or used by other departments. Inspection Reports and other quality-related reports are examples. Buyers need to know about rejected material to either inform suppliers or to be aware if other departments have informed the suppliers.

The Purchasing Process

PLACING THE ORDER

Except in small companies, the need for material is usually determined outside of the purchasing operation. Purchasing is informed of the need from an engineering function that designs items for manufacturing and resale, or from any department that needs material or services to conduct business. Requests for the purchase of material used in manufacturing often are received from a production control or inventory control department.

Inexperienced and timid buyers accept requisitions and then try to place orders for the material or services without scrutinizing the written request or asking the requestors for clarification. In many cases, the suppliers need missing information or further clarification of what is needed. Consequently, the buyer must then contact the requestors to obtain additional information and contact the supplier a second time to place the order. As the buyer becomes more knowledgeable about the organization's needs and the idiosyncrasies of the users, he or she either knows enough to clarify the requisitions or asks the users for all the required information before contacting the supplier the first time. This improves purchasing efficiency and speeds up the buying process. Perhaps more importantly, it gives the supplier a better image of the buyer's ability and knowledge and therefore improves the results from negotiating efforts.

Initial contacts with suppliers to order material are usually made by telephone, but requests for bids can be made by telephone, FAX, letter, or the Request for Quotation form described previously. In some cases the first notification a supplier gets of an order is receipt of a Purchase Order form.

In any case, when there is a formal purchasing department, purchase orders are almost always issued as confirming documents after the order has been placed orally. Exceptions are often made for very small expenditures, reimbursed out of petty cash, or employee reimbursed travel expenses.

Whether orders are placed by phone, in person, or otherwise, good purchasing requires a discussion with the supplier of terms, conditions, and prices. It is up to the buyer to ask for a better deal than is first offered. Seldom do suppliers voluntarily give their best offer first unless it is requested through the bid process. Even then, the most favorable transactions for the buyer come through negotiating. More on this in Chapter 6.

One of the most important steps in any transaction is to properly document the agreement. Including all facets of the agreement in a written form such as the Purchase Order is essential if enforcement of the agreement becomes necessary. Most transaction terms can be written down quickly and easily, especially if there are standard terms printed on the front or back of the Purchase Order. However, if a purchase involves a complex item or large sums of money, enough time should be taken to make sure the documentation is accurate and complete.

ENSURING SATISFACTORY TRANSACTIONS

Those with little or no knowledge of business purchasing activities may mistakenly believe that once the order is placed the job is all but done. Order placement is only a small fraction of the buyer's job. Good purchasing practice involves many steps before the order is placed, including planning, shopping, specifying, analyzing, and negotiating. After the order is placed the buyer must make sure the goods or services that were ordered are delivered as specified. That means the goods must conform to the description of what was ordered or the service must be performed as requested. The order must be delivered to the proper place and at the proper time.

A great amount of time is spent by the average buyer either making sure that the suppliers perform as agreed, or trying to get them to correct the situation when they have not. The percentage of time spent on these aspects varies from organization to organization, but generally the more time spent on the steps prior to order placement, the less the percentage of time that is required after order placement. In other words, problems with the purchases can be minimized if sufficient effort is given to qualifying the supplier and adequately communicating purchase requirements.

Typical problems after order placements include late deliveries, material received damaged, incorrect material, and incorrect quantities received.*

RECORD AND FILE RETENTION

Keeping adequate purchasing records before the widespread use of computers and database management was very time-intensive. Now nearly every business can afford to maintain historic purchasing files with little effort. Data about transactions can automatically be saved in a database for reporting purposes when the computer generates purchase orders. However, this writer still recommends keeping a hard copy of transaction records, primarily for legal reasons. Copies of purchase orders are necessary to satisfy the requirements of government tax regulations. Copies of bids, supplier specification forms, warranty statements, correspondence, and even supplier sales literature may be needed if any litigation develops.

CANCELING ORDERS

Occasionally all organizations need to cancel purchase orders or other contract forms. The number and frequency of these cancellations depends on the type of buying organizations, the planning that is made prior to the purchase agreement, and the capabilities of the suppliers selected. They may become necessary because the buying organization made an error or because the selling organization failed to perform adequately. Following are some of the reasons for cancellations by the buyer and caused by the buyer's organization.

---

*Fcr a full discussion of follow-up methods, expediting methods, and how to obtain on time deliveries, see *Handbook of Buying and Purchasing Management*, by Hough and Ashley, Chapter 12, "Obtain Delivery When You Want It," published by Prentice Hall, 1992.

Buyer's Responsibility

- Buyer's sales forecast was too high.
- Buyer's customer canceled an order.
- Buyer ordered the wrong material.
- Production schedule was changed.
- Engineering changed specifications.

In practice, most suppliers will accept cancellations of these types without penalty providing they have not invested in order to fill the order and cannot use or dispose of the material or product without taking a loss. For example, if the order was for proprietary material made especially for the buyer, it may not be possible to cancel without paying a price. Orders for standard products available on the supplier's shelf for many customers are normally cancelable without penalty and without argument. However, occasionally a supplier will claim that the order cannot be canceled, or that the buyer must pay a substantial portion of the cost of the item or items. It is doubtful that the seller could obtain such a fee legally unless an actual cost was incurred.

Sometimes a seller will claim goods have already been produced to fill the order or that they have already been shipped. Buyers have successfully challenged such statements by saying they are going to visit the supplier to see the physical products or requesting the names of the carrier and the billing of lading numbers for the shipment. It is only then that the supplier realizes that the goods have not actually been made or the goods have not actually been shipped.

Following are some of the reasons for cancellations made by the buyer but caused by the seller.

Seller's Responsibility

- Seller could not deliver on time.
- Seller could not produce proper quality or meet specifications.
- Seller refused to meet terms of the contract.
- Strike at the seller's location.

It is a different story when the supplier has failed for one reason or another. The buyer can cancel for good cause because the supplier has failed to perform. Nevertheless, reasonableness is called for. It is only prudent to give a supplier the opportunity to correct errors or improve performance before cancellation. The product requirements and any errors or problems should be carefully documented in writing to make sure there is no dispute about what is right or wrong. Make sure discrepancies, errors, or problems are reported to the supplier. Keep a record of what was done to correct the situation and how quickly it was done. Record as many details as possible, including dates, quantities, and description of the errors. Then when you cancel, you can be fairly confident that you will win your case if the supplier decides to take legal action, it is doubtful that the supplier will decide to go to the expense of using a lawyer unless the amount of the canceled order is large.

In most cases suppliers will accept cancellations, especially from a regular customer, because they hope to receive business in the future and they don't want to alienate the buyer or cause any ill will. Even when the cancellation might involve some cost to the seller, it may be accepted without much of a penalty. The supplier may figure that he or she has done a favor for the buyer who will be obligated to return the favor by more business later or by excusing some minor error in the future.

Summary

This chapter discussed how small and large businesses structure their buying activities, from informal operations with no established purchasing department to the formal operations that clearly define buying responsibility. The differences between centralized, decentralized, and modified organizational structures were explained. The importance of establishing a formal system with proper documentation of each purchasing transaction was covered.

Each of the usual forms used by purchasing operations was described and then the normal purchasing process for business was explained. Finally, the reasons for cancellation of orders were discussed as well as when you can and when you can't cancel an order without penalty.

Chapter 4

Keeping Transactions Legal

Understanding Business Law

The good news is that you don't need to know anything about the law to place an order. Anyone can buy products or services in the marketplace without any formal or informal training in law whatsoever. Surprisingly, half of the people who buy for business have never attended any law course or seminar. Most of them don't realize that knowledge of the law has value to any buyer, let alone a buyer for business. Human resource managers and general managers who are responsible for hiring purchasing personnel seldom concern themselves if the applicant has any legal training. They rarely ask if the potential buyer has had even one course in business law.

More good news. You can place thousands of orders and spend millions of dollars without ever encountering a legal problem. Companies can and do exist for decades without any disputes about a purchase contract.

The bad news is that a company can incur serious financial setbacks when its buyers have no knowledge and understanding of the law that applies to purchasing transactions. When a dispute occurs, millions of dollars may be at stake. Although serious disputes are rare in most business circles—considering the number of business transactions—there are still thousands of disagreements that require the services of legal counsel.

Minor disputes are often ignored or buried simply because either the buyer or the company attorney becomes aware that their company's position is too weak to solve the problem to the company's advantage. Lacking knowledge, the buyer may have not documented the transaction properly or may have committed to unfavorable terms or conditions without realizing the consequences.

So although you may obtain a position as a buyer for business without any knowledge of the law, it is to your advantage and that of your employer if you know some fundamental business law. It is to your benefit as well as helpful to the company because you, personally, can be held responsible if you ignore certain principles.

AREAS OF LAW THAT CONCERN PURCHASING

Now let us examine the different areas of the law that may apply to what you do as a buyer and what areas of the law with which you should be concerned. The law can be divided into two broad categories, statute law and case law. Statute law is the law that has been written and passed on or voted on by some legislative body such as the city, county, state, or federal government. Case law is the law that results from the interpretation or ruling of a case or dispute held before a judge.

Case law derives from English common law where the king or other ruler heard each side of an argument and made a decision in favor of one of the parties in the dispute. The next time a similar case was heard, either the judge or one of the parties would use the previous ruling to support their position. Sometimes different rulings were made by different judges or in different locations, and the parties would refer to the rulings that most favored their case. Attorneys today use the same method to support their arguments before the court. Rulings made closer to geographical area and time have greater impact than those that are more remote, but an attorney will use whatever precedents can be found to support his or her case. The body of law created by judicial interpretation is immense and far more problems are resolved using the common law and precedent than by referring to statute law. Knowledge of this principle and the decisions that have been made regarding contracts is of paramount importance for the well-qualified buyer for business (see Exhibit 4-1).

Exhibit 4-1.
The American Legal System and the Basis
of Legal Decisions for Commercial Activities

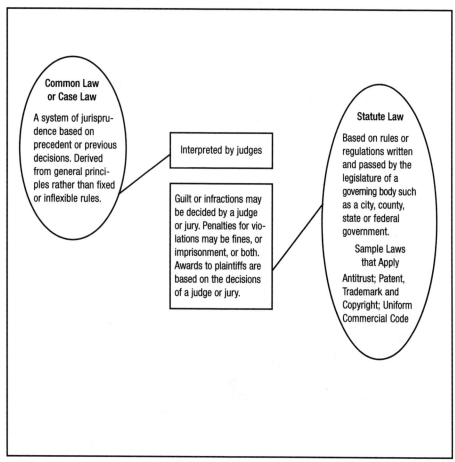

Common Law or Case Law

A system of jurisprudence based on precedent or previous decisions. Derived from general principles rather than fixed or inflexible rules.

Interpreted by judges

Guilt or infractions may be decided by a judge or jury. Penalties for violations may be fines, or imprisonment, or both. Awards to plaintiffs are based on the decisions of a judge or jury.

Statute Law

Based on rules or regulations written and passed by the legislature of a governing body such as a city, county, state or federal government.

Sample Laws that Apply

Antitrust; Patent, Trademark and Copyright; Uniform Commercial Code

Understanding and Making Contracts

WHAT IT TAKES TO MAKE A CONTRACT

If you are a buyer for business, you routinely make contracts. It is a common belief that a contract is a piece of paper with a lot of legal jargon on it. That is not what makes a contract. Every time you place an order, get delivery, and pay for an item, regardless of how small the dollar amount, a contract has been made and concluded. Buyers for business are making contracts all day long, day after day.

What is a contract? What does it take to make one? There are some very basic requirements for a legal contract and only a legal contract can be enforced. Here is what they are:

1. The agreement must involve legal subject matter.
2. Parties to the agreement must be capable.
3. There needs to be an offer.
4. There needs to be an acceptance.
5. There must be consideration.

This means you can't have a valid contract to steal something or be involved in some other illegal act. A capable party can't be insane or intoxicated when they make the agreement. An offer does not have to be in writing. An offer can be accepted in various ways, but it doesn't have to be in writing either. The problem with not getting an offer or acceptance in writing is that if there is a dispute later, the terms and conditions of the offer are very difficult to prove. Nevertheless, just shaking your head at an auction can be interpreted as an acceptance of an offer. If a supplier ships you a product and you keep it and use it, even though you may not have ordered it, your actions can be interpreted as an acceptance of an offer.

Consideration is required to establish a contract. Consideration is the something that is given in return for whatever is obtained. Normally it is the payment in cash or a check or a credit card for the purchased goods or service, but the consideration you give may be in the form of a service or of another product you give to the supplier.

HOW PURCHASING TRADITIONALLY MAKES CONTRACTS

After the buyer negotiates with the seller and all terms and conditions are believed to be settled, the buyer prepares a purchase order form adding any unique clauses that were agreed upon. The description of the product or services required is inserted, indicating the quantities and prices. Once the form is signed, it is then handed to or mailed to the seller. If the seller has previously submitted a bid or other writing, that bid or writing constituted an offer. If the purchase order contains all the terms of the submitted bid or the seller's offer, exactly as written, the purchase order then becomes evidence of the acceptance of the offer. All that is necessary for completion of the contract is delivery of the goods as specified and payment by the buyer's organization.

If, however, the buyer decides to change some of the terms and conditions of the offer and writes the changes on the purchase order, then the purchase order, rather than an acceptance, may be considered a counteroffer which too must have an acceptance in order to form a contract. If the answer to the counteroffer has terms or conditions different from the previous counteroffer, then they become another counteroffer rather than an acceptance, and there is still no contract. This situation can continue until one or the other of the parties either agrees to all terms or conditions or gives up and walks away from further discussion. This is the way all agreements were either made or not made in many states when this writer began his career in purchasing. But today, in the United States, this method applies primarily to transactions for services. Now, in the U.S., transactions for tangible products, referred to as "goods," fall under the provisions of the Universal Commercial Code.

Provisions of the UCC Affecting Purchasing Activities

The Uniform Commercial Code, referred to as the UCC, was the ruling law in some states over two decades ago. Gradually, each state has adopted its provisions, although there are minor variations from state to state. A committee of the American Bar Association recommended the creation of the Code, as lawyers refer to a law, to eliminate the confusion caused by different state laws affecting business transactions or legal interpretations.

The UCC applies to "goods" or tangible products involving a transaction between merchants in the amount of $500 or more in value. Note that it only applies to merchants. You may not be aware that as a buyer for business you are considered a "merchant" or an authorized agent for a merchant in the eyes of the law. It does not apply to sales or purchases made by consumers who are covered by consumer protection laws. Even if you are a buyer for business, no doubt you also buy as a consumer. When you buy for your employer, the UCC may apply. When you buy as a consumer, it does not.

In addition to covering the typical transaction made by business purchasers, the UCC also covers various types of transactions that never involve most buyers. The Code covers approximately one hundred pages of legal language that is sometimes difficult to understand, but the average business buyer need only be concerned with Article 1 and Article 2. Article 1 simply defines terms. Article 2, entitled "Sales," should be read at least once by every business buyer. These two articles amount to only thirty-three pages as reprinted in the appendix. Some of the sections are exceptionally important for purchasing professionals to know. Although the law is always open to interpretation by various jurisdictions and depends on the particular circumstances involved, the following paragraphs describe a few of the things you should remember.

Documenting the Contract in Writing

With certain exceptions a contract for the sale (or purchase) of goods for the price of $500 or more is not enforceable unless there is something written indicating that a contract has been made and signed by the parties to the agreement or by their authorized agents. The written document does not have to be in any particular form. It need not be a purchase order or sales acknowledgment. However, in most business transactions by organizations of more than a few people, either purchase order forms and/or acknowledgment forms are used. But keep in mind this paperwork is not the contract itself, it is only written evidence of the contract and may be the only proof available of what was agreed upon.

If the written documentation of the contract is received within a reasonable time, but does not include all the terms and conditions agreed upon, and the parties to the agreement have reason to know its contents, they must object within 10 days after receipt of the document. For example, if you issue a purchase order for goods at a certain price that you believe was agreed upon by the supplier, who then disagrees with your interpretation of what was said, the supplier has 10 days to voice an objection after receipt of your purchase order document. Or, if the seller gives you a sales order with information that is different from what you thought you agreed to, you also have 10 days to object.

As the authorized buyer, your organization is responsible for goods ordered and manufactured especially for you or for the work that was done in making those goods. If you are going to cancel an order for non-stocked material, do it as quickly as possible before the supplier orders raw material and before any work is performed. Otherwise your company must pay for materials or labor, even though you don't need it, unless the supplier is able and willing to try to sell the goods elsewhere.

The agreement, as evidenced by the signed document such as the purchase order and intended as the complete agreement, does not include terms or conditions of previous agreements or discussions. If a dispute arises and you or the seller remembers a conversation about items not in the written agreement, or even subsequent to the signed agreement, those terms are not part of the contract. Additional terms or conditions may be accepted as part of the contract if they are normal and usual for the particular trade involved, unless the writing shows that it contains the complete and exclusive terms of the agreement. For this reason, many purchase orders now contain a standard preprinted or a customized inserted clause such as: "This order expressly limits acceptance to the terms of the order and any additional or different terms proposed by the seller are rejected unless expressly assented to in writing by the buyer."

A CONTRACT CAN EXIST EVEN IF CERTAIN TERMS ARE MISSING

A contract may be established simply by the conduct of both parties. For example, if a supplier delivers goods and the buyer knowingly accepts and uses the goods, a contract is apparent. There may even be a contract if certain terms are omitted. If both parties agree, there can still be a contract even though no price is mentioned. If that is the case, then the price is a reasonable price at the time of delivery. If the place of delivery is not agreed upon, it is the seller's place of business, or if none, the seller's residence. But if the specific goods at the time of the contract are in some other place that is known to both parties to the agreement, then that place becomes the place of delivery. As the buyer, it is almost always to your advantage to specify the place of delivery. It may also be wise to discuss the mode of transportation that will be used to transport the goods, and possibly the name of the carrier that will be used.

If the time for delivery is not specified in the agreement, then it becomes a reasonable time. Relying on this principle may be troublesome. It is better to obtain a specific delivery date from the supplier even though you may not be happy with how soon you can obtain the material. One way that this writer handles this problem is to indicate to the supplier when you would really like the material, but then establish the agreed date. Show these two dates on the purchase order indicating the first date as the requested date and the second date as the agreed date. The idea is to keep the supplier aware that you are not happy with the agreed date and provide an incentive to ship earlier if possible.

If there is no delivery time mentioned and no indication that the supplier has failed to perform, a reasonable notice must be given to the supplier before canceling the order. An agreement that no notification of cancellation is required may be invalid if it is viewed as being unfair.

All goods that are purchased are for delivery at one time unless otherwise agreed. If the agreement is for partial deliveries then payment may be required for the delivered portion unless otherwise agreed.

Prior to the UCC the offer and acceptance of offers had to match. But under the UCC there may even be additional or different terms unless acceptance is expressly made conditional on agreement to the additional or different terms. The additional terms are to be construed as proposals for additions to the contract and become part of the contract unless the offer is expressly limited to acceptance to the terms of the offer; unless the new terms significantly change the agreement; or unless the new terms were previously objected to or are objected to within a reasonable time after notice of them is received.

Different Types of Warranties

There are different types and uses of warranties, particularly when the UCC applies. A warranty may sometimes be referred to as a guarantee by a layman, but the correct term for assurances about the quality or specifications of a product in business is referred to as a warranty. The UCC includes a warranty that the seller is conveying title to the goods and not subject to a lien or claim by a third party. In other words, the buyer becomes the true and only owner of the goods.

EXPRESS WARRANTIES

The two major types of warranties are express and implied. An express warranty is a statement either oral or in writing that either describes the product, tells what it will do, or gives specific details about it. The statement need not mention the words "warranty" or "guarantee." For example, if the seller says the product will be 134 inches long, an express warranty is made that it will be 134 inches long. If a sample is submitted, there is a warranty that the delivered goods will match the sample. For this reason, it is extremely important that buyers take notes on what is said by the sales people or other representatives of the supplier. Record the dates and who said what.

Likewise, it is important to keep printed product descriptions that appear in brochures or specification sheets. Mark the receipt date on brochures or other sales literature and correspondence, and either attach them to the back of the appropriate purchase order or include them in an appropriate file for the particular purchase order involved. Make a separate file for the supplier if more than one order will be given for the products described.

Samples should be kept in a safe place and tagged or marked so that they can be identified with a particular agreement or purchase order. To make sure that samples are not mixed with stock that will be used up, keep them in a location far removed from regular inventory. If there is a discrepancy with the delivered product and it does not match the sample or what you believe was the sample, you will have no way of proving it if the sample is misplaced or mixed with other goods.

Not all statements by a seller about products offered for sale are express warranties. Those that purport to be fact or that would normally be construed as facts are interpreted as express warranties, but those that are very general or mere opinion are not. A salesperson may claim a product as the best available without making an express warranty. Such statements whether orally given or in writing are considered "puffery." The law expects merchants to brag about their products and perhaps exaggerate their worth.

IMPLIED WARRANTIES

The other type of important warranty is the implied warranty of merchantability. The UCC provides that if you buy goods from a seller that usually deals with a particular type of merchandise, there is an implied warranty that the goods must be of a quality normally acceptable in that type of business, that they are fit for ordinary purposes for which they are normally used. The goods must be within the tolerances or variations permitted by the agreement, must be adequately packaged and labeled as specified by the agreement, and conform to the descriptions on the label (if there is one). Other implied warranties may apply as a result of the way you conduct business with a supplier over time or by the way business is conducted by other suppliers in the same business.

There is an implied warranty that the goods are fit for the purpose intended if the seller knows at the time of the contract the purpose for which the product will be used and the seller knows that you are depending on his skill or judgment to recommend or supply the right product. In such a case you are sometimes better off giving a potential supplier a functional specification so that you can rely on the supplier's judgment to furnish the proper product.

When your engineering department or a requestor from another department gives detailed specifications about a product without mentioning what the product should do, or not do, then the seller may not be responsible if the product does not perform as expected. Of course, if the seller is aware that a buyer's specifications will not do what the buyer wants, the supplier has the responsibility to point out the problems or render an opinion. But if the buyer insists on his own specifications in spite of a supplier's warning, then it is doubtful if there would be any implied warranty.

Suppliers try to escape or limit their obligation to provide warranties by language written on their bid forms, on acknowledgment forms, in brochures, and on product labels. Buyers under pressure to place orders and obtain material to meet schedules may not take the care that they should in reading statements that limit the seller's responsibility. This can be a serious mistake although the UCC tries to protect buyers by not allowing exclusions that are unreasonable. If a seller wishes to exclude the implied warranty of merchantability, the statement must mention merchantability and any writing must be conspicuous.If the seller wishes to exclude the implied warranty of fitness for a particular purpose, then the exclusion must be in writing. Generally, all implied warranties are excluded by expressions like "as is," or "with all faults."

Protection from unreasonable action is a common thread in the law. Contracts that are forced upon a buyer are termed "unconscionable," meaning they are unfair. Such contracts may not be enforceable. Another example of the law's concern for fairness is the disregard by judges and courts of language printed on either buyers' or sellers' forms that is so faint or so tiny that it is all but impossible to read. If you want your purchase order terms to be acceptable, make sure the type can be easily read. However, don't depend on this idea to think you can ignore reading sales forms or contracts written by the seller. You can never be certain how a judge or court will rule. If you have trouble reading faint or fine print, get it enlarged. What may seem to be too small or faint by one judge may be deemed acceptable by another.

The Place and Time Where the Buyer Takes Ownership

Important sections of the UCC define where and when ownership of the goods passes from the seller to the buyer. Normally, unless otherwise agreed, that ownership referred to as the "title of the goods" goes from the seller to the buyer at the point of delivery of the goods. This is the case even though the title document is not delivered at that time and even though payment for the goods may not have been made, and the seller may still have a security interest in the goods.

The usual place of delivery for most business transactions is indicated by the use of what is called the F.O.B. term. While there are other terms and abbreviations, by far F.O.B. is used more than any other. The initials F.O.B. stand for FREE ON BOARD and are accompanied by a named location such as: "delivered," "Detroit," "shipping point," or any other named place. A typical use would be "F.O.B. Delivered" where the delivery point is indicated in the agreement or on the purchase order form. Most purchase order forms used have a space or box especially used for the F.O.B. term.

If you learn nothing else after reading this book, understand the meaning and use of the F.O.B. term. It is continually misunderstood in spite of the efforts of educators. Knowing what it means and using it properly clearly separates the competent professional buyer or purchasing manager from others.

Somehow the initials have been misconstrued to mean "freight on board." This is probably because the F.O.B. point determines who normally pays for transportation of the goods unless there are words that indicate otherwise. The reason for this is clear. If the F.O.B. point is where title to the goods passes from seller to buyer, why should the other party pay for transportation of the goods that they do not own? For example, assume you, the buyer, are in Chicago and the seller is in Detroit. The supplier ships from Detroit and the term is F.O.B. Seller's Plant. Then you, the buyer, become owner in Detroit even though you are physically in Chicago. You are responsible for payment of any freight charges and responsible to buy insurance if it is desired; there are no agreements for the seller to buy such insurance. If the agreement stated "F.O.B. Chicago," the seller would be responsible for charges for delivery and insurance, if any, to someplace in Chicago. Obviously it would be better to specify the delivery point you want.

Another term used when shipment involves water transportation, primarily ocean shipping, is "F.A.S." which means FREE ALONGSIDE; in other words, alongside the ship or vessel. However, F.O.B. is still often used if transportation over land is also involved.

Less frequently used are the terms "C.I.F." and "C.& F."; "C.I.F." meaning cost, insurance, and freight, and cost and freight respectively. These terms mean that the price includes the cost of the goods, the insurance, and the freight.

Agency: Who Has the Authority to Buy or Sell?

The portion of the law concerned with authority of buyers or sellers is called the Law of Agency. It establishes the rules regarding how a person becomes either a buying or selling agent. It also deals with the general rules regarding an agent's authority and responsibility as well as that of the principal. The principal is the organization hiring or assigning duties to the agent. Some new buyers are concerned about what they have authority to do and their level of responsibility. They should be! Seldom do organizations spell out the details. Much is assumed by the boss as well as the new employee when a person is hired for a position in purchasing. This writer and others who work in purchasing based their authority limitations to some degree on what was previously done by their predecessors. Some of us simply took as much authority as we could until someone said we should obtain approval for that amount of expenditure or for those items. But experience has taught us that if you don't get something in writing detailing your authority limitations, you should write it yourself and send it to your boss for approval. Keep a copy of the memo in case you never get a written response.

There are different types of agents. A special agent may be given authority to conduct only one transaction, while a general agent has authority to handle many transactions. A universal agent handles various types of duties for the principal. Buyers are normally considered general purchasing agents.

Obligations of the Agent and the Principal

There is often confusion over the term "purchasing agent" because it can have two different meanings. The first meaning is the legal one, and it means a person who has the authority to buy for someone else or for some organization. The second meaning refers to the title of an employee. Confusion arises because people with various titles may still be purchasing agents. For example, the V.P. of Purchasing, the Purchasing Manager, and those with the title of Buyer are all purchasing agents as well.

In the not-too-distant past, most purchasing department heads had the title of Purchasing Agent, but because of both the expanded responsibility of supervision and planning and to avoid confusion, most companies now use the title of Purchasing Manager. Formerly, in many cases, the person with the title of Purchasing Agent was the only person authorized to sign orders. In most companies this is no longer true.

A purchasing agent, regardless of title, is responsible to look after the principal's interest. The agent is not permitted to use the position to promote personal interest. Any money or property collected for the principal must be kept safe and turned over to the principal promptly.

The principal also has obligations. Contracts made or transactions conducted by the purchasing agent must be honored by the principal. In other words, when an authorized buyer purchases goods that conform to the contract, the organization must pay for those goods in accordance with the terms of the agreement. The principal has the duty to pay the purchasing agent for services provided.

The principal has the obligation to defend the purchasing agent providing the business was conducted legally and did not exceed authority limitations. As you can see, it is therefore important to ascertain what those limitations reasonably are in the event that there is any legal action against you.

WHAT A SALES AGENT IS

The law of agency also applies to sellers. A salesperson only has as much authority as his boss, the principal, has delegated. The buyer should ascertain if the salesperson has the authority to negotiate and agree to all the terms and conditions that the buyer wants or to change prices or terms. If not, that person is simply a messenger relaying the buyer's offers to a superior and then coming back with answers or counter proposals. While this may be one way to negotiate and could be a part of a strategy, you should know up front if you are dealing with someone who can make decisions. You may not want to waste time on someone who has no authority to make a commitment or to change a supplier's so-called standard sales agreement. You may want to insist on only talking to someone who can make such decisions.

Antitrust and Unfair Trade Practices by Buyer or Seller

Unfair dealings can be perpetrated by either buyer or seller and are often considered illegal under U.S. antitrust laws. While the buyer's chances of being accused or indicted for violation of these laws is small unless you work for a large company, every buyer should be aware of the implications of antitrust. The reason is that not only do you want to avoid breaking the law, you can also be a victim of violations. If you break antitrust or fair-trade laws, you can be indicted and if found guilty may even be imprisoned. Conversely, if your company, through you as the buyer, is a victim of violations, your company can bring charges against the guilty seller and be compensated for resulting losses.

It is beyond the scope of this book to go into many details about the laws, but the Sherman Act, the Clayton Act, and the Robinson-Patman Amendment are the major laws that constitute antitrust legislation. Basically, they make it illegal to enter into agreements that restrict competition, or to conspire to restrict competition by price fixing. It is illegal to have tie-in agreements that require the buyer to buy certain items in order to purchase other items. It is illegal to demand a price concession or more favorable terms than other buyers receive in the same market. A producing supplier who can affect the competition must offer the same prices and terms to all buyers in a particular market. That is why a supplier may ask you to divulge the price or terms you receive and, if you do so, will match those terms and price. The law allows this. However, if a supplier matches a lower price, then that same price must be offered to other customers.

Realize that the buyer is not required to disclose any prices or terms that are received from another supplier. But beware, never tell a supplier that you are receiving a lower price or better terms if it is not true. If you are challenged in court and unable to prove you told the truth, you would be in violation of antitrust.

Reciprocity is illegal. That is, a buyer cannot offer to purchase from a seller if the seller buys the buyer's products. When I was a buyer, I had several executives ask me to buy from certain suppliers because they were good customers. In one case, the instruction was only to buy if the customer was competitive. Suppliers who try to pressure customers by promising to buy the customer's products usually have inflated prices or poor quality.

An analysis and comparison of the offer with those of other suppliers often indicate that the cost of changing sources or awarding business in this fashion usually exceeds any profit that is obtained from the sales to the source. This makes the argument against breaking the law doubly powerful.

Patent Infringement or Unauthorized Use of Trademarks

A patent is issued by a government to allow the patent holder a monopoly to make, sell, or use a product or to license another party to make, sell or use a product. A trademark or servicemark is issued by the government to allow the holder exclusive use of a design or certain words on products or advertising. Various governmental bodies including the states, the federal government, and foreign countries have their own rules and regulations for issuing patents and trademarks. Patent and trademark holders may register their products or designs in one or more jurisdictions. For example, a manufacturer may hold a U.S. patent but it may not apply in Canada or Japan. The buyer must be concerned with buying products that infringe on a patent because such products may be confiscated by the government, and the buyer may not recoup any money paid for the product. In addition fines are possible for infringing on patent rights or by inappropriately using marks or words that are protected.

HOW A BUYER CAN INNOCENTLY VIOLATE PATENT RIGHTS

You might be surprised to learn you are guilty of infringement even though you only purchased the goods and were not personally involved in the manufacture of the product. But that doesn't matter. If you buy or use a product that is protected by a patent, it is a violation if the use was unauthorized. The manufacturer may have either wittingly or unwittingly infringed. At the discretion of the patent holder, the manufacturer may have to surrender to the patent holder all revenue earned from the sale of the product in addition to the value of any inventory, or obtain the return of all product sold and destroy all inventory. As a purchaser of the product you may have to either surrender or destroy the product.

OTHER INFRINGEMENTS

It is easy to place an order innocently for printing or packaging and then find that another supplier wants to be paid for the work in addition to the one to whom you gave the order. This might happen if a previous order was placed for a package with a design made by the supplier. That supplier can easily claim a right to compensation on any future order for the same thing based on his creation of the design. The way around this is to make sure you have a clause in any orders involving a design that either states you are the creator and owner of the design or that the work is given out for hire. A "work for hire" clause means that the supplier only produces the item but retains no ownership of the design.

Legal Differences in International Trade

Today more and more supplies are being purchased from international sources. Even if you don't get involved in buying from overseas right away, sooner or later you probably will. Although some aspects are the same, many are different. One that may not always be obvious is the law. Law in the U.S. is based on English law; law in other countries may be based on French law, or a system that is totally different. There may be different and unique rules that you must obey when dealing with foreign countries.

You can't expect to get the same treatment in obtaining compensation when you are wronged. If your operations are primarily in the U.S. and you must resort to a lawyer to get help, the attorney in the U.S. will need to work with a lawyer who is licensed or permitted to practice law in the foreign country. Therefore it will take more time and expense to settle a foreign problem than to settle any domestic problem.

You can't make assumptions about international contracts that you can in the U.S. You should be cautious when dealing with foreign sources. You should check out suppliers more carefully than you would in the U.S. simply because it will be harder to resolve problems.

The High Risk of Consequential Damages

A term that appears in most standard sales agreements excludes the seller from consequential damages even though the supplier will warranty the product. The cost of consequential damages may far exceed the product cost. Consequential damages are those that result from failure of the product to be delivered or to perform as expected. For example, when a product fails it can cause a fire that destroys a building; a part of a machine may break off, fly through the air and put someone's eye out or kill someone. The resulting lawsuit could cost millions of dollars. The broken part could be a bolt that costs only a few cents.

While it is important for the buyer to be aware of the potential problem with this exclusion clause, often there is little the buyer can do. The seller will seldom want to take the risk of being responsible for consequential damages. Nevertheless, attempt to get this clause removed or at least modified if it is in the contract. You are probably better off not to mention it, if it is not already in the agreement.

Other Statutes Affecting Purchasing Operations

Although there are not many statutes that affect a buyer's activities, there are a few that should be learned. The buyer should understand the general regulations regarding sales and use taxes applicable to his or her geographical area. In most states sales taxes are not applicable to raw material used in the manufacture of products for resale. Sometimes a supplier sends an invoice that includes the sales tax even though the item should not be taxed. It is up to the buyer to be alert to this possibility and inform the accounts payable department both to deduct inappropriate sales taxes and inform the supplier to issue a correcting invoice.

The buyer should understand the implications of the federal occupational and safety requirements of OSHA. If the buyer's company is a contractor or sub-contractor for the government, it is particularly important to abide by the federal equal opportunity laws by making sure that the suppliers who are selected also follow the government's guidelines.

Ways to Avoid Legal Problems

Knowing some law helps the buyer avoid legal problems. Attending a seminar in the law that pertains to purchasing is recommended, but keep in mind that this does not make you an expert. Talk to your company attorney if you anticipate a problem. It is better to get advice before you get in trouble. If a problem develops that you are not certain how to handle, your company attorney can often minimize the damage or eliminate any harm altogether. In most cases you will not need counsel if you operate with the guidelines on the list shown.

USE THESE TEN PRACTICES TO AVOID LEGAL PROBLEMS

1. Keep good written records. Document what is said by salespeople as well as what you, the buyer, say. Make sure the records are dated and contain the correct full names of people involved in conversations as well as where the conversations took place. Keep all correspondence in files that are cross-referenced by subject and date.

2. Keep sales literature in an organized manner so that it can be retrieved easily if and when necessary.

3. Clearly identify supplier samples when an order is placed for that material and store and protect the sample for retrieval if and when necessary.

4. Make sure that only those properly authorized within your organization order material or services. If an unauthorized individual places an order, notify the supplier immediately and instruct the individual to work through the proper channels. Instruct the supplier not to accept orders from anyone other than an authorized buyer.

5. Read all terms and conditions on sales proposals and sales acknowledgment forms. Delete or amend unacceptable terms or conditions before signing. Instruct non-authorized, non-purchasing personnel never to sign sales proposals or acknowledgment forms.

6. Notify suppliers of rejected material promptly.

7. Notify suppliers of cancellations in writing.

8. For purchases involving large dollar commitments, obtain references and financial statements from potential suppliers and evaluate the information before using the supplier.

9. Carefully document ownership of any tooling or inventory held or used by the supplier. When purchasing any material requiring tooling such as plates for printing, dies for packaging, molds for plastic or metal parts, or any other items, make sure that ownership is clarified. Make sure such tooling is returned to the buyer if the supplier is changed.

10. Keep good records of purchased raw material or inventory material held by the supplier.

Compensation for Supplier Failure

The simplest buyer's remedy when a supplier fails to deliver on time or delivers unacceptable goods is to cancel the order and obtain the goods elsewhere. However, both timeliness and acceptability of goods are subject to interpretation. If the goods are one or two days later than the scheduled delivery date, they could still be considered on time unless the contract specified that time was "of the essence" and it was clear that the goods had to arrive on or before a particular date.

Specifications indicating the requirement for acceptable goods must be clear. If the goods do not meet the precise specifications, it is easy to reject them. Nevertheless, the supplier may want to replace the unacceptable goods with better quality goods that are acceptable. Normally, this should be allowed if the other terms of the agreement can be met, such as the required delivery date.

Once in a while a supplier will try to change the terms of the agreement at the last minute by raising the price or changing the product. This is a breach of the original agreement and the buyer has the right to "cover" if the supplier refuses to honor the original agreement. This means that the buyer may purchase goods from another source and obtain any difference in price from the original supplier. In practice, you are not likely to enforce payment from the supplier for a small difference. If it is a major contract, it may be well worth while to do so.

Summary

This chapter explained why it is important for business buyers to know the law that affects purchasing transactions. It covered the elements of a contract and indicated that all purchases involve some type of contract, written or otherwise. It discussed the Uniform Commercial Code and its importance. It described the types of warranties. It described the most common business terms. The law concerning agents was covered including the rights and responsibilities of business buyers and principals.

There was a discussion of antitrust and unfair trade practices. The importance of buyer awareness of patents was covered. The differences in the law regarding international transactions were mentioned. A warning about consequential damages was given. Awareness of various laws and knowledge of the tax implications on purchases was discussed. Finally, suggestions were made on how to avoid legal problems involving purchasing operations.

Chapter 5

Buying for a New or Small Company

Establishing Priorities and Implementing Purchasing

Unless they are given very specific instructions, inexperienced buyers and purchasing managers may well wonder where to begin when they are thrust into a new position in a purchasing department. Seldom are specific instructions given. More likely the new employees are given a desk and told to begin work.

How well organized the department is when they assume their new duties determines how soon they will begin receiving requests for materials or services. Sooner or later requestors will start submitting their requirements. Often, the new employee gets a stack of requisitions within a short time.

It is important for the new buyer or manager to learn the way things were done before his or her arrival. If someone had been doing the buying there may be a very good system, or a poor one, or there may be little evidence of any organized system. The new person must try to find out how transactions were made to avoid conflicts with personnel from other departments, to avoid conflicts with suppliers, and to determine what changes, if any, might eventually be necessary.

The surest way to get off on the wrong foot is to get into arguments with personnel from other departments. Changes to the old way of doing things should be made cautiously, unless top management has mandated drastic and immediate improvements and gives full support and authority for such changes.

These words of caution are not to imply that you should not develop a better system. They are simply warnings to make sure that any changes will not conflict with other policies and procedures within the organization.

Obtaining Needed Materials and Service Is the First Priority

A primary responsibility is to obtain required material and services. That cannot be neglected. You must see that orders are placed quickly enough to obtain the material when needed. If it is determined that the requestors are not allowing enough time to do so, that problem must be addressed quickly. There are various solutions. Some are short-term; others have more permanent results. In the short term, it may be necessary to add to inventory, work overtime, or hire help. The long-term solution requires a thorough investigation into the causes of the problem, which may be poor sales forecasting, poor scheduling, poor stock handling, poor inventory control, or other failures in the system.

Beginning Cost-Cutting Efforts

After obtaining material and services to fill requestors' needs, the next major objective of the purchasing function is to reduce costs. Again the question is the same: Where to begin?

Some suppliers will help, especially if they are nervous or uncertain about their competitive position in the marketplace. A supplier may voluntarily offer a price reduction rather than let a new buyer discover that they have been overcharging. While this appears to be a good thing and the new buyer usually earns credit for such price reductions, be careful not to make any long-term commitments in return for the reduction unless you know the market or until you see if the new offer is worth accepting on a long-term basis. There may be much better opportunities with other suppliers.

More likely, suppliers will wait for the buyer to initiate a request for lower prices. Some suppliers might even test a new buyer by raising prices. The increases may be justified if the supplier has not had any increase for an extended period. A former buyer, planning to leave the organization, may have managed to maintain the price level or postpone any increases until leaving. Don't stand still for these increases. Notify the suppliers that you want to sit down and discuss the situation in detail. Schedule a meeting as far in the future as they will accept to give yourself time to gather your ammunition. If they insist that the increase is necessary and they don't want to discuss it, tell them you will be shopping and going out for competitive quotes. Ask them to hold off for ninety days or the end of the year or whatever other time period you can negotiate. There may be nothing you can do for the moment if they refuse, but they will have been put on notice that you are not going to accept every price increase without doing anything. Unless the amount of business that they receive from you is insignificant, they will probably think twice about making the next request.

One excuse a supplier may give for requesting an exorbitant increase is that prices had remained constant for several years or more in spite of inflation and high added costs that were absorbed. The logic of this argument is suspect and might be countered by pointing out that if the supplier asked for no increase for such a long time, then the price must have been too high when established and profit must have been excessive for a long time.

Concentrating Efforts on Big-Dollar Items

Novice buyers may spend too much time trying to negotiate on every item regardless of its cost or the volume that is purchased. If an item only costs twenty-five cents and you are able to reduce the price by half, you have made a 50% saving. But if only a hundred pieces are purchased, the total saving amounts to $12.50. Take another item that costs $10 and ten thousand pieces are purchased annually. Let us say that, in spite of all your best negotiating efforts, you can only reduce the cost to $9.90 or by merely one percent. Nevertheless, you have still saved $1000. The point is that you only have so much time available; spend it where you can obtain the best results. Incidentally, it has been said that a new buyer should be able to reduce the total cost under his or her responsibility by 10% or more. Note that a reduction may not be possible on every item, but an average 10% reduction is not unusual. That means that on some items the percentage reduction will be much greater and on some there may even be cost increases. This writer's experience corroborates that. And keep in mind, we are talking about cost reductions, not simply price cuts.

If you are going to concentrate your efforts on the big-dollar items, you first must determine what those big-dollar items are. Note that they are not necessarily the high-priced items. If an item has sufficient volume it can fall into this category even if the unit price is a fraction of a cent.

There are several ways to learn what the largest expenditures are. A good computer-based purchasing system will automatically tell you. You get a print-out of total annual expenditures by item or item category or by supplier in descending dollar value. All of these reports will be helpful. If the organization does not have purchasing computerized or the system will not generate such reports, you may be able to obtain the same information from a computer-generated report of accounts payable records. More than likely the data will not be available for each item, but will only show what was spent with each supplier. This will usually narrow down the data because the suppliers with the largest dollar volume often only supply a small number of different items.

Another possibility is getting the information from an inventory control department. In this case the data will more than likely be available by item, but no information will be available on expenditures by supplier. Since inventory control is usually more concerned with quantities available for production if the organization is a manufacturer or available for users in other types of organizations, the item data may not have prices assigned, but rather quantities only. However, it should be relatively easy to assign prices to the high-usage items in order to get the amount spent on those items for the year.

Concentrating Efforts on Major Suppliers

When you obtain a report of dollar expenditures by supplier you have a ready tool to negotiate where it counts the most. Obtaining an across-the-board price reduction from a major supplier has a tremendous effect on your company's profits. Even a small percentage reduction can produce enormous benefits.

Requesting a price reduction on all items purchased from a particular supplier is only the reverse of the common practice of suppliers asking for a certain percentage increase on all items purchased. Although the buyer should vehemently object to that approach by suppliers and insist on details of cost changes by item, there's nothing lost by trying for a blanket reduction. If successful, you have saved much time discussing each item and analyzing the costs from suppliers and bids from other suppliers. There are at least seven reasons why a supplier might be willing to grant a blanket decrease:

1. Economic conditions may have significantly changed since the individual prices were established;

2. Technological advancements or new equipment may have reduced the supplier's costs;

3. New competition may have entered the market place forcing the supplier to accept a lower profit margin to retain the business;

4. The supplier may have changed its costing system and profits are much higher than originally thought;

5. The supplier may have new general management with a different, more competitive pricing policy to prevent other suppliers from obtaining its business;

6. The supplier might wish to obtain a larger percentage of your business;

7. The supplier might be aware of alternative products that threaten its business and its management hopes to make it less attractive to switch to another type of product.

Time permitting, it may be better to look at all the items supplied by the major supplier. By look at, I mean determine the amount spent annually on each item by multiplying the quantity purchased for a year by the price. This will give the necessary data to estimate the potential cost reduction on each item and to compare it with any across-the-board decrease. A significant price concession on one or two high-volume items may amount to more than a small percentage decrease on all items or the reverse may be true. Incidentally, the buyer may find it important to discuss potential cost reductions with the buyer's own sales management or other members of management. Reductions for some items may be more desirable than for others. For example, reducing the price of a particular item may help increase sales and profits significantly, while a reduction on other items may be of little consequence. Buyers have worked hard to obtain a price reduction of a particular product only to find that the company no longer intended to buy that product.

Asking for Concessions and Being Prepared to Compromise

A good buyer always attempts to obtain the most favorable transaction whether buying a new product or one that was previously purchased. However, when you are starting out, you usually don't have the time to obtain the best products or the lowest cost every time. You have to settle for a reasonable effort while you are working on the major items. Your objective will be to eventually establish long-term agreements and blanket orders so that a low cost and good terms and conditions are established ahead of time for repetitive orders.

Every supplier and every product has some weaknesses. Try to discover them and let the supplier know you are willing to make a purchase in return for something in particular that you would like. You may want a discount for early payment. You may ask for a lower price. You may want to receive the material sooner than usual. Some buyers ask for an extended warranty. Others want a trial supply of an item. You decide what is important for your organization. But be prepared to compromise and to give something in return.

Qualifying New Suppliers

To assure that you will receive the goods or services you want, you must qualify every supplier. How and to what degree you do this depends on the type of product, the amount of the expected expenditure, and whether you foresee a continual need for the product.

Even when you are able to obtain a very low price from a new supplier or you calculate a low cost considering other factors in addition to the price, you have no certainty that the supplier will deliver the quality you want. Unless you investigate a supplier's capability, you have no way of knowing if the supplier will deliver the product or service on schedule. Unless you check the supplier's reputation, there is no evidence that the supplier will provide service when you need it. Without checking financial strength there is no way of knowing if the supplier will still be in business to supply repair parts when they are required.

If there is little risk of damage if improper quality is received, only a minor inconvenience if delivery is not made on time, and the unlikelihood that any repair items will be needed, an investigation of the supplier may be more costly than it is worth. This is especially true if the item will not be repeatedly purchased. Conversely, the more important it is to obtain precise specifications and on-time delivery, the wiser it is to check the supplier's ability to produce. The higher the cost of the item, the more important it is to make sure the supplier will be there to deliver repair parts or services when they are needed.

Conducting the Investigation of Suppliers

Ask the supplier for customer references. Most suppliers are happy to give you the company names, addresses, and telephone numbers of what they believe are satisfied customers. For less important purchases a couple of names should suffice. For others, you may want to get three or more. If the supplier also gives you the names of individuals within the companies, try to obtain their titles as well so you can assess the responses you will receive. A quality control manager may have a different opinion of the supplier than a purchasing agent or a manufacturing manager. Remember that once you have the name of the customer company, you can contact various employees within that company to gather different types of information about the supplier. That does not mean they will always be willing to provide information. They may simply refer you to the person who has the authority to respond.

Keep in mind that the supplier will be inclined to give you the names of individuals that are likely to give a good reference in addition to companies that will respond favorably. However, that does not mean that you won't get honest answers to your questions or that you won't get negative comments if you ask the right questions.

Make a list of the questions that you want to ask before you contact the reference. Try to ask open-ended questions that require more than a yes-or-no answer. If a reference seems to avoid answering your question or is vague with the answer, rephrase the question. Be suspicious if the vagueness continues about a particular aspect of the supplier's performance. Most people dislike giving negative information unless the performance was extremely poor.

Establishing Objectives by Understanding the Business

If you are in a high tech business, quality is very important. If the business is to provide products to consumers at the lowest possible price, then the price you pay for products must also be very low. If the business is involved in providing quick service such as overnight or same-day delivery, then it is essential that you obtain needed goods quickly. Price, quality, and on-time delivery are important for all purchases, but you may have to sacrifice the maximum good of one of these variables to obtain satisfaction in one of the others. Some suppliers specialize in quick delivery, but they want high prices in return for this service. If you must use short lead times, then you may end up paying more. You need not immediately divulge your highest priority when negotiating with the supplier, but stay aware of your objective when you make your supplier selection. For example, less quality at less cost may be a better buy if necessary to get quicker delivery or to conserve cash for other needed material.

Finding the Appropriate Source

First, use the suppliers who have been doing business with your company first. Get to know their capabilities and their strengths and weaknesses before you give business to new sources of supply. Learn what your company needs in terms of quality, delivery, and cost. Learn about the products your company sells and about the products that are purchased. Take your time in looking for new suppliers if your internal requestors are satisfied with the status quo. In any case don't be pressured into making a quick move to an untested supplier.

Eventually, there will be a time to try a new supplier. In many, if not most cases, they will come to you. Nevertheless, there is always a need to locate suppliers for products never purchased before or to replace or supplement existing suppliers. Usually, it is easy to find the suppliers who make a particular product by using directories such as the telephone Yellow Pages, the Thomas Register of Manufacturers, MacRAE'S Blue Book, or any of the other supplier directories that specialize in particular industries. To find a source in these books is simply a matter of defining the product category where those suppliers are listed.

To find less common items, ask existing suppliers of related items. Industry associations sometimes print listings of suppliers and will assist buyers in locating them. Attending trade shows and reading industry magazines sometimes provide clues to help you find a source. Many commercial departments of foreign consulates maintain lists of suppliers eager to export their products to the U.S. The largest countries have consulate offices in major U.S. cities; all have offices in Washington, D.C.

Qualifying Suppliers in Other Ways

Locating suppliers, investigating their reputation with customers, and checking their financial stability may not be enough for some buyers' requirements. A physical inspection of a supplier's facilities can reveal problems that can be discovered no other way. For example, suppose the supplier's major customer is the buyer's major competitor. A physical inspection might disclose the competitor's products in process or cartons addressed to the competitor. The buyer might not want his product information available to the competitor, a risk which giving orders to that supplier might involve.

Different Types of Suppliers

Using the right type of supplier is important to obtain the best product or service you need at the lowest cost. Suppliers differ in their financial resources, the kinds of equipment they have to produce products, and in the capabilities of their personnel. One supplier may produce a product cheaply because of loose tolerances and low-cost material. If that product serves your purposes, it is simply a waste of money to buy a better-made product from another source that costs more.

A small company will not have the proper equipment to produce high volumes but their prices on low quantities will tend to be lower because the equipment they use is less expensive. In addition, their facilities may be less costly and their wage rate may be lower than that of large companies. On the other hand, if you need a high volume the large company may sell the product at a lower price because they use machines that can produce it faster and perhaps with less labor.

If you try to order low volumes from a high-volume producer, your order may be either refused altogether, or there may be a minimum charge, or the price may be much higher than what you could obtain from a smaller company.

Another way companies differ is in their structure or type of ownership. Proprietorships or partnerships tend to be small. Corporations may be either small or very large. Large corporations can have an interest in a small company; that interest may not be apparent, or it may be promoted to give the buyer the impression that he or she is dealing with a well-qualified organization. This impression can be deceiving and if there is a problem the parent organization may ignore any request by the buyer for help in solving it. Subsidiaries and divisions of large corporations often operate almost independently except for financial reporting.

Experience has shown that you get more attention and better service when dealing with a small organization unless your purchase volumes are relatively high. When you are dealing with a small company, you may be dealing with the owner, president, or vice president of sales. Again, unless your volume is very large, when your business is placed with a big company, you normally deal with the lowest sales level. The person may be an order taker, or an entry-level salesperson. Owners and executives usually are more concerned about satisfying their customers and providing good service. Obviously there are exceptions, but generally buyers do better when transacting business with management level people.

Finding the Right Type of Supplier

Use the telephone book, supplier directories, and the Internet to learn which suppliers sell the product you want. Narrow down the selection by asking for a description of each supplier's facilities and basic financial information. Approximate annual sales volume is the best indicator of size and is usually given without argument. Companies with less than five to twenty million in sales are small. Some would even say that anything less than a one hundred million in sales is small. To supplement this information ask the number of employees. Fewer than a thousand employees is probably small for a manufacturing organization, although these figures vary depending on the industry. Companies listed on any exchange tend to be medium to large. Most companies listed on the New York Stock Exchange are large. Obtaining an annual report and visiting a supplier's operations is the best way of evaluating a company's size.

Making the Initial Contact

Initial discussions with a supplier may be made by using a Request for Quotation form, by telephone to the sales department, by letter, by FAX, or by using the Internet. If the amount of your anticipated purchase is large, either for a one-time buy or over an extended period of time, contact the sales manager or vice president of sales or marketing. This is better than talking to just anyone who happens to answer the phone. Sometimes, if you only indicate that you are interested in talking to someone in sales or that you want to discuss a possible order, a secretary or telephone operator will ask where you are located so they can then transfer your call to the sales representative in that area. It might be OK to talk to such a person if you only want preliminary information, but it may be difficult to work past that person later when you want to talk to management about large volume business.

Establishing Close Relationships

Some suppliers welcome any buyer who represents the opportunity for new business, but others are restrained until they get to know you and learn how you do business. Suppliers may be cautious with new buyers because they don't know if you are sincere about giving them orders or if you are just looking for information that can be used to negotiate with their competitors. They are cautious because they don't know if they can believe your predictions about how much business potential you have to offer. They are cautious until they know your company's creditworthiness. Once they get to know you and your company better, they are more likely to be more open and more likely to present attractive offers.

In recent years, purchasing management has embraced the concept of "supplier partnerships." This means working closely with a supplier to achieve common goals that benefit both buyer and seller. It normally involves teams of employees from both organizations communicating needs and information. The selling organization is supposed to honestly reveal all its plans and costs as well as the buying organization. Then both sides sit down and determine how they can work together and compromise so that everybody gains. This concept, like so many other techniques, works and is helpful in certain circumstances, but it doesn't apply to every purchasing transaction. It probably won't succeed when buyer and seller are unfamiliar with each other. It is first necessary to get to know your supplier. This is particularly true when dealing in international trade. With Far Eastern suppliers, in Japan for instance, it is often difficult to get information and get a good agreement before the supplier gets to know you well.

This is the reason for a few minutes of non-business conversation before a sales presentation. It breaks the ice. It creates a more congenial atmosphere in which to conduct business. As long as the conversation steers away from controversial or confidential topics, a few minutes on personal information or common interest is routine and helpful. Improving relationships is also one of the reasons for so-called "business entertainment." It can go too far and it is unethical and often even illegal to accept gifts and lavish entertainment from a supplier, but that is not the same as having a lunch or dinner together. To avoid any appearance of impropriety, the buyer should pay or at least reciprocate. For a further discussion of this topic see "How Close Is Too Close?" in Appendix I.

Obtaining Financing or Credit

Obtaining credit for purchases is not of much concern to buyers for large- or medium-sized companies. The people in the finance departments of those businesses obtain loans when necessary or arrange financing in various other ways. The buyers place the orders and the bills get paid, for most part, on time without the buyer ever even hearing about it. The only exception is when a bill is overlooked or the company has serious financial difficulties.

This is not the case with small organizations. Not only are buyers asked for credit references, they sometimes approve bills for payment after it is certain deliveries have been made and the goods are satisfactory. Approval by purchasing personnel is not good accounting control and most companies make sure that invoice checking and payment is handled by accounting as soon as there are enough people to handle the work. When purchasing personnel check invoices they are diverted from their other normal duties, and effective purchasing activities are sacrificed.

The normal or minimum usual business terms are "Net 30," but small companies may have to pay cash upon delivery (C.O.D) or pay in advance or provide a substantial deposit unless adequate credit references can be given to the supplier. Once good credit is established and there is a good relationship between the buying and selling companies, it may even be possible to improve upon the Net 30 term. A discount may be offered by the supplier if paid within ten days. For example, "1% 10, Net 30" is a common term that means the buying company is entitled to a one-percent reduction in the invoice if paid within ten days, but after that time the full amount of the invoice must be paid and the total is due in thirty days. The discount amount and the number of days are negotiable contrary to what the seller or the seller's accounting department might have you believe.

One way the buyer can get credit that may take the place of a bank loan is by negotiating extended payment terms. It is not unusual for buyers to negotiate Net 60 or Net 90. Even if the buyer's company has the cash and could pay earlier, using extended payment terms is equivalent to a price reduction. The average cash on hand is increased and can be used for other purposes in the business or invested to earn interest.

If necessary, when first starting a business or first doing business with a new supplier, pay net or in advance, but gradually improve upon the terms. Increase the order size in return for longer terms or a payment discount. Offer an annual commitment or a commitment to buy a certain percentage of your requirements in return for longer terms. Make sure the supplier does not report longer terms as late payments when answering credit bureaus or bank references.

Another way a small company or new corporation can get credit is for the owner or owners to personally guarantee payment by co-signing the purchase agreement. Banks require this when making a loan to a small business, particularly where one person or family holds all the common stock.

A buyer can obtain credit and a lower price for a higher volume of goods by getting the supplier to produce enough stock for a longer period of time but only invoice for the amount actually shipped or used. In return, the seller may want a letter of intent or contract for the full amount. With this arrangement, without receiving an invoice for the full amount, and assuming the order is cancelable, it may be possible to exclude the purchase from the buying company's financial statements. This would allow for increased credit elsewhere. However, if the full amount of the order is non-cancelable, potential lenders may require reporting of any outstanding orders.

Leasing is a good way to obtain much needed capital equipment when cash or other financing is unavailable or difficult to obtain. There are various types of leases that give greater or fewer benefits to the buyer. Companies selling the capital equipment may either handle the lease themselves or go through financial institutions with which they have made arrangements. The buyer or business manager should evaluate carefully the cost of obtaining the lease through the capital equipment seller or through lease companies that they contact on their own. Sometimes it is less costly to go through the supplier. At other times it is less expensive to obtain your own lease.

What is referred to as a purchase lease allows the company to own the product at the end of the lease upon payment of a small percentage, compared with the full purchase price. Some leases only require 10% or less of the original price. Others require the depreciated market value at the expiration of the lease.

In addition to being able to acquire goods without full payment, leases are used for tax purposes. You can avoid the need to dispose of obsolete equipment, and thus alter the appearance of financial statements.

Obtaining a loan from a bank for the purchase of products or inventory usually requires more paperwork, but it is the frequent choice of all types of business. Rates for loans vary widely so it is wise to shop around. It is much easier to obtain loans for tangible goods and property than for marketing or operating expenses unless other tangible assets are available as collateral. The banks are able to recoup some of their investment by taking possession of those assets if the company fails to pay back the loan.

One way many new and small businesses obtain financing is by using consumer credit cards. Consumer credit is relatively easy to obtain because the interest rates are high. The amount of interest may not be significant if the business can pay off the balances quickly, but keep in mind that the individual holding the card is responsible for the full amount due.

Another type of credit card is now being marketed to business. These cards issued by Visa, MasterCard, and American Express—and supported by many banks throughout the U.S.—are offered to minimize the paperwork connected with traditional purchasing activities, particularly for M.R.O. items. The cards are usually issued to employees who would otherwise be asking the purchasing department to make the purchase. The cards can only be used with sellers who are authorized to accept the cards and those sellers pay a percentage of the purchase price to the card companies. Consequently, the price must be inflated to compensate the seller for this additional cost.

The card companies claim that this added cost is more than offset by a reduction in labor cost from the purchasing operation. I believe those purchasing costs could be reduced by internal efficiencies and improved methods without the need to pay higher prices for the goods obtained by the use of credit cards. But using the purchasing cards might provide a temporary credit source for companies in need.

Finding Enough Time

It is important to establish priorities by using the methods described earlier because there is a limited amount of time available in any company to make purchases. This is particularly true in a small- to medium-sized company. Using wisely the time available for purchasing is essential in order to obtain good results in terms of cost and service. Here are some ways to save time.

- *Develop and use a "Welcome to Purchasing" brochure.* This type of brochure describes what the buying company does or the products that it sells. It lists the names and titles of the buyers and other purchasing personnel. It indicates what products each buyer handles. Most important, it includes various purchasing policies and procedures. It is advantageous to prepare and use such a publication so that every potential supplier can read it and know what the ground rules are. It saves repeating all of the information to each new supplier or forgetting to tell new suppliers about certain policies. If properly prepared, it may help eliminate the need to talk to some salespeople who may not know what the company does and have no product that would be of interest to the company.

- *Develop and issue a "Requestor's Guide."* This type of brochure provides instructions to employee requestors. It tells them how to prepare a request and what should and should not be included. It eliminates many questions and telephone calls from requestors and reduces the amount of time needed for clarification (although no system will entirely eliminate this).

- *Use blanket order.* A blanket order for one or more products needed over time eliminates the need to negotiate and prepare a new agreement every time a new quantity of the same item is needed. For example, assume you need ten cases of paper towels every two months. Without a blanket order you might call for prices and negotiate a purchase six times during the year. By placing a blanket order you negotiate for sixty cases and prepare one order for that amount and indicate on that order that ten cases are to be shipped on a specified date every two months. Negotiating time is saved, order preparation time is saved, and filing time is saved. Incidentally, you would probably get a better price also because of the larger quantity, and you may be able to lock in a lower price in a rising market.

- *Use the Traveler System.* The requestor indicates a new amount needed and due date using a card or computer-generated record of each order. The same form includes the price history and supplier information as well as all previous quantities purchased so the buyer doesn't have to look up the information every time the same product is needed. The information card is returned to the requestor or stored in the computer for use the next time needed.

- *Use a "Systems Contract."* A systems contract is basically an extension of the blanket order idea. The difference is a selection of a limited number of suppliers for certain product categories chosen by the bid process. It is made on the basis of those suppliers having a total low cost for many items and the assurance that those items will be in stock when needed by the buying company. For example, there might be one supplier for all stationery supplies, another for all plumbing supplies, and another for all electrical supplies used by the buyer. One contract with one supplier may cover hundreds or even thousands of items needed during a year or more. Such a system can eliminate the need for hundreds or thousands of purchase orders and the clerical work connected with them.

- *Use well-designed forms to save time.* Proper spacing with requested or supplied information in the proper sequence and corresponding to other forms reduces eye movement and reduces fatigue. A sufficient number of copies of each form, but no more than necessary, eliminates redundancy and saves filing time. Combining form purposes while striving for clarity and efficiency will save time.

- *Use well-designed computer screens and databases to reduce processing time.* Minimizing the number of screens required for frequently needed information can save an enormous amount of time. Recent studies have shown that updated faster hardware and software save far more in a year than the required additional investment.

Summary

Various aspects of buying for a small company were discussed in this chapter along with how to set priorities for purchasing operations. Immediate attention must be given to obtaining needed material and services before attempting to reduce long-term costs. Then concentrate cost-cutting efforts on the high-dollar items and the major suppliers. Ask suppliers for lower cost, but be ready to compromise. Qualify new suppliers by investigating their reputation, financial condition, and capabilities. Establish objectives to achieve better results.

It is important to recognize the differences between different types of suppliers so that those selected will be appropriate for the planned purchase. Small suppliers are often better suited for low quantities than large suppliers because they may have lower cost equipment and offer lower prices. It may be better to use large suppliers when high volumes are needed because they have larger machines that can reduce labor cost.

Initially, suppliers may be contacted at any level but it is important to talk to sales managers or executives to obtain the best terms and conditions. So-called supplier partnerships can be established to maximize the benefits of purchases for both buyer and seller, but such partnerships are more successful after dealing with a supplier for a period of time. International suppliers want to get to know you before they will give you the best offer.

New or small companies can obtain credit or financing by negotiating longer payment terms and by using credit cards. Leasing is also a way to conserve cash. Finance leases allow the buyer to purchase the goods at the end of the lease period for the depreciated value or the market value. Leases can often be obtained directly through the supplier of capital equipment or through other financial institutions.

Buyers can make efficient use of time by using "Welcome to Purchasing" brochures for suppliers and "Requestor's Guides" for users. Well-designed forms, blanket orders, systems contracts, and travelers are helpful in giving buyers more time to meet with suppliers and negotiate better purchasing agreements.

Chapter 6

Obtaining the Best Possible Agreement

Communicating and Selling the Seller

Buyers in purchasing departments of all but the smallest of companies are requested to make purchases by other employees in their organizations. They are told what to buy either in general or very specific terms. It is up to those buyers to find the proper supplier and obtain the goods, which can range from simply placing the order to analyzing bids and conducting lengthy negotiations with the supplier.

This description is slightly different for buyers in retail organizations. Those buyers decide what items they should purchase and those decisions are based on what they believe the retail customer will buy. Thus, they are merchandisers in addition to being buyers. But buyers for manufacturing companies may also buy goods for resale in addition to buying material going into the manufacture of products.

The type of buyer doesn't really matter. In fact, the person may be a buyer of businesses or real estate. All buyers, and sellers too, must communicate clearly in order to get what they what. Then they must convince the other party to revise their opinions or objectives to help reach agreement. They do this by convincing the other party that there is more to gain by accepting the offer than by walking away from any agreement whatsoever. This chapter will discuss the way buyers do this.

Using the RFQ System

Most businesses at one time or another ask suppliers to submit bids. A bid or quotation is simply an offer to sell a product or service. It includes a description of the product that may be general and brief or it may involve many pages providing great detail. The bid usually includes prices or price formulas and payment terms. There may be many other terms included to protect the seller's interests.

Governments (local, state, and federal) traditionally use bids to obtain competitive offers. The "request for bid" or "request for quotation" may be oral or written in a letter or, more commonly, on a form called a Request for Quotation (RFQ). Many businesses, especially those in manufacturing and of a larger size, routinely send out RFQs for the same item periodically. The items selected are those that are purchased repeatedly over an extended period. The objective is to determine if the current supplier is still competitive in the marketplace and to negotiate a possible lower cost.

Other items that may only be purchased once in a very long time, if ever again, ideally suited for the RFQ system, are capital equipment or construction work. Some companies go even further and obtain competitive bids on almost everything they buy.

DIFFERENT PURPOSES OF OBTAINING BIDS

Bids are not only used to compare prices and costs, but also to compare products offered by different suppliers. Buyers use the Request for Quotation method to obtain more information about what is available or what a product will do. The information supplied by a half-dozen different suppliers may be evaluated and then a specification or description of what seems the most appropriate is used to obtain a price based on those specifications.

In some instances, most suppliers will be able to provide the desired specification or a suitable substitute. In other cases, only a few suppliers, or even just one, will be able to come up with the specifications desired. The buyer should try to provide specifications that allow more than one supplier to be competitive; otherwise, the buyer's negotiating position becomes weak. To do this, a range of tolerances should be provided rather than narrowly defined specific data that only one supplier can produce. Although the other suppliers may have the technical ability to produce to the desired specification, it may require an investment in tooling that they may not be willing to make. Buyers should be aware of this problem and work with any engineering or production departments who may be unduly influenced by either supplier advertising or by suppliers' salespeople to ask for restrictive specifications.

It is a courteous and good business practice to let suppliers know if an RFQ is for information only or if an imminent purchase is the purpose of the request. The request may only be to help establish what is really needed and to compare approximate costs of one type of product with another. Requests may also be made for planning and budgetary purposes, but the costs cannot always be relied on for six months or a year. Nor should they be. Not only do costs go up; they may also come down, and it is a foolish buyer who will pay a higher price for a product simply because that was the price used to make the budget.

There are two possible ways of handling submitted bids if the purpose of the RFQ is to obtain a price for a prompt purchase. Perhaps the most common (and some believe the most ethical) way is to accept the lowest bid without any further negotiations. The second way is to negotiate with the lowest bidder to obtain an even more favorable agreement. Some buyers will even pick several of the low bidders, especially if their bids were very close.

Keep in mind that price is not the only determining factor in making sourcing decisions and some of the other factors, unfortunately, are somewhat subjective. For example, suppose the lowest bidder's references were good, but not as good as the second lowest bidder. If the obvious cost factors are the only criteria, then the lowest bidder should receive the business. But there is also a hidden cost factor called risk. The buyer may justify going with a slightly higher price in order to avoid any risk of problems or product failure.

There are two opinions on the ways to handle either of these methods. One says that you should tell the suppliers which method is being used. The other says only the winners need to know. Those of the former opinion print a statement on the RFQ form that says, "Your first bid is your final bid." This means there is no opportunity to discuss or revise the bid. The other prints a statement that says, "All bids received are subject to further negotiation."

The theory behind the "first bid, final bid" idea is that a supplier will keep the price as low as possible and the terms as favorable as possible because he knows he will not get another chance. Thus the buyer will save time and be reasonably certain that the costs are near bottom. Those with this idea criticize the method that says all bids are subject to negotiation by pointing out that a supplier who knows that he may have to negotiate is not going to offer the lowest price immediately. They say he will include a little cushion to offer during negotiations.

Those who favor negotiating bids counter by indicating that if the bids are not sufficiently low, the supplier may not be included in any negotiation.

INFORMAL REQUESTS MAY DO THE JOB

It is not always necessary to use RFQ forms to get information. Simply telephoning suppliers and asking for catalogs, brochures, or data sheets is often sufficient. Depending on the product, some suppliers will provide samples, trial products or demos. All of these may help to establish what you want to buy, but be careful. Acceptance of samples or demos may be interpreted as a commitment even if you don't intend it as such. Serious argument or even legal actions can result. Make sure that you read anything carefully before signing for a product. It is probably better to pay for samples, or write a purchase order that indicates you are paying for rental or use for a limited time, not for purchase. Make sure the amount you are paying is clearly specified. Remember that few things in this world are free. Usually, offers of free samples or demos are given to make you feel morally obligated. What is worse, you may run into a seller who intends to make you legally obligated as well.

CAREFUL PREPARATION OF FORMAL RFQS

If you really know what you want, you can prepare an RFQ with all the details that the supplier needs to make a proper bid. Attached blue prints, engineering drawings, sketches, or other written specifications should be referenced on the front of the RFQ form. Make sure you indicate drawing number, drawing dates, revision numbers, and revision dates. Otherwise, you may receive a bid based on the wrong version or engineering level. If you don't have the engineering specifications, but you really know what you want the product to do, you can write a functional specification. In other words, describe in as much detail as you can what you want the product to accomplish.

Whether you use a letter, or a standard or customized bid request form does not matter as long as all the necessary information is included. What is important is a specific date when you want a reply. Usually such a date is given as a deadline and it is normally interpreted as such even if you don't call it that.

Make sure you allow enough time for the supplier to get the answer to you before the deadline. If what you are asking for is a stock item or a standard item, chances are prices are available and the supplier will be able to answer quickly. However, if what you are requesting must be manufactured to non-standard or custom specifications, then it can take considerably longer. If the supplier must obtain raw material that is not in stock or that has not been purchased recently—if ever—then he must contact his suppliers to obtain a current price of raw material needed for his product. If there are many components and many labor steps involved in what you are asking for, it may take a considerable length of time to develop a cost. The person who estimates the cost may need to have it checked and approved by several people before submitting a bid. Simple price quotations, especially for standard or shelf products, may be received within minutes; complex bids may require weeks or even months to prepare. The point is, you must be realistic in establishing a deadline if you really expect a valid answer.

What if You Don't Receive an Answer to an RFQ?

There are various reasons why you may not receive a response to either a request for information or a price. You may not have given the supplier sufficient time to prepare the request. To get an idea of approximately how long it should take, contact a few suppliers by telephone and ask how long it normally takes to prepare a response to an RFQ. The amount of time will differ by the type of product as well as from supplier to supplier. A supplier simply may not be interested in your business for one reason or another. For example, a supplier may be "at capacity," unable to produce any more product to meet the customer's needs. That doesn't mean that he or she may not be interested in your business in the future. Usually, good sales departments realize this and will return your request marked NO BID, but others will simply not respond. Possibly, you may have chosen suppliers that don't produce the type of product you want. Again, some may answer and tell you this, but others will simply not reply.

Still another reason, and perhaps a more critical one, is that the supplier believes that you are just "fishing" for information and there is no real opportunity for business. The supplier who believes you are just using the information to negotiate with another regular supplier is not going to give you ammunition to help you. In some cases, a supplier will submit a ridiculously low bid and risk taking a loss just to test you to see if you are really interested in using its services. If it gets the business then it may try to jack up the price or recoup any loss through future business with you.

If you send out six requests and receive five bids, you probably don't have to think you did something wrong, although it might still be helpful to call the supplier who did not bid to find out the reason. However, you definitely should call if you send out six and only receive one reply. You simply want to know the reason. It may be you didn't allow enough time. Or you may have picked the wrong type of suppliers. In the worst case, it would be because the suppliers thought there was no chance for the business.

If you picked the wrong type of suppliers, a telephone call may be all that is needed to get a suggestion of one or more suppliers who deal in that type of merchandise.

Writing clearly and with enough detail helps establish good communications with the supplier from the start of the buyer-seller relationship. It is essential to do so as discussions progress in order to obtain the maximum result from negotiating efforts.

One more word about RFQs. Inevitably you will find a supplier that calls with various excuses to ask for an extension of time beyond the deadline, even though you are sure you allowed enough time and all the other suppliers responded within the allotted time. You have several choices when this happens. The simplest, most common, and most ethical thing to do is to say sorry, better luck next time. Another method that some buyers use is to allow the supplier a specified amount of extra time, but then notify all the other bidders that the time limit has been extended, and they are free to submit a revised bid until the new deadline.

How to Analyze the Bids

There is a tendency to quickly look at the prices on the bids received and make hasty decisions about which suppliers are competitive and which are not. But what the competent buyer should do is compare total costs, not prices. This is easier said than done, because total costs are seldom revealed on the submitted bids which usually show prices only. They may show component prices and even total prices for all components. They may break down labor and material and show totals for each. They may even show separate prices for setups and tooling. All of this information is valuable and the more detail that you receive the better. Suppliers should be encouraged, if not required, to submit such detail. Even so, the information is still basically price information rather than cost information.

To convert price information to cost information requires evaluating all the elements of costs. Some of those elements are represented by price information on the bid, some are not. For instance, suppose you are buying a printer for a personal computer. Assume the price of two different printers is the same, but one prints eight pages per minute, whereas the other prints six. Obviously, if everything else is equal, the eight-page-per-minute item is a better buy. Seldom is everything else equal and seldom is it easy to see the differences. The buyer's job is to sort out those differences and evaluate them. This example illustrates the differences in costs associated with different product specifications. However, even if the buyer is providing the specifications for the product, it cannot be assumed that product specifications from different suppliers will be exactly the same. (See Exhibit 6-1.)

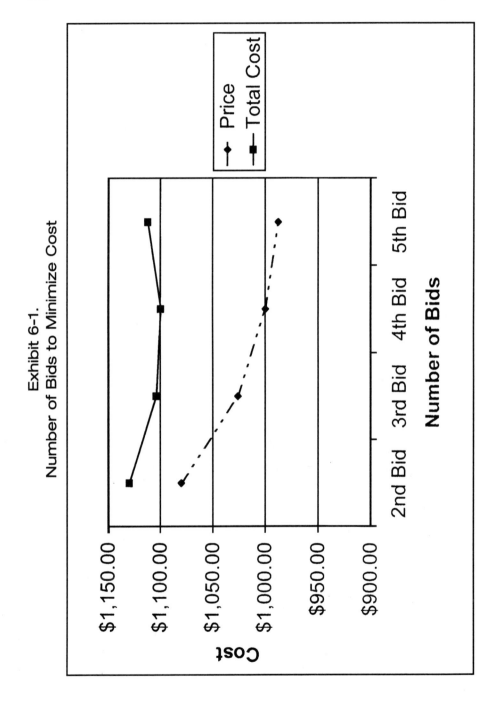

Exhibit 6-1.
Number of Bids to Minimize Cost

Bargaining With a New Supplier

It is not uncommon to have no previous contact with a supplier before sending a request for quote or receiving a bid. If the anticipated value of the purchase is fairly high, many buyers prefer to get to know the supplier before asking for a bid. They become acquainted in various ways. They may look at brochures or catalogs received in the mail. They may interview salespeople who make a "cold call" or they may call the supplier and ask to speak to a sales representative. Interviews may be conducted on the telephone or in person. A buyer may make a request to Dun and Bradstreet or other financial reporting services for information about a particular supplier.

Cold calls are made by salespeople who stop to see the buyer without being asked or even without obtaining a prior appointment. Most buyers discourage such calls as an interruption to their work and many refuse to see salespeople without an appointment. Exceptions are made by some if time is available, or if the supplier is from out-of-town or from a distant location. Buyers often learn about interesting and valuable products if they are receptive to these unplanned meetings.

The stage for future business is often established at these initial meetings. First impressions by buyer or seller can be lasting impressions. Personal physical appearances and office and other facility surroundings, as well as the conversation, affect the image that the seller takes away. For example, if a salesperson observes that the facilities are clean and neat, the conclusion may be that quality products are important. If papers are piled up everywhere without apparent organization, the opposite conclusion may be made. Courteous treatment of the salesperson will be remembered as well as rude behavior. Too many buyers discount this important stage of the negotiating process.

Gathering Preliminary Supplier Information Quickly

The initial interview with a sales representative is the time to weed out quickly most unqualified suppliers. There are salespeople who will try to sell their products to companies that haven't the remotest possible use for the products. Such salespeople are simply wasting the buyer's time as well as their own. The first thing the buyer should do to prevent this is to get some general idea what product is being sold and to quickly dismiss the salesperson if the product has no possible use or advantage to the organization. This writer even experienced a salesperson trying to sell us a product similar to a better product that we manufactured at less cost.

Sellers give you calling cards with their name, title, company name, address, telephone, and FAX number. The information on these cards can be entered into a database file in the computer, or entered on a Rolodex or other manual record, or simply inserted in a case or book available from any stationery supply store. Many such cards are collected over a relatively short period of time, therefore some thought going into the method of storage is worth the effort. You'll save time in the long run. The best methods will allow insertion of new cards in some order without having to re-sort all the cards. The computer provides the advantage of being able to sort or index by salesperson's name, company name, and product offered.

The salesperson gives the buyer brochures and catalogs with descriptions both of the supplier and of the products being offered. The size, the amount of information, and the attractiveness of the brochures and catalogs vary from the sparse and inadequate to the immense and superfluous. Nearly all the so-called selling literature contains overblown exaggerations of the merits of the products or services provided. The buyer should be very careful in accepting statements of alleged facts in these writings. Look for specification sheets and compare the information with your needs or the competition rather than the general sales text produced by sales and marketing professionals. The engineering specifications are normally a better indication of what the product will do. However, even this data may be exaggerated, misleading, or simply in error. Check it out if much depends on its accuracy. If the product may be purchased, make certain that any brochures containing statements of alleged facts are kept on file for future reference and use in case of product failure.

It is always a good idea to find out how long the firm has been in business. Although new suppliers have innovative products and may offer lower prices to become established, there is much greater risk that they will not survive. Most business failures occur within the first few years.

There is no need to obtain much additional information about the supplier if any anticipated purchases are of little value or if the buyer feels there is no likelihood that any purchase will be made from the supplier. This is especially true if the supplier is a distributor or a middleman of a product or service that can be obtained from many sources.

Obtaining In-depth Supplier Information

One method used to obtain supplier information quickly and with little expense is to ask salespeople who wish to do business with your company to fill out your Supplier Information Forms (see Exhibit 6-2). Although the forms should be carefully reviewed by the buyer for completeness and accuracy, you can save a lot of time by asking for all of the information during the interview. However, having a printed form improves the chances of getting all the information wanted. It acts as a checklist and having the supplier write the information helps ensure the facts will not be exaggerated.

Salespeople may not be able to answer all of the questions, especially about financial capabilities. In those cases, they should be instructed to take the forms back to their office to obtain the information from management.

Information requested should include the legal name of the organization, the addresses of its facilities, telephone and FAX numbers, and Web and e-mail addresses, if any. Whether the organization is a proprietorship, a partnership, or a corporation should be indicated. If it is a corporation, the supplier should state if the stock is privately held or publicly traded.

The year the business was started is important as well as the names and titles of management and officers and where they are located. If it is a large company with many branches, it will probably be a stock-exchange listed public company. In such cases, an annual report should be available that lists the names of the officers. That should suffice, along with the names of the key local or divisional management.

Exhibit 6-2.

SUPPLIER INFORMATION AND QUALIFICATION FORM

FULL SUPPLIER COMPANY NAME

OFFICE ADDRESS   CITY   STATE   ZIP

TELEPHONE   FAX   E-MAIL

WEB SITE ADDRESS

SHIPPING LOCATION OR LOCATIONS

SALES CONTACT

SALES MANAGER

TOP SALE OR MARKETING NAME AND TITLE

PRESIDENT OR TOP LOCAL MANAGER NAME AND TITLE

NAME AND LOCATION OF PARENT COMPANY

☐ PROPRIETORSHIP   ☐ PARTNERSHIP   ☐ CORPORATION

TYPE ORGANIZATION

YEARS IN BUSINESS

ANNUAL SALES VOLUME FOR PAST THREE YEARS

ATTACH THREE CUSTOMER REFERENCES INCLUDING COMPANIES, ADDRESSES, PHONE NUMBERS, AND CONTACTS

ATTACH THREE CREDIT REFERENCES INCLUDING COMPANIES, ADDRESSES, PHONE NUMBERS, AND CONTACTS

NAME OF BANK REFERENCE WITH CONTACT AND PHONE NUMBER

GENERAL DESCRIPTION OF PRODUCTS OR SERVICES OFFERED FOR SALE

Please continue answering questions on back.

American Purchasing Society Form 060198A

Exhibit 6-2. *cont'd*

SUPPLIER INFORMATION AND QUALIFICATION FORM

Continued from front.

GENERAL DESCRIPTION OF FACILITIES

DESCRIPTION OF EQUIPMENT

PLEASE SUBMIT CURRENT ANNUAL REPORT IF A PUBLIC COMPANY OR IF NOT, CURRENT FINANCIAL STATEMENTS

PLEASE SIGN AND PRINT NAME NEXT TO SIGNATURE   DATE

THANK YOU FOR YOUR INTEREST IN DOING BUSINESS WITH US

THE SPACE BELOW IS RESERVED FOR BUYER'S USE

BUYER'S OR PURCHASING MANAGER'S ANALYSIS AND COMMENTS

PRICE/COST

DELIVERY

QUALITY/SPECIFICATIONS

STABILITY/FINANCIAL

BUYER/ANALYST   DATE

American Purchasing Society Form 060198A

Descriptions of the products offered and physical facilities are important. The type of equipment available helps the buyer determine if the supplier is capable of producing what is needed.

A separate sheet may be appropriate for various references including bank and customer names and addresses. Financial information, capabilities, quality, customer satisfaction should be checked with these references by phone or mail. Many organizations are reluctant to put anything in writing so a telephone call is usually more likely to get the information you need. If the reference check is done this way, the buyer should make sure the information is carefully recorded and becomes part of the supplier file.

Checking financial information is important to ascertain the stability of the organization. While the number of years in business is a helpful indicator that the organization will be around, many old companies do go out of business, sometimes without warning. Obtaining an annual report of a publicly traded company makes it easy to check its liquidity by comparing the cash on hand with accounts payable. You can immediately see if the company is profitable.

For other companies, a bank reference will usually tell you the approximate balance in the checking account. For example, the bank might say balances average in the high five figures or low six figures. Another source of information is Dun and Bradstreet, a financial reporting organization. You must pay a fee to obtain a D & B report, but it will show you if the company has been paying its bills on time. Incidentally, it is a good idea to obtain an annual financial report on a public company and/or a D & B report on any company periodically if you continue to do business with a firm over an extended period. Conditions change, and a review of these reports will help avoid stockouts because a company closes its doors unexpectedly.

INSPECTION OF FACILITIES

A physical inspection can be done by the authorized buyer or by people from various other departments within the buyer's organization, such as quality, engineering, plant operations, or any other department. It is nevertheless much preferred that the buyer tour the supplier's facilities to get direct knowledge of the many facets of the supplier's operation. Sometimes a team made up of representatives of several departments visit initially. Subsequent visits are often needed to check material being made or to solve particular problems with the supplier.

During these visits, the buyer should meet with and talk with the supplier's production, quality, and accounting personnel, and general management, in addition to any sales or marketing people involved. Record the names and titles of these individuals so that they may be contacted later as needed. Future discussions with them will be easier and more productive if you can remind them of your previous meeting.

Pay attention to what equipment is available. This will help determine what the supplier can produce and how quickly it can be produced. What equipment is being used? This will give you an idea of how busy the supplier is and if the supplier has idle capacity. The supplier is more likely to offer better terms and conditions if added sales are needed and can be absorbed easily.

A supplier that has all equipment in use and is working three shifts must either accept orders for future delivery or re-schedule another customer's order. A supplier who chooses the latter option may do so because your business is more profitable and you are being charged a higher price. If the supplier is willing to do this for you, he may be willing to do it for someone else to the detriment of your order.

Make sure you ask to see what type of equipment is used to measure quality. Manufacturing organizations should have various measuring devices including gauges, calipers, Rockwell Hardness Testers, Brinell Testers, microscopes, X-Ray machines, and spectrographic equipment. Laboratories are often present to analyze chemicals, raw materials, and finished products. Much production machinery now includes features that measure the products as they are produced and automatically rejects unsatisfactory pieces, sending them to one side.

Negotiating Method

PLANNING AHEAD

It is far better to plan any negotiation than go in cold and hope to achieve whatever you can. Planning involves knowing the supplier and the supplier's competitors, knowing the industry and knowing the state of the economy. "Knowing the supplier" means being familiar with what type of facilities it has, its history and reputation, and the individuals with whom you will be negotiating. When you plan a negotiation you need to evaluate costs and establish the targets that you want to achieve (see Exhibit 6-3). You should list the items that you must have and list separately concessions you might make as well as the minimum that you would be willing to accept. Your targets could include the price, payment terms, F.O.B. point, type of packaging, delivery date, warranty, and details about service and service parts after delivery.

Plan where the negotiating meeting will take place— your office, the supplier's office, or a neutral site. Each has advantages and disadvantages. When the meeting is in your office you have all your data available and you can call in other employees to answer questions or give assistance. But you may be interrupted by your boss or others who need your input. However, you may plan to be interrupted and this is easier when its your office.

When the meeting is at the supplier's office you can leave any time you are ready. An important disadvantage is the time required and the expense of travel, especially when more than one person is needed or the site is in a foreign country.

Timing the sessions is important if pricing of products is seasonal or if the economy is a factor. Some negotiators deliberately plan meetings late on Friday or on the week-end when most people are anxious to be home. They do this hoping the other side will give in on more than they otherwise would.

Who will make up the negotiating team is a very important consideration. You want people that are capable, knowledgeable, and will not speak out of turn. The negotiator may only be the buyer or any number of people from other departments may participate. Team buying is a popular technique today, but it is not always appropriate. A one-on-one session will often produce better results more quickly. Teams may prolong the negotiations, can be expensive, but often can be carefully coached to produce good results. While they are expensive in the use of time, they are commonly used and very helpful in complex and major transactions.

Who will negotiate for the supplier is just as important as who will be there for the buying organization, if not more so. Usually, it is best to

Exhibit 6-3.
Action Plans for Different Types of Negotiations

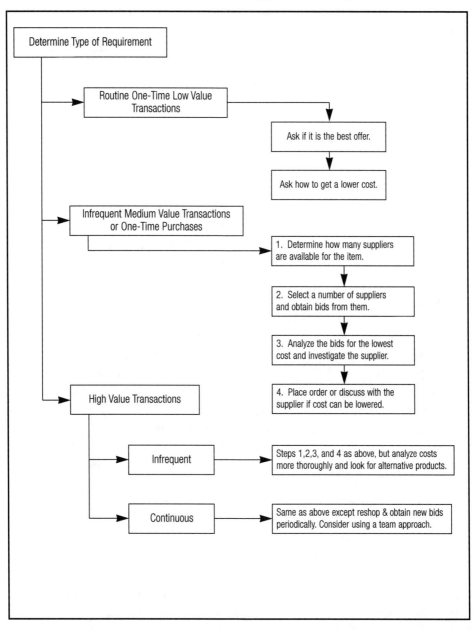

make sure that whoever attends will have the authority to make concessions, set price, etc. Otherwise any effort by the buyer will be a waste of time. The only exception is when your strategy is to send a message back to those in authority.

You must rehearse regardless of the size of your team. Make sure each person knows what to say and what not to say. An ill-timed or inappropriate bit of information can destroy the chance of obtaining any major concessions.

CONDUCT AT THE MEETING

It is tempting for a buyer to spell out a list of demands at the beginning of a negotiation meeting. But listen to anything the salespeople have to say first; otherwise you may be demanding something that they already were willing to offer up front. Silence and listening carefully are powerful negotiating tools. Too often buyers talk too much and too soon. Even when no one is speaking and the room is quiet, it is often beneficial to just wait. It is difficult for most people to tolerate this total silence very long, and salespeople will often break the quiet by offering a little more.

One of the best tools during any negotiation is the use of questions which have two purposes: giving information as well as getting it. For example, if you say, "Do you know your competitors have lower prices than you do?" you are really giving information by telling the supplier that you are knowledgeable about the competition.

Another valuable tool is the observation of body language. Someone who avoids looking you in the eye may not be trustworthy. When a person's eyes blink at a rapid rate you might be hearing a lie. Many mannerisms and gestures can be interpreted to provide clues to the negotiator's true feelings. See the bibliography for books that cover this topic.

Pay attention to the meaning behind commonly-used words and phrases. If a salesperson says, "Believe me. . . . ," you may have reason to doubt him. When people ". . . doth protest too much . . ." we recognize that they are probably guilty. You may well be suspicious when a salesperson modifies his or her speech with words such as "truly" and "honestly." Beware of proposals that begin with, "You can trust me."

DIFFERENT STYLES OF NEGOTIATING

Some modern observers of negotiating methods recommend the "Win-Win" style which differs from the old belief that one party must gain at the expense of the other. Proponents of the "Win-Win" style claim the older method didn't achieve the most for either party in the long run. The stronger party tended to win more in the short run and the weaker party lost more. In the end, however, the weaker party often got even or stopped doing business with the stronger party.

With the Win-Win process, both parties disclose more facts concerning their needs, and through truthfulness, full disclosure, and sharing real needs, both achieve their most important objectives. Negotiations are based on principles. No attacks are made on the other person or on the other person's positions.

The Win-Win system is an ideal to be strived for. It is the best way for long-term relationships. There are problems, however, if the one side wants to make a quick killing and run. Fortunately, most businesspeople want long-term relationships and repeated sales. But the buyer must be alert to the few who will take every advantage because they are not concerned about a continuing relationship. Some of these might be salespeople with large, reputable organizations. They may simply want to make a sales quota or close a deal to get a promotion and move on.

Buyers can take advantage of sellers too. If you know you have a strong position you might be inclined to push your demands to the limit. Some buyers do this by jumping on every tiny supplier mistake. Some plant managers want the supplier to pay double for less-than-perfect material and then they still use the material. They expect to be reimbursed for the material and for overtime labor used by the plant. This approach can backfire. The supplier can later raise prices. It can lose interest in obtaining more business and force the buyer to look elsewhere to satisfy material needs. It can restrict supply during periods when goods are put on allocation. It can serve other customers first and delay shipments.

There is a fine line between permitting too much profit and being greedy. Allow the supplier to make a reasonable profit. If you don't, you end up with a supplier that either goes out of business or eventually gets even.

PLACING THE FIRST ORDER

The first purchase order given to a supplier may be for a small sample shipment, for a one-time purchase, or for a long-term major purchase. Orders for long-term material needs should require a sample shipment whether it is requested by a separate order or is in a single agreement with continuous shipments contingent on the acceptability of the sample. Clearly indicate the criteria to be used in accepting the sample. Many disputes arise because the definition of acceptability is too vague.

NEGOTIATING WITH EXISTING SUPPLIERS

Buyers should remember two principles about negotiating. First, anything can be negotiable. It is just a question of what the other party must have in return. The second is that negotiating is a continuing process. As time passes, circumstances change. Personnel move on and new people have different policies. The economy moves up and down, and good buyers keep track of it so they can obtain lower costs in declining markets and lock in low costs in rising markets. Technology changes. New companies enter the marketplace. Better products sometimes cost less. New companies are hungrier than older well-established organizations.

These facts send a clear message to buyers. You must re-shop, obtain new bids, and continue to negotiate with existing sources. You don't reward suppliers because they have been suppliers a long time; you reward them with business because they are competitive and continue to be so. If you don't follow this advice, your own organization will soon become non-competitive and may not survive.

WHY NEGOTIATIONS SOMETIMES FAIL

Probably the major reason for failed negotiations is improper planning. It is likely that there is inadequate information without a plan, and objectives are cloudy. Negotiations also fail because the parties allow insufficient time. Major negotiations sometimes take months to reach a satisfactory conclusion. Arguing positions rather than principles prevents agreement. Ignoring the give-and-take principle and being unwilling to compromise makes failure almost certain.

Some buyers don't realize they have other things to gain besides a price concession and other things to give the seller besides the terms and conditions that the seller proposed. To get what you want, the trick is to find out what the other party wants. It may be quick payment or a long-term agreement, or a change in scheduled delivery, or endorsement of his product. It often takes a lot of work and questions to get beneath the apparent objectives.

Summary

Proper communication with suppliers is one of the keys to successful purchasing. You obtain information by requesting bids or quotations either informally or formally. When no bid is submitted, it is a good idea to find out why. Bids must be analyzed to determine the lowest cost supplier. Information should be gathered about the capabilities of the suppliers and a physical inspection of the supplier's facilities conducted.

The first step in major negotiations is planning. There are different styles of negotiating, but the best is the Win-Win system if the supplier is interested in a long-term business relationship. Continuous shopping and negotiating with existing suppliers is essential to remain competitive. Negotiations fail because of poor planning, not allowing sufficient time, and not being willing to compromise.

Chapter 7

Using the Computer for Better Purchasing

The use of the computer is so widespread that nearly everybody assumes the advantages of its use far exceed the disadvantages. True, but be aware that there are problems involved. One is that you must have certain hardware and software and be willing to pay the expense of obtaining both. The good news is that the cost of very powerful equipment and software has been going steadily down and probably will continue to do so.

Another problem is that either hardware or software or both may fail to perform as expected. Steps need to be taken to minimize the hardships this may cause, whether you are using the computer for purchasing operations or any other important function.

Small companies may start up and run the business without computerization, but they have a hard time competing and it gets worse if the company grows.

There is a need for training to use any computer equipment, even if it is self-training, and sometimes the amount of time required seems inordinately long. Indeed, the investment in time may exceed the investment in the hardware and software. Nevertheless, it is an investment that will need to be made sooner or later if the company grows to any appreciable size.

The computer is more useful for certain business functions than others, and purchasing applications are among the extremely useful for most organizations. The larger the number of purchasing transactions, the more beneficial it is to computerize the purchasing operation because it has always been a paper-intensive function, and the computer either eliminates or minimizes much of the paperwork. It follows that a young person getting a job in purchasing should be able to use a computer or understand that such knowledge should be acquired quickly.

Purchasing Applications Using the Computer

Although purchasing duties using the computer vary from company to company, there are basic applications in common. They can be performed on simple personal computers (PCs), on mini-computers, or on main frames. The computer can be a "stand alone" or part of a network. The software may also differ, but all basically accomplish the same thing.

WORD PROCESSING FOR PURCHASING

Word processing software using a computer and printer has replaced the typewriter in most organizations. Buyers need to communicate with suppliers often by letter. While some buyers rarely write a letter to a supplier, they would be better off to do so to document discussions and certain agreements.

Word processing eliminates the need to re-type entire documents because of errors. The errors alone can be corrected and the revised document printed. Better yet, if you need to send similar letters to many suppliers, all you have to do is change the address or other variables. Names and addresses can be stored in a separate computer file and merged with the master document in predetermined sites in the letter. Envelopes can be generated from the same file, eliminating the need to re-type. Form letters, such as those that might be used to announce plant closings for vacation or holidays, may be stored and re-used annually by changing the dates. These types of letters are necessary to alert suppliers to avoid shipping material when the plant is closed.

The word processing software is also used to send FAX messages. It can be used for forms and other types of documents, although certain specialized software is also available.

A document prepared with word processing software can be electronically saved on a disk, which eliminates the need to file every piece of paper. Admittedly, some managers prefer to retain a hard copy of correspondence as well as the stored electronic. Electronic data can be easily sorted and retrieved by subject or date.

SPREADSHEETS AND STATISTICAL SOFTWARE

Analysis of bids can still be done manually on columned sheets of paper, or paper forms and graphs and charts can be done by hand on graph paper; however, it is much easier to use the computer with appropriate software programs. Spreadsheet programs such as Lotus 1,2,3, Excel, and QuatroPro are well suited for bid analysis. Such programs usually have mathematical and statistical functions as well as charted or graphing features.

These programs are useful to record and compare supplier performance, purchasing budgets, and other purchasing activities. Office 97 by Microsoft and Corel Suite even have built in forms to generate purchase orders. Data can be linked to other files.

Spreadsheet programs accept each piece of information and store it in an individual cell. Mathematical operations can be automatically performed on data entered in a cell by pre-assigning formulas to a cell. Thus, for example, a unit price in one cell can be multiplied by the quantity specified in another cell to produce the extended amount in still another cell. All of the extended amounts for each item can then be totaled at the bottom of a screen to give the value for a purchase order. This is all done automatically once the system is set up. These programs have purchase order templates already established to perform this operation, but they may be revised for your own company's needs.

Spreadsheet programs minimize various types of errors and eliminate repetitive work. It is easy to copy cells and formulas to other areas and a simple matter to insert additional spaces between columns or rows if needed. It is easy to make the columns wider if necessary to accommodate longer entries. All these are impossible with manual paper sheets without re-copying the entire sheet.

PURCHASE ORDER GENERATION

The purchase order form spreadsheet program templates can even incorporate your own logo into the form. While this is adequate for small companies, it may not be enough for larger organizations that want a comprehensive purchasing system. In such cases, buying a software package designed especially for the purchasing operation may be the choice. There are a dozen such programs that produce purchase orders and do many related jobs. Contact the American Purchasing Society for a current list of such companies and their addresses.

An alternative is to develop your own system or hire a software company or programmer to develop a proprietary system. Not many years ago, this was the choice of larger organizations because no canned software did what they wanted. Today's canned programs are much better.

DATA STORAGE AND RETRIEVAL

A major advantage of the computer is the ability to store data for later retrieval, analysis, and reporting (see Exhibit 7-1). Both the requisition and the purchase order contain information that can be stored and later retrieved in various formats. Data may also be entered from other sources. For example, a supplier may fill out a supplier information sheet with the name and address of the company, the contact people, and perhaps the names and titles of management. The information sheet or accompanying sales brochures or catalogs can provide information about the company's products and even specifications about products. All of this can be stored in the computer for later use.

A buyer may use stored data to generate an order. For example, entering a supplier code number for the name of a supplier may be all that is necessary to select the supplier. By entering the code, the supplier's name and address are automatically printed on the purchase order. By entering a part number and quantity, a product description, a price, and a total amount for that quantity are also printed on the order.

The buying company can have its own standard inflexible terms and conditions either printed on the back of blank purchase order paper forms fed into the computer or have them printed on the form from a separate file

Exhibit 7-1.
Computerized Purchase Information Flow

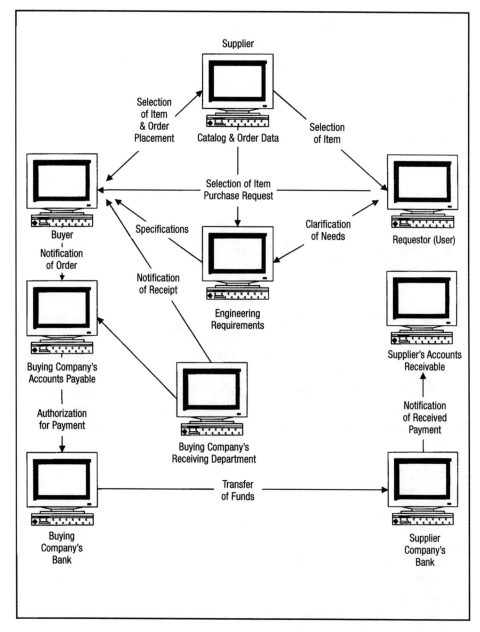

stored in the computer memory. Much software now allows the buyer to revise terms and conditions to correspond with the negotiated agreement made with the supplier. Certain items may automatically insert "default values" unless the buyer changes them. For example, the point where title passes from buyer to seller might have a default entry of F.O.B. Delivered. If the seller does not accept an order with such a term and insists on F.O.B. Shipping Point, the buyer can simply change the entry. Some software lists a number of different choices for various terms; obtaining a particular term only requires clicking the mouse or placing a screen pointer and pressing "enter." Usually there is an "other" category that requires typing the full term.

Storage of product specifications can be used to fill in an accurate description of the product without laboriously typing and re-checking large amounts of text. Engineers can even update the latest product information or revisions, especially for proprietary items, if the system is networked and allows such changes. In this case, the descriptions or engineering design level used on purchase orders with older designs are stored either by design date, revision date, or both.

Paper files can be lost or damaged by fire or other hazards. But computer files are vulnerable, too. Data can be lost when a hard disk "crashes," or erased by a power loss. Software problems can raise havoc with data. Because all hard drives eventually fail, good computer management requires all data to be routinely backed. Some back up daily, some weekly. The frequency depends on the amount of data entered and the risk you are willing to take. If only a few changes are made per day and there is some paper record of recent changes, backup may not be as frequent as those with dozens of changes a day. Backups are made to tape or disk using special software and drives.

REPORTS AND USE OF DATA

Before computer storage of data it was so time consuming and costly to obtain certain reports that it was uneconomical to obtain them. Consequently, the buyer was working with limited information. The ability to negotiate to the best advantage was restricted simply because of lack of information. Buyers got around the deficiency by bluffing or settling for less than they may have obtained with adequate information.

Purchasing managers based budgets on a "gut feel." They measured buyers subjectively. They estimated results and forecasted changes based on memory and experience rather than on recorded history and mathematical calculations.

Now, with the accumulation of price histories, supplier performance records, expenditure records by product, and total expenditures by supplier, buyers have the raw data to produce reports and conduct their negotiations based on actual records. With actual accurate figures regarding total expenditures by buyer, and purchase volume records, managers have the information to prepare better budgets and estimate costs.

Price action reports may give details about price changes during a specified period of time. A buyer is much better equipped to negotiate with a supplier who is requesting a price increase if the duration of time is known since the last increase and how much prices have changed for that product over a given time period. For example, assume a supplier wants a price increase of 3%. Modest. But not so modest if the supplier has had two other increases of 3% each during the last fourteen months.

Supplier performance reports can include the number of times a supplier shipped either late or shipped early and by how many days. This can be compared with other suppliers of a similar product or with various other suppliers. It can be compared with a previous period and indicate an improving or failing trend. If the same item is split-sourced among two or more suppliers, a better performing supplier could be awarded a higher percentage of business in a future period and failing suppliers could be penalized by fewer orders or eliminated altogether.

Storage of information about quality rejections should also be included in the supplier performance report. Quality problems include failure to meet product specifications, quantity shortage, and billing errors.

Sales and inventory information available on computer screens help buyers negotiate the proper quantity purchase. Even when quantity is specified by a requestor or a production control department, the buyer is better off when he or she knows actual usage and the inventory on hand. Although the present order may be as requested, the buyer can estimate future usage to the supplier and thus be able to obtain cost reductions or help the supplier plan the buyer's needs. The supplier may decide to order a larger quantity of raw material in order to reduce his cost. Or the supplier may reduce raw material inventory if the information points to a reduction in orders. Buyers who work with the supplier in this way may obtain significant help from the supplier when it is needed.

RECEIVING RECORDS

With any network or online system, it is advantageous to tie the computer operation into the receiving operation. Of course, the receiving operation should be locked out from receiving price information or other information that may be restricted to outside sources.

The receiving function should enter items as received along with any noted discrepancies. This alerts the buyer and eliminates the need to follow-up with the supplier on material already in-house. Too often, buyers used to be embarrassed after calling a supplier to find out why certain items were not delivered only to find out the items had been sitting in the receiving department for two days waiting to be put away or delivered to the using department.

ACCOUNTS PAYABLE

With a network system, the buyer can see which invoices have been paid and which have not. Another embarrassment that buyers encounter is to learn from a supplier that payments are delayed or are always late. Buyers need to know if it is better to negotiate for longer payment terms or for discounts for early payments. What is the point of obtaining a 2% discount for payment within 10 days if the bills are not going to be paid for 45 days? The accounting department may ask programmers to lock out payment information for anyone outside of the accounting department, but it is better if buyers know the true payment status when dealing with a supplier.

EDI AND THE INTERNET

Many companies are now using electronic data interchange (EDI) or the Internet to conduct business transactions. Catalogs are now "on line" and a buyer can determine what to buy and the cost without seeing a salesperson. Orders may be placed electronically with the use of a modem and a telephone line.

EDI links buyer data to seller data. Specifications, scheduling, and shipping information are shared. Billing is done electronically, and payment is transferred from buyer to seller at the speed of light.

There are still some unresolved issues surrounding the use of electronic transactions including FAX communications as well as EDI and the Internet. One purchasing manager recently asked this writer if terms and conditions need to be sent with every electronic order. Right now it is not clear what the courts will accept in place of written hard copies. At present, it is better to err on the side of caution and include all the "boilerplate" with the order. An alternative would be to develop a formal hard copy contract to last for a specified period, perhaps one year. The contract would include the desired terms to be applicable to all orders issued during the same period and have the document signed by both authorized buyer and authorized seller.

INFORMATION AVAILABLE THROUGH THE INTERNET AND THE WEB

With only a PC, a modem, and some inexpensive software anyone can find helpful information for making informed purchasing decisions. More and more companies are establishing Web sites that provide information about the products and services they provide. Companies are placing their catalogs on the Web and are providing interactivity to place orders.

Supplier Directories on Line

The information from long-time publishers of hardbound supplier directory books is now available through the Internet. Thomas Register and MacRAE'S Blue Book have sites. There are services that provide information about particular order categories such as electronics.

You may visit the Thomas Register of American Manufacturers at http://www.thomasregister.com to find suppliers that make a particular product. There are 155,000 U.S. and Canadian companies listed for 57,000 product and service headings, and 3,100 online supplier catalogs that give the buyer 44,000 pages of detailed buying and specifying information.

You type in the product category you are looking for in a box that appears on the computer screen. For example, if you typed in the words "stainless steel" a report appears on the screen showing there are 270 headings for that search and goes on to report that it includes 62 companies in stainless alone, 7 in stainless steel bar, 9 in stainless steel coils, etc.

You can obtain sales literature by FAX and visit individual company Web sites. Company addresses, telephone numbers, and FAX numbers are provided.

Price Indexes and Economic Information

The Bureau of Labor Statistics Producer Price Index (PPI) information and news releases are available on the Web. Using a WWW browser, enter the Bureau's homepage address, http://stats.bls.gov. After clicking the "DATA" button on the home page you may retrieve index data in any of the following six ways:

- Most Requested Series—provides Producer Price Indexes for the most commonly requested information including "All Commodities" and the stage-of-processing indexes such as finished goods.
- Selective Access—for users familiar with the PPI coding structure.
- News Releases—contains the most current press release produced regarding the PPI program.
- Series Report—uses PPI commodity or Standard Industrial Classification Codes (SIC) to obtain information for specific data ranges.
- Economy at a Glance—contains current data on various economic indicators produced by the Bureau of Labor Statistics (BLS).
- Gopher—a link to the BLS for those who require an extensive amount of data.

USE THE INTERNET TO FIND FINANCIAL INFORMATION

There are many areas of the Internet and the Web that give financial information. Although much of it is aimed at investors, the buyer can also use it to learn about a company's financial status. Go to America Online's business section and enter the Company Research area. From there you can ask for financial statements on over 22,000 U.S. and international companies.

LEARN NEWS ABOUT COMPANIES AND COUNTRIES

Dow Jones News by Company, Inc. Magazine Archives, and America Online Company Research all give the latest news about company activities. You can search for recent news releases for the company that interests you or you can go back in time to earlier news releases.

When you want to find out about doing business in a foreign country, visit the site of The Economist Intelligence Unit. It will give you information about doing business in Eastern Europe or elsewhere. It will give you world statistics.

TOTAL ONLINE TRANSACTION PROCESSING

Fully automated purchasing is illustrated by the computerized purchase information flow diagram shown. Computers are networked between the buyer's and seller's organization and include the user or requestor of material, purchasing operations, engineering, accounting, receiving, and the buyer's and seller's respective banks. Funds are transferred from the buyer's company to the seller's company once the ordered material is received. This network illustration could be expanded with additional space by including other departments such as the buyer's marketing department, inventory control, quality assurance, and production control.

TRAINING AND EMPLOYMENT INFORMATION

Look at the American Purchasing Society's web site if you are looking for a job in purchasing or you want to hire purchasing personnel. The site also includes helpful tips and problem-solving information about purchasing. The address is www.american-purchasing.com.

What is Needed

SOFTWARE REQUIREMENTS

Computer experts claim that you should select the software you need before buying the hardware. That is at least in part because the software may require a minimum amount of memory or a certain operating system designed for the hardware. Generally speaking, a small purchasing operation can get by with inexpensive word processing, spread sheet, and database software. All of this can be obtained for under $1000. If there is more than one buyer, you will either need to duplicate everything or go to a network system. Software dedicated to purchasing operations runs from a few thousand dollars to many thousands. Mini and mainframe computers require much higher-priced software.

HARDWARE REQUIREMENTS

A simple PC can now be purchased for under $1,000, but an investment of closer to $3,000 is probably more appropriate for any business or purchasing operation. This includes the processor, an adequate amount of storage for data, and an average size monitor. A printer will be an additional charge as well as devices for large backups. Multiply this amount by as many PCs as are necessary.

Printers come in a large variety. Impact printers work by striking the paper and therefore can produce carbon copies. Inkjet and laser printers simply lay the ink on the paper and therefore will not produce a carbon or NCR copy; however, you can obtain an exact copy by printing two sheets or using a copying machine.

Printers also have different widths for wide sheets. Some printers have sprocket gears that allow the use of continuous form paper. This is advantageous for heavy output. The forms may be blank or pre-printed with headings or boilerplate on the reverse. Obviously, this is an added cost and these pre-printed continuous forms need to be purchased from specialized printers. The continuous form may be interleaved to contain carbon and extra copies.

BACKUP DEVICES

You need to make a backup copy of your transactions to avoid losing records. Backup hardware devices and software use various types of disk and tape. The devices are priced on the speed and amount of data that can be stored. Individual PCs can have small tape drives that are fairly inexpensive for one unit, but as the number of PCs increase so does the cost. Network systems can depend on the server to back up the data on one drive or multiple drives such as RAID systems that are relatively expensive.

The type of hardware affects the cost. Faster output for the computer or printer means a higher price. It is not always necessary to have the latest or fastest equipment and settling for slower speeds can save money.

NOTEBOOK COMPUTERS

While most buyers and managers now have PCs, few use notebook-sized computers except at the executive level, because they are relatively expensive and easily stolen. Nevertheless, a buyer who is able to obtain approval for the use of these smaller tools will find them useful. Taking a notebook computer along when visiting a supplier is a good way of finding the status of current orders and making notes about facility tours. If the notebook is equipped with a modem, FAX messages may be sent back to or received from the home office. Prices range from under $2000 to over $6000, but the high-end machines are only necessary for graphics work and audiovisual presentations.

Notebook computers' vulnerability to theft is particularly true if you are traveling to certain foreign countries. Another problem is that battery life is fairly short even on the best of notebooks and if you are going to use them for an extended period, you will need to take along a charging unit. Be careful connecting the notebooks and chargers to electrical sources that are not compatible in foreign countries.

When to Upgrade

It is important to keep up-to-date to be competitive, but it is not necessary to have new hardware or software the minute it becomes available. New hardware models or software versions are often more expensive in several ways. The newest hardware is priced high because it is new and many buyers want the latest technology. Gradually, competition forces prices down. The latest software may be introduced at deep discounts, but the expense frequently comes in trying to learn the new versions and trying to eliminate the bugs or problems that new versions often carry. It is best to wait a while until others have tested the software and any problems have been corrected.

Old equipment and software that is working well should be upgraded with caution. Expect problems when you obtain new equipment and software. It might be a good idea to keep one or more machines and old software while learning to operate the new.

How Computers Will Change Purchasing in the Future

There is little doubt that purchasing operations will become ever more dependent on the computer as a buying tool. Every professional buyer will be required to have good computer skills; they will be needed to obtain information about suppliers and products. Companies will prefer to provide information through the Internet rather than send salespeople and bear the cost of expensive in-person visits. Orders will be placed electronically, and billing will be done the same way to reduce administrative costs and speed up transactions.

Some companies are doing these things now, but it will soon be standard for all but the smallest organizations. If this forecast is accurate, then it is apparent that anyone considering a purchasing career, or most business careers for that matter, should make certain that they learn and keep up-to-date on computer technology.

Summary

It is important to use the computer to facilitate purchasing transactions. Even so, the buyer must consider the expense involved in the purchase of the equipment and the software as well as the possibility of failure of those products. There is an additional cost for training in order to use new computer equipment or software. Although small companies may still use a manual system for purchasing, today it is essential for the growing organization to computerize its operation if it wants to be competitive. There are various types of software and applications used by purchasing. They include word processing, spreadsheets, purchase order generators, and database packages. All kinds of information to help the buyer is available on-line or through the Internet. There is little doubt that the computer will continue to play a bigger and bigger part in buying and purchasing management.

Chapter 8

Purchasing Management Concerns

Different Methods for Organizations
of Different Sizes

This chapter discusses the management of purchasing and how management styles differ between large, medium, and the smallest of businesses. It covers the ways purchasing effectiveness and efficiency are measured. There is a discussion about ethics and how dishonesty is prevented. The importance and advantages of establishing standard purchasing policies and procedures is included. Finally, there is a discussion of the needed qualifications for buyers and how some companies select them.

How Large Purchasing Organizations are Run

Large organizations have the luxury of having more people in purchasing and consequently each person can more or less specialize in a certain facet of the purchasing operation. For example, certain people may only have the duty of expediting orders. The largest operations can have a person who concentrates on finding and hiring purchasing personnel.

BUYER SPECIALIZATION

Buyers are responsible for the purchase of a limited number of products and items. One buyer may be assigned a certain product category such as packaging material. Another buyer may be responsible for purchasing office supplies only. There may be a specialist who is in charge of negotiating and making contract agreements.

However, there are no hard-and-fast rules about how assignments are made. Much depends on the overall organization structure and perhaps the type of industry that is involved. A highly decentralized company may delegate all of the purchasing to the local level. If local plants or offices are small, one person may handle all aspects of purchasing even though the size of the company, as a whole, is huge. In some cases, the person in charge of purchasing at the local level may handle other functions as well. It is not uncommon to be responsible for inventory as well as purchasing, although such a position might have a different title. Materials Manager is frequently used, although this may include a number of other related responsibilities as well.

AUTHORIZATION FOR PURCHASES

Placing purchasing orders with suppliers is usually delegated to buyers when an organization has two or more buyers in addition to a purchasing manager or purchasing director. However, in many cases the purchase orders must have one or more additional approval signatures if the amount of the dollar commitment exceeds a specified amount.

While selection of suppliers is the rightful responsibility of purchasing personnel, large organizations in particular often require elaborate approval criteria from other departments. Engineering may need to qualify suppliers' technical capabilities. Quality Control or Quality Assurance may want to assess suppliers' ability to meet the desired level of quality as evidenced by needed test equipment and measuring devices.

A strong buyer or purchasing manager sometimes has authority to make decisions without the approval of these other departments, but disregarding the wishes of other functions is a risk that few will take. If things go wrong when advice has been ignored, the buyer will be hard pressed to justify a decision.

DEGREE OF AUTOMATION

Large companies can afford and usually have well-designed computer systems. On the negative side, some of these systems are now outdated. They were installed years ago when purchasing was not viewed as an important function and software was designed primarily for other areas, particularly accounting and sometimes manufacturing. Programmers assigned to the system design were knowledgeable about accounting or manufacturing but usually were ignorant of purchasing methods or needs. Consequently, the purchasing portion of the software was an afterthought that was a module of the primary function.

Many of these old systems did little more than generate purchase orders. Others stored data about suppliers. The ability to retrieve certain data was limited and the speed of operation was slow. Today, some companies are improving their systems by installing stand-alone purchasing software or are revising their old system to better accommodate purchasing needs.

EASIER CREDIT APPROVAL

Buyers for large, well-known, or stock exchange-listed companies rarely need to discuss credit approval with new sellers unless the order amounts are very large. Salespeople assume that the company has the ability to pay, although the supplier's accounting personnel may obtain a Dun and Bradstreet report or look up the D & B rating before authorizing order fulfillment. The buyer may not even be aware of this credit check.

This occurs even when the company is experiencing financial difficulties. The few salespeople who want financial information are often satisfied if the buyer gives them a copy of a recent annual report, probably because information is readily obtained through the D & B listing.

Be aware that this is a general discussion; there are numerous exceptions in both large and small organizations. Managers and buyers may be given limited authority in a small organization if that is the operating style of the executive in charge. Buyers may be given much broader authority in a large organization if that is the wish of general management.

AMOUNT OF PURCHASE CONTROL

Large organizations have more formal controls than most small organizations. Authorization for a purchase may be given to purchasing orally by a general manager, whereas a larger organization requires a written, approved budget well in advance for certain types of purchases, such as capital equipment. A written requisition form is normally required in a larger organization and the requisition must be signed by a person authorized to order material or services. Sometimes several approval signatures are required on the requisition form. Similar controls are used for purchase orders. The buyer may be permitted to sign the purchase order up to a certain dollar limit. Above that amount, one or more additional signatures may be required on the purchase order or any other document that places an order with the supplier. Formal legal contracts often require the signature of an officer of the buying company. Such a requirement is not to satisfy the law, as an authorized agent can issue the contract legally, but the buying company and/or the selling company may simply require it as part of their policy or procedure.

Large companies often delegate product selection to special departments. These departments are variously named Engineering, Product Development, or even Marketing. Although in practice they are not supposed to name or select the supplier, they often do. This is contrary to what most purchasing managers believe to be good practice as it weakens the ability of the buyer to negotiate. Salespeople contact the buying company's engineers or any other personnel outside of purchasing if they believe those employees have an influence on which supplier will be selected for an order. They may even ignore the purchasing department altogether if they believe that the sourcing decision is made outside of purchasing. A strong purchasing manager will try to overcome the situation by gaining the support of general management in enforcing appropriate policies and procedures for good purchasing practices.

It is logical that more internal purchasing controls are usually in place with larger companies. Not everyone knows everyone else when there are thousands of employees. Any one employee may not know what another employee is supposed to be doing or is authorized to do. Purchasing may keep a record of who is authorized and to what extent.

In a small company it is much easier to know everyone and to be aware of what they are authorized to do. A buyer may be on a first name basis with the owner, whereas a buyer in a large company may not even have met any of the officers. Nevertheless, purchasing people are usually more visible to internal and supplier management than personnel from any other business function.

CONTROL OF PROCUREMENT CARDS

Procurement cards are special credit cards such as Visa, MasterCard, and American Express that are especially designed for use by business. The business issues the cards to its managers or other employees who need material and supplies that would otherwise be directly obtained by their purchasing department. The card companies sell these cards to businesses on the basis of saving paperwork and time. They contend that the purchase is delayed because requisition forms must be made out and submitted to the purchasing department and then the buyer must contact the supplier and place the order. The card companies say that the administrative cost of this system often far exceeds the cost of the goods. Using the cards instead eliminates order handling by purchasing and eliminates the necessity of accounting checking and paying many invoices. The card companies are able to code the cards so that only certain suppliers may be used and so that the individual cardholder is limited to a certain amount or type of purchase. Reports are issued to the buying company by the card companies monthly showing who made purchases, the amount of the purchases, and the names of the suppliers. Accepting the credit cards is sold to the suppliers on the promise of improving cash flow by receiving payment almost immediately. Nevertheless, most manufacturers do not accept the cards so cardholders are mostly limited to retailers and some distributors.

If numerous users are issued the procurement cards, or improper amounts are authorized for each holder, or if too many of the wrong suppliers are permitted when the system is installed, then there are insufficient controls and purchasing cost is likely to rise significantly, especially in the long run. Some companies make sure that purchasing controls who receives the cards and who the authorized suppliers are. The monthly reports are reviewed and individual expenditures are compared with budgets. Unfortunately, this happens after the purchases have been made.

Further drawbacks to the cards are:

1. The supplier must pay a percentage from 2% to 3% on each transaction. Eventually, that cost must be passed on to the buyer and any saving in administrative costs under the old system is offset by this amount.

2. Allowing many employees to be in direct contact with salespeople at the suppliers weakens Purchasing's ability to negotiate prices and other terms.

3. Allowing inexperienced employees to buy helps the supplier charge what the market will bear.

4. Many suppliers simply do not accept the cards and see no reason to do so.

There is little doubt that procurement cards lighten Purchasing's workload, especially for MRO items, but not all purchasing managers or general management think their benefits outweigh their disadvantages. Even though they have been around for almost ten years, an American Purchasing Society survey indicated that as of mid-1998, only about 27% of purchasing departments say they are used by their company.

LARGE COMPANIES SHOP

In contrast to small organizations, large companies are always searching for better suppliers. Buyers for large organizations develop so called "partnerships" with their suppliers, but that does not mean that they are not looking for other possibilities. There are often established written policies and procedures that specify when and how often competitive quotations should be obtained. Competitive bids are usually required for items never before purchased. Competitive bids are requested periodically for items that are purchased on a continual basis unless there is a long-term contract or "partnership" agreement. There is a tendency for buyers from large companies to check suppliers located in distant geographical areas. Higher transportation costs are factored into the total acquisition costs and compared with suppliers that are closer to the user's location.

LARGE COMPANIES ANALYZE SUPPLIER CAPABILITIES MORE THOROUGHLY

As indicated previously, buyers should check references of potential suppliers and analyze their financial stability, but in practice, few from smaller companies do so either because of lack of time or knowledge of how to do so. Perhaps they also feel the risk of supplier failure is not great enough to warrant the cost in time and effort. Buyers from large companies either take the time or delegate it to specialists who do the job for them.

The management of a large organization usually insists on a careful analysis of comparative costs between suppliers, even including the make-or-buy decision. Both internal auditors and public accountants check to see that this is done and are quick to criticize if it is not. The buyer must be able to justify the selection of one supplier over another by showing documented proof of cost or other differences.

LARGE COMPANIES NEGOTIATE MORE AND ON A REGULAR BASIS

Although it is this author's contention that all types of communication, including oral, verbal, and non-verbal, are or can be forms of negotiation in the broader sense, formal, face-to-face negotiations are planned and more frequently used by larger organizations. Buyers from small companies often feel they are in a weak negotiating position compared with larger organizations and therefore don't try. Those that do find they have more power than they thought and achieve far better results than their competition.

LARGE COMPANIES USE TEAM APPROACHES

Teams made up variously of employees from departments such as Quality Control, Finance, Engineering, Marketing, Inventory Control, Production, and Purchasing are particularly used by large companies to plan, negotiate, and transact business with suppliers. Employees from departments other than Purchasing in smaller organizations usually feel that they cannot spare the time to do what they feel is a purchasing job and they don't appreciate the advantages derived from the team approach. Smaller companies that do use the team approach often feel that it is the only way to go and they fail to understand that there are times when using a team is best and times when one-on-one discussions are more appropriate. Both systems have advantages and disadvantages. (See Team Buying).

LARGE COMPANIES AUDIT PURCHASING ACTIVITIES

In general, audits of purchasing activities are few and far between, but buyers and purchasing managers never know when they will be conducted. Public companies, especially those listed on a stock exchange, probably have more purchasing audits than proprietorships, partnerships or privately held corporations, but all well managed companies of more than a few people should have them. Because it is costly, ISO certification is more frequently obtained by larger companies and such certification depends on the outcome of audits. Among other things, the ISO audit checks to see if there are written documented policies and procedures and compares them with actual activities to determine if they are being followed. ISO approval is only obtained if there is agreement between the written policies and procedures and actual practices.

LARGE COMPANIES USE VALUE ANALYSIS

The automobile companies disassemble their own products and their competitors' products and mount each item on a board next to its corresponding competitors' item. Analysts then figure out how each separate item was made and the cost associated with that process. By doing so, they learn which method produces the lowest-cost product. A value analysis or value engineering committee decides on what function the item serves and then "brainstorms" to come up with various other ways to accomplish the same function or task. Sometimes an item can be entirely eliminated by changing another item so that it will accomplish more than one task. Sometimes they change the material or the way it is manufactured. The objective is to lower the cost or produce greater value. The value analysis process can be applied to services as well as products. Large companies, especially in the aircraft manufacturing and automotive industries, have used VA for many years. The process can be used to great advantage in any manufacturing environment, but it could also be used in any other type of industry or service organization. Unfortunately, few small companies utilize this highly profitable cost-saving technique.

LARGE COMPANIES PROVIDE INTERNAL SPECIALIZED ADVICE

Purchasing managers and buyers who work for a big company have the advantage of getting informed help from various specialists. They don't need to know everything about many functions. The buyer's job is narrower in some respects because responsibility lies within those other areas of the company. For example, a small company may have no separate traffic function and the buyer will have to figure out the least expensive mode of transportation or the best routing for a shipment from the supplier. In larger organizations, the traffic department may pick the type of carrier and routing desired.

Once in a while, a buyer or purchasing manager will have a problem concerning an agreement with a supplier. Large organizations usually have an in-house legal department who can provide advice on how to handle the problem. Company attorneys will usually review proposals or contracts from suppliers and offer suggestions, if not rewrite the contracts. In some cases, purchasing managers and buyers feel these legal departments go too far by requiring that all contracts or certain types of purchase orders be submitted to them for review or approval. Qualified purchasing agents should not need such scrutiny if they have sufficient knowledge of business law (see Chapter 4). Buyers in all types of businesses of all sizes write contracts regularly without needing legal advice or approval.

Nevertheless, information about new laws that affect purchasing can be very helpful, if not essential. Many internal legal departments can and do keep purchasing and other departments informed about new legislation. Purchasing people in small organizations are usually on their own to find out new legal requirements. Fortunately there are seldom new laws that affect purchasing to any significant degree.

There are even product design and engineering departments in small companies, but there are fewer graduate engineers and those that are employed cannot be technically familiar with all types of products. They may not even become involved in wide product areas that need to be purchased. For example, they may not concern themselves with capital equipment or MRO purchases. It is therefore left to the buyer, technically trained or not, to decide on proper specifications for the products involved. Not so in big companies. Separate engineering departments may be in place for maintenance items, capital equipment, and for products to be manufactured or purchased for production. Detailed written specifications are given to the buyer or discussed with the supplier. Even when the supplier's engineering department provides the specifications, the buyer's engineering department may review them or approve them for use.

A similar situation exists for the quality function. A formal quality control or quality assurance function in a large organization helps the engineers establish specifications and monitors products received to make sure they meet those specifications. Sometimes an inspector or other members of the buyer's quality assurance function will visit a supplier's facility to check what quality measures are in place, or to approve products during the manufacturing process or before they are shipped. In certain cases, a buyer's quality representative will stay at the supplier facility on a semi-permanent basis. Smaller companies simply do not have the manpower to operate in this fashion and it would be uneconomical to do so with the lower quantities involved. An exception would be for highly technical products requiring a high degree of precision such as in certain military applications or in the medical equipment field. In these cases the product cost, potential liability, and associated risks of unsatisfactory products justify more quality control expense for the smaller company.

BUYERS FROM LARGE COMPANIES DO MORE INTERNATIONAL SOURCING

Although many small companies buy foreign goods either directly or indirectly, most do not. Buying internationally requires more knowledge and more effort than buying from domestic sources. In addition, the administrative cost and the product cost from international sources may be higher for lower quantities. The lead time is normally much longer. Most large companies buy some items from international sources because the costs for them are lower. In some cases, where split sourcing is used, a portion of the requirement is purchased domestically and a portion is purchased internationally. There are also certain items that are only available in the international market.

Purchasing Is Often Involved in Top Management Discussions and Decisions

The top purchasing officer in most large organizations has the title of Director of Purchasing, Vice President of Purchasing or a title conveying similar responsibility and authority. The holders of these titles are executives in every sense of the word. They attend management meetings and are asked for their input and advice on important management decisions. They are involved in setting corporate policy and usually have complete authority to conduct purchasing operations as they see fit as long as their methods are legal and do not conflict with general management policies or procedures. This type of authority is rare in small organizations.

Using Supply Chain Management

One of purchasing management's latest interests is what is called supply chain management. It is an extension of the materials management organization that includes various additional functions of business from the planning stages to the delivery of the product to the final customer. A materials management type of organization usually, but not always, includes the purchasing function. It also includes inventory control, receiving, warehousing, and shipping. It may also include production control and traffic. The supply chain management organization includes external as well as internal organizations. It includes one or more of the suppliers and carriers. The idea is to promote communication among all of the functions of business, wherever they may be, so that no particular one is working at cross-purposes with any other. Every party involved in fulfilling the customer's requirement is working toward the same objective. The management of what is included in the supply chain may differ from industry to industry and from company to company, but the concept is full coordination and cooperation to achieve the common goals.

If the supply chain were carried to its extreme, it would include various functions at each supplier as well as the link with the supplier as a whole. See the illustrations of component links in the supply chain.

- Internal—Planning
- Internal—Product Development
- Internal—Engineering
- Internal—Sales/Marketing
- Internal—Accounting/Finance
- Internal—Scheduling
- Internal—Inventory/Production Control
- Internal—Purchasing
- External—Supplier and all supplier departments
- Internal—Quality Control
- Internal—Traffic–Inbound

- External—Inbound Carrier
- Internal—Production
- Internal—Warehousing
- Internal—Traffic–Outbound
- External—Customer

Does Size Difference Really Matter?

Many of the differences between small and large organizations are simply a function of resources. The bigger companies have more people to devote to special duties. In addition, because the dollar volumes are so much larger, the administrative cost becomes a smaller percentage of the total cost. But that is a general picture. Many large organizations don't spend much time on purchase analysis or don't shop continually or in any systematic way. There are also small organizations that somehow are able to make time to shop regularly and use every known purchasing technique to minimize their material and outside service costs.

If you are a buyer for a small company you shouldn't be intimidated by salespeople from a big company. By showing confidence and asking for what you need in a polite and professional manner, you will get the same respect as a buyer from a large organization. When you are with a small company you often have more authority to make agreements without others' approval than a big company buyer. Salespeople know this. In order to sell large companies they may have to call on a dozen different people and meet with them many times. They appreciate it if they are able to obtain an order in less time and with less effort.

Back Door Selling

Purchasing management is concerned about more than organization structure. What is referred to as "back door selling" is a continuing problem. It is when sales people either ignore the authorized buyer completely or spend minimum time with purchasing personnel. Most of their sales effort is with requestors, engineers, or others within the company. They try to get requestors to specify their brand name on the requisition. They try to get engineers to use their product's proprietary specifications so the buyer will be forced to purchase their product.

Although it may be necessary for salespeople to discuss their product's advantages with the ultimate user, it is better if an authorized buyer is present. Some companies require salespeople to always see purchasing first before visiting any other employee. They also require suppliers to send copies of all correspondence to purchasing. Employees other than buyers arc prohibited from discussing pricing and terms with the supplier. Suppliers are notified of these restrictions and told not to accept any order not issued by the authorized buyer.

Preparing and Using Budgets

Organizations use budgets to control different types of costs. Any particular company may use any or all of the following budgets:

- *Headcount.* This sets an authorization limit on the number of employees within a department.
- *Capital Equipment.* This establishes a limit on how much may be spent for specific capital purchases.
- *Raw Material or Production Components.* A budget for these items may either be a limitation on price or a limitation on quantity purchased.
- *Expense Item Budget.* This budget is for supplies, telephone usage, travel expenses, training expenses, or any other expense item.

Budgets may be fixed or variable. A fixed budget sets a specific amount that should not be exceeded regardless of any changes during the budget period. A variable budget fluctuates with changes in circumstances, usually sales volume or production volume. Companies sometimes make a firm or fixed budget for items with costs that are likely to vary with changes in volume. It is difficult to control a budget made in this manner. Budgets for prices are established to set objectives for the purchasing operation, but in practice, the products must be obtained even if the price exceeds the budget. When costs exceed budget, this is called a negative variance and buyers may be questioned closely when they appear on a report. They are asked to explain why and what they did to prevent the variance. Although a positive variance is desirable, if it is too high it indicates that the budget was not based on a realistic cost forecast.

Buyers may be asked to help prepare one or more kinds of budgets related to purchasing activities. This assignment can be a burden since proper preparation takes time. Nevertheless this assignment should not be taken lightly because buyer performance and compensation may be closely connected with the ability to work within the approved budget.

Manufacturing companies often use what is called a standard cost system. This establishes a price or cost for every purchased or manufactured item. This cost is the basis for establishing a price for the finished product. Once in a while, purchasing performance is measured against these standard costs. This is unrealistic unless purchasing takes part in establishing the standards and is only evaluated by the closeness to the standard. A negative variance means the company is losing profit, a positive variance means the product could have been priced lower and would have been more competitive.

Matching Proper Staffing to Workload

Purchasing managers are concerned about the headcount budget in order to have enough buyers or other purchasing personnel to do a good job. They usually have to justify the number of people in relation to workload. This can be a problem because it is difficult to measure purchasing workload accurately. Neither the number of items purchased, the number of purchase orders issued, nor the total dollars spent give an accurate indication of how busy a buyer is. A combination of this data is helpful, but a better indication might include how long it takes, on average, to place an order or how many supplier discrepancies need to be resolved.

Evaluating the staffing level and workload in comparison with other organizations is also difficult because of differences in responsibility.

Some buyers are assigned the accounting duty of comparing invoices to the purchase order, a very time-consuming task. Other buyers have more responsibility to establish product specifications. Still others must keep inventory records. Another variable is the number of requestors. More work is required if a buyer must deal with a higher number of requestors even though the number of items or the dollar amount spent is equivalent. A better evaluation of workload should compare the history of purchasing volume to the history of sales volume or production volume.

Even so, measuring work volume in these ways does not consider the effectiveness of the buyer. A true measure would include counting the number of deliveries made on time compared to those that are late. It would include the total cost of goods purchased compared with the total cost of similar goods and quantities purchased by another company, a figure almost impossible to obtain.

Using Benchmarking

Managers like to compare their activities and performance with other managers, other departments, and other companies. Today, these comparisons are referred to as "benchmarking." Looking at two sets of figures only helps the ego if the other organization is worse off than you are. If it is doing things better it then provides the information needed for improvement. Comparisons are made both within the same industry and outside of the industry. The aim is to find the best operations in order to learn the most successful ways. The American Purchasing Society provides benchmarking help by conducting an annual Benchmarking Survey of more than two thousand purchasing managers throughout the U.S.

Honesty and Ethical Conduct Concerns

Honesty and ethical conduct is a concern of every thoughtful purchasing manager for several reasons. First, lack of honesty probably leads to unprofitable purchasing. Periodically, businesses discover that buyers or other employees have taken "kickbacks" or have been compensated in other ways by suppliers. Sometimes these buyers go to jail; at the very least they are shamed and fired. The amounts taken may be small and not worth the loss of a good career. Unfortunately, once an instance of dishonesty is discovered, it is too late to avoid the consequences. Anyone who feels that he or she might be tempted should avoid the purchasing profession.

Managers worry for another reason. Whether they are aware of the misconduct or not, they are responsible for the operation of their department. Some are fired when the problem is discovered. At the very least, they fall under suspicion of being involved. Taking personal kickbacks in the form of gifts or cash has been prosecuted by employers. The guilty parties can be and have been investigated by the IRS for tax evasion because they have not reported their gains. The message is clear. Make sure you refuse or return all so-called "gifts" from suppliers. Keep in mind that these items are only given in order to obtain orders, not because the supplier particularly likes you.

There is a small exception. Token promotional gifts that carry advertising or that may be immediately consumed are permitted by some organizations. These items include key chains, pens, calendars and such. Salespeople from the major companies give few items of significant value and are usually prohibited from doing so.

Managers try to avoid dishonesty by screening and investigating potential job candidates well. They observe their buyer's standard of living in comparison to his income. They are wary of those who take alcohol beverages to excess or who gamble since such people would be more susceptible to bribes.

A good purchasing policy helps prevent unprofitable business by requiring documentation of the bid process. The policy requires three or more bids to be obtained on major purchases periodically. The buyer is required to write good and valid reasons whenever business is not awarded to the lowest bidder. These records are randomly selected and audited periodically for any indication of wrongdoing.

Poor ethical conduct is a lesser offense but is of concern because it reflects badly on the company and badly on purchasing. Furthermore, suppliers are reluctant to make their best offers to unethical buyers or unethical businesses. Poor ethics includes agreeing to certain terms but deliberately not honoring them. For example, it is unethical if a buyer agrees to pay in Net 30, but accounting routinely takes 45 or more days to send the check. It is unethical to ask for a bid from a new supplier just to use it to get a lower price from an existing supplier when you know you would never buy from the new supplier. It is unethical to tell the competition the price you receive from another supplier. It is unethical to "bad mouth" one supplier to another. If not unethical, it is certainly bad manners to keep salespeople waiting, whether they have an appointment or not, without telling them the reason for any delay and how long they may have to wait.

Disclosure of Confidential Information

The prices a buyer pays and the names of the sources of supply for products is of great interest to other suppliers. It gives them the opportunity to bid just low enough to make you interested, but no lower. It may not even be for the same item. By knowing what you pay someone else, suppliers can calculate the competition's cost or profit margin and adjust their bids accordingly. They can also use the information against your supplier with other customers. For this reason, it is important to limit who gets the information internally. Records should be restricted and not exposed on desks or computer screens so other people can see them. Don't leave a ready-to-sign purchase order on your desk when a salesperson from a competing company is present. Salespeople learn how to read upside down.

Information about prices, names of suppliers, order terms, and specifications should be restricted to those who need to know to do their jobs. If someone needs a certain price and is allowed to receive it, only give that specific price. Don't give them free access to all files or records.

It is not only suppliers that find certain information useful, your own competitor may like to know what you are doing also. Make sure that your suppliers keep your proprietary information secure and away from your competitors. I once discovered a potential supplier making an item for our competitor that my company had just developed and engineered. There was no way that they could have obtained the design so quickly except through one of our suppliers.

To help avoid this there should be a confidentiality term in your agreements with suppliers. Print or stamp something similar to the following on all engineering drawings. "This drawing contains confidential information that is the property of the buyer. It must not be shown to or disclosed to any third party or sub-contractor without the written consent of the buyer."

Summary

Large organizations use buyers that specialize in certain products or categories. Such organizations require several authorizers for purchases. Obtaining credit from suppliers is easier than it is for small organizations. Big companies have more controls on purchasing. Buyers for big companies negotiate more, analyze suppliers more thoroughly, and negotiate more on a regular basis. They use team approaches. Purchasing audits are more frequent. There is more use of international suppliers. Purchasing is more involved in top management decisions.

Good communication with all internal and external elements in the supply chain management reduces problems and improves service to the final customer. The differences between small and large companies are not that important to the buyer. Management is concerned about the detrimental effects from back-door selling. It can be controlled by not permitting conversations about price by anyone but the authorized buyer and supplier. Budgets used by purchasing include those for capital equipment, production material, and expense items. They may be fixed or variable. Headcount budgets are based on workload and must be justified. Measurement of purchasing workload is difficult and approximate. It is best to consider historical records and compare changes in sales revenue or production volume to changes in the purchasing staffing level. To improve operations, managers use "benchmarking" techniques to compare the best practices of other departments and other companies. Honesty by buyers is a concern of purchasing managers because dishonesty can reduce or eliminate profits and the manager may be held responsible in addition to the buyer. Price and other information about purchasing should be restricted to those who need to know. Such information must be guarded carefully as suppliers and competitors find it useful.

Chapter 9

Buying the Quality Needed

Quality Defined

What is quality? Some people equate quality with highly-priced products or services. They feel "you only get what you pay for." If this were true you would not need a professional buyer. Anyone would do. All someone would have to do is look for the highest price if they wanted the best quality.

Other people equate quality to durability. This definition would reject some of the most expensive fur coats that wear out easily. It would reject certain gem stones that break easily.

Economy automobiles transport people from one place to another just as the most expensive limousine does, although not as comfortably. If extreme comfort is not as important to you, then the added luxury may not be worth the higher price. This implies that quality is really what you expect from a product. In other words, it is how well something is made in relationship to what is asked for or needed. Good quality means that products match or exceed the specifications.

Modern manufacturers have learned to design products to fulfill their purposes without exceeding the necessary level of quality. For instance, the thickness of steel in automobiles over the past decades has steadily declined. Present day steels are stronger and more rust-resistant and the added thickness adds only weight that reduces fuel efficiency.

Machinery years ago had castings components or assemblies that were probably twice as thick as needed. The extra weight did nothing more than add cost without adding any benefit to the users. There was a time when most machinery was made in the U.S., Germany, or Great Britain. Practically nothing came from Japan. My employer at the time needed new lathe machines to expand our manufacturing operation. Those from Great Britain looked like heavy-duty tanks, while those from Japan were lighter, better-designed, and more efficient. But the deciding factor was the price, and total costs of the Japanese products were significantly less. It was no surprise to see the machine tool industry go into a sharp decline in Britain while skyrocketing in Japan. Today, intelligent buyers are more interested in the speeds and feeds of the machinery rather than how bulky the machine looks. They are interested in the mean time before failure (MTBF) rather than the appearance.

The durability of a product may or may not be important. The product may not be required to last a hundred years. With today's fast-paced technology items often become obsolete long before they wear out. Why pay for goods that will last longer than needed?

The Customer's Definition of Quality May Differ

Buyers normally think of themselves as the customer that needs to be satisfied about product quality. But they should think the real customer is the requestor or user of the product being purchased. Buyers receive varied requests from other employees within their organization to buy goods to meet certain needs. Although the buyer may feel that the quality of the purchased item is just about perfect, the user may not feel the same way. There is more than one reason why there is frequently a difference of opinion on this issue. Here are some:

- The buyer and requestor are not communicating properly on what the user requested.
- The buyer and requestor differ on what really will do the intended job.
- The buyer is more concerned about price or special features of the product than the user is.

- The user changed his or her mind about what is needed.
- The user did not realize how much was going to be charged to his or her budget.
- The user was convinced that another supplier had a better product.

You can help avoid disagreements about quality if you make sure you completely understand what the requestor wants (see Exhibit 9-1). Clear up any fuzzy descriptions before you order an item. Make sure you inform requestors about alternative products and the charges to their budgets if that might be an issue. Do what you can within company policy and procedures to limit back door selling so competitors will not sabotage purchasing activities. Some buyers take the radical step of telling suppliers that they will not be considered for future orders if they contact other employees outside of purchasing without purchasing's knowledge and approval.

Measuring the Quality of Proprietary Products

Buyers of their company's proprietary items don't have to worry how long something will last. They rely on the specifications provided by their engineers or designers. As long as the received products match those specifications, the quality is satisfactory. If they don't match, the products are rejected. There is sometimes a problem agreeing on how closely the products must match the specifications. A definition of what matches and what doesn't is often required. Products that fall within a certain range are considered satisfactory. If they fall outside that range they are rejected.

The range may be specified by what is referred to as a tolerance. Thus, a cast wheel may be acceptable if a certain dimension is within plus or minus 0.005 of an inch. Low-tech items have wide tolerances. High-tech items may require very narrow (sometimes called tight or close) tolerances. These differences are very important for the buyer to understand.

If you are a buyer for a low-tech item you may be able to use almost any supplier that produces that type of goods. However, you will more than likely pay much more to a firm that specializes in producing goods to close tolerances. One reason may be because they have more expensive

Exhibit 9-1.
Relative Importance of Quality

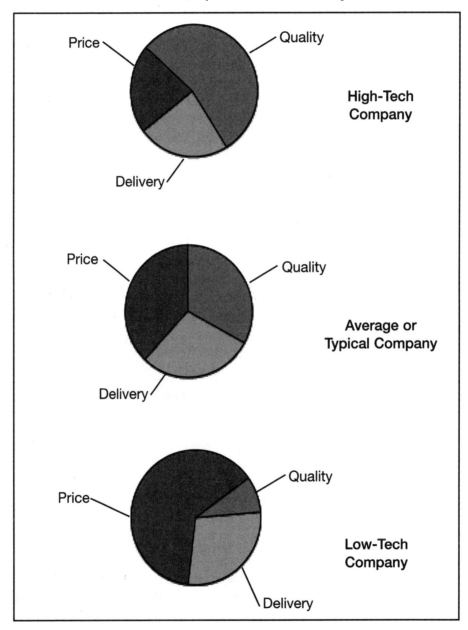

equipment that is needed for the closer tolerances. Another may be because they employ more highly skilled and therefore higher-salaried workers necessary to produce higher quality goods.

Conversely, you will more than likely have trouble getting good quality from a company that doesn't normally make goods requiring close tolerances. Companies that produce precision goods to narrow tolerances usually have different types of equipment. They usually have more ways of measuring and controlling output to meet high tech requirements, and as mentioned above, they usually have higher skilled workers. None of this matters if the goods produced by a low-tech organization meet your requirements. You will more than likely get what you want at a lower price.

It is only easier to buy the right quality with proprietary items if the specifications are in sufficient detail and reflect on what is actually desired. Any buyer will have difficulty satisfying requestors if the specifications are inadequate or inappropriate. This is why it is helpful for the buyer to know something about the design and engineering requirements of the product. It is helpful, but not necessary as long as the specifications are proper. If they are improper it may take much effort and time to discover why rejections are being made, why suppliers are failing to deliver acceptable goods, and even why purchasing is being blamed for buying poor quality.

Where Quality Begins

It is common business practice to begin checking products only after they are received. Many companies do better in catching faulty material by checking the items during the manufacturing process at the supplier's plant. The best way to obtain the quality you want is to begin the "quality assurance" process the first time you meet with the supplier.

You must communicate the importance of meeting your standards. This is accomplished in a number of ways. The image you create by a neat and orderly office, plant, and dress is not inconsequential. The supplier who sees that the buyer has a sloppy environment is not likely to believe you when you say you require the highest levels of quality.

If you need products requiring a high degree of precision, your instructions will carry more weight if your purchase order and specifications are carefully and accurately written. Misspelling, poor grammar, typos, and vague statements are more likely to be mirrored by the supplier's performance. You can't expect accurate invoices if your purchase order has many errors.

If you keep a salesperson waiting an inordinately long period of time even though she had an appointment, you are sending a message that meeting schedules is not important. How can you complain then when a supplier ships a few days late?

Letting the supplier know up front of the need to meet your specifications in order to obtain and keep business is of major importance. Questioning the supplier company about what quality levels it has produced and is capable of is necessary if your requirements are important. References should be obtained and checked. The higher your standards are, the more it is necessary to do a thorough investigation job. If the anticipated purchase involves any substantial dollar amount either directly or indirectly and either in the short term or long term, then it is advisable to conduct an on-site review of the supplier's facilities. At least a full description of equipment and, in particular, measuring devices and inspection tools should be obtained.

The buyer should ask for a description of the supplier's quality policies and procedures. A lack of any formalized procedures should raise a warning sign. One supplier indicated that every employee was responsible for quality, but could not provide details of how the employees assured any particular degree of quality. Statements of this kind are similar to typical puffery that salespeople use when they say their product is the best available. Essentially it is meaningless and has little value in determining the capability of a supplier.

Areas of Quality Concern

Whenever you buy you should expect the product that you selected will have the quality you need, but you also want quality in service from the supplier. Good product design helps achieve total quality. Proper material and construction helps achieve the durability specified. A good design helps assure that the item will do the job intended. Even if all product concerns provide good quality, total quality may still be less than desired.

Supplier quality is unsatisfactory when the supplier consistently fails to make delivery as agreed and scheduled. Quality is not acceptable if the supplier continues to deliver the wrong quantity of goods. There is evidence of poor quality if the supplier packages the goods in such a way that the goods are damaged. Quality is lacking if invoices are incorrect by showing the wrong quantity, or the wrong price, or other errors. Supplier quality is to blame if repair or maintenance of an item is needed and it takes an excessive amount of time to obtain service.

Concealed discrepancies are a common and sometimes difficult problem to resolve. A concealed discrepancy usually involves shelf items that are pre-packaged. For example, there may be a dozen boxes packed in a corrugated container; each is supposed to contain a dozen small pieces. Inspection may only go as far as determining that the quantity of corrugated containers is correct. More careful inspection may indicate that there are twelve boxes inside each corrugated container. Later, it may be discovered that there are only ten pieces inside the boxes instead of twelve. That amounts to a 17% shortage. The quicker the shortage is discovered after receipt of the goods, the more likely the supplier will be willing to issue credit. The supplier is likely to argue that the goods were used or taken by someone if the shipment was received more than a few weeks prior to discovery. Nevertheless, checking every internal box may be cost-prohibitive. The answer is to randomly spot check several cartons and keep good records. Repetitive offenses may indicate the shortages are not accidental.

Establishing the Quality Level

The user of a product or service may provide the buyer with the desired level of quality. For example, there may be a request for carpet for an executive office, and it should be of the highest quality or should last at least ten years. Often quality levels established this way are vague and open to different interpretations. Design engineers or other product designers need to be more precise. Much depends on the type of product, its complexity, and its intended use. Component parts for an airplane need detailed specifications and require closer tolerances than parts for consumer home use. Items used by hospitals and surgeons have strict quality guidelines dictated by the product designer or even by organizations whose purpose it is to develop standards. Government bodies frequently mandate certain requirements. For example, the AAR (Association of American Railroads) sets standards for components and the D.O.T. (Department of Transportation) provides its own requirements for railcars.

Although some standards are not required by law, the buyer is almost forced to abide by them for various other reasons. For example, electrical components may or may not be approved by the Underwriters Laboratory (UL). If approved, they are entitled to carry the UL seal of approval; if not approved, no such seal. One company found that it could purchase an electrical cord assembly delivered from the Far East for less than half the cost of that from the domestic supplier it was using. Although the item from overseas appeared exactly the same as that produced domestically, it did not carry the UL approval. The company's marketing and legal department decided not to use the foreign source because of the risk of possible legal action in case of an accident and the possibility of lost sales since potential customers would favor the competition that carried the UL seal on its product.

Incidentally, companies that want the UL seal must make application with Underwriters Laboratory and pay a large fee to cover the cost of testing and administrative costs. This often prevents small companies from making application and precludes them from becoming competitors to larger or well-established organizations.

Standards are established by independent associations and organizations for all types of products. Following are just some of the organizations that produce standards:

- AISI American Iron & Steel Institute
- ASME American Society of Mechanical Engineers
- ASTM American Society for Testing and Materials
- FAR Federal Acquisition Regulation
- ISO International Organization for Standardization
- MIL U.S. Military
- SAE Society of Automotive Engineers
- UL Underwriters' Laboratories

These organizations usually assign a specification number to the standard for any given product. Engineers or anyone interested may obtain copies of the standard for a fee. Such standards help designers establish specifications in less time and with less difficulty.

Both users and engineers often attempt to establish a certain level of quality by using a brand name in the specification rather than providing more detail. This is done to save time and effort, but it is based on several assumptions that are frequently not valid. Companies spend millions of dollars familiarizing the public with their brand names. Brands are supposed to establish a level of quality, but the products themselves may be changed over time as well as the company that sells those brands. Companies use every selling technique they can to get brand names used in engineering specifications. When they accomplish this, it usually locks in the buyer who must purchase that brand without much negotiating ability to do so.

The defined quality level is closely associated with the limits of acceptable and unacceptable quality. Sometimes those limits are incorporated into the specification; for example, so many bad parts allowed per thousand good parts. The allowance may be a percentage of pieces or a percentage or number out of tolerance. It then becomes a matter of checking the goods to determine if they are within the acceptable limitations.

How Quality is Measured

Some type of checking or monitoring system is usually employed once the level of acceptable quality is established. The checks may be done by a formal quality control department or by various other functions within the organization.

CHECKING GOODS RECEIVED

The receiving function normally has the responsibility to make sure the correct number of packages is received. Receiving clerks may also be responsible for counting separate items to make certain that the quantities shown on packing lists match the physical quantities being received. Accounts Payable normally checks invoices to see that they are in agreement with what the receiving function reports as being delivered and verifies that the quantity billed or received corresponds to the quantity shown on the purchase order issued by the buyer. All matching, formerly done by hand, is now facilitated by the computer.

The verification of product specifications may be done by one or more operations. Receiving inspection, warehousing operations, quality control, engineering, and the user may all take part in making sure the items received are the items ordered or identified. Once in a while, items will be mismarked and it is important to catch these mistakes before goods are stored or used. Mislabeled goods that are placed in stock will cause two errors to be recorded. The inventory record of the correct item will show a higher amount than actual, and the inventory record of the item actually received will show a lower amount than is on hand.

IN-PROCESS CHECKING

Buyers can take the seller's word that quality checks are being made as the goods are being manufactured or being done before the goods are shipped. However, if the specifications are difficult to achieve or if accuracy is of paramount importance, buyers may send inspectors or go themselves to check the goods before they are shipped. Some purchasers have quality control people stay at a supplier's plant on a permanent basis as long as that supplier is producing parts for the buyer.

USING SAMPLE TESTING

In many if not most cases, products and services are measured or tested by checking a small number of items. It is more meaningful to select the sample randomly throughout the batch rather than picking the samples from a restricted area such as the top or the bottom. True random numbers can be obtained from a random number table or generated from a computer program or a function built into some calculators. The samples are then chosen by using those random numbers.

Sample testing substantially reduces checking cost and has a high degree of reliability. The reliability of the total shipment (population) is a function of the size of the sample in comparison to the size of the population. The probability of acceptable material based on the sample size can be calculated by statistical methods.

A variation of the sampling method can be used to determine counts of very small inexpensive parts. For example, it would take a very long time and be cost-prohibitive to count a shipment containing ten million screws. Instead of counting every screw, you can count a hundred, weigh them, and then weigh the total shipment. There are now electronic scales that will allow you to place one piece on the scale and then tell you how many pieces are in the total shipment.

DESTRUCTIVE TESTING SOMETIMES NECESSARY

Some items are used up or destroyed when they are tested. Obviously, this type of item requires sample testing if you are to have any material remaining for regular use. Other items may be tested for various properties, but it is more economical to select samples for destructive testing. Let us say we want to test a shipment of steel. A chemical test can be conducted to determine the chemistry of the steel. We can check to see how much iron, carbon, and sulfur it contains. The steel can be put under a microscope to look for imperfections and to observe its crystal structure. With this information a metallurgist can predict various properties of the steel. Another way of testing is to take a sample and pull the steel until it breaks. We will then know the strength of that, but that piece will have been destroyed. In some cases one type of test or the other is more suitable. In other cases we may want to do both.

Measuring and Quality Control Tools for Testing

Organizations use many different types of equipment to determine if products meet specifications. Some measure distances, others measure weight, others magnify the surface so that visual inspection is easier or possible. For example, a microscope may be used to check for imperfections in the surface of a metal product.

Other types of equipment such as the Brinell or Rockwell machines test for hardness. A well-equipped quality inspection laboratory has ultrasonic devices, x-ray equipment, spectroscopes, and other sophisticated tools to determine if a product meets specifications. Highly-qualified suppliers not only have the equipment, but also use it on a regular basis. When visiting a supplier's facilities, a buyer is well-advised to ask to see what type of equipment is available for quality control and where inspections are conducted. It is not out of line to ask for a demonstration of such equipment.

Some suppliers have measuring devices built into the manufacturing process or assembly lines. The partially-completed products are automatically measured either mechanically or electronically and compared with the expected standard. Those items failing to meet the standard are flagged or shuttled off to a reject bin. Any buyer who is having difficulty getting acceptable parts from a manufacturer should suggest the supplier obtain such equipment. Who pays for the equipment may be negotiable. The buyer who has other potential sources of supply is in a strong position to influence the seller to make the investment if a significant amount of continuing business is at stake. Alternatively, the buyer may wish to make the investment to improve quality performance if the supplier is reluctant to pay for the measuring equipment.

Obtaining Quality Internationally

If obtaining quality goods is difficult domestically, it is even more difficult when buying from foreign suppliers. The problems are compounded by communication difficulties associated with language and cultural differences. Obtaining on-time delivery is more likely to be an issue because of distances and the cost of transportation. Determining the responsibility for damage is harder because of longer transit times and more people involved in handling the goods. While inspection prior to actual shipment is not impossible, it usually involves extra costs. Nevertheless, a well-informed and capable buyer should not avoid buying from an international source as long as proper care is taken regarding quality issues.

If foreign suppliers are evaluated prior to placing any orders and sufficient attention is given to communicating quality requirements, there is little reason to avoid using them as long as the risks are weighed and the total costs including the risk factors are considered. It is unwise to eliminate international sources because of some problems associated with using them. Sooner or later your competition will certainly use them if those sources provide the lowest overall cost. Avoiding the use of foreign material will eventually make your company non-competitive.

Solving the International Inspection Problem

It is not much of a problem to inspect material before shipment from Canada or Mexico. Suppliers are not that far away and it doesn't take much time or expense for a buyer or assigned inspector to take a trip to the supplier to check the goods before they are shipped. It costs significantly more in time and money to travel to a supplier in Asia. Unlike the purchase of material from a domestic supplier, products purchased from suppliers located in foreign countries are usually paid for before they are delivered to the buyer's site. Payments are made through the use of letters of credit and after all the paper work is properly completed and proof of delivery to an ocean vessel is provided, the foreign bank pays the amount forwarded to them from the buyer's bank. Therefore, unless some type of inspection is made prior to or at the time of shipment, any discrepancies or quality problems are not discovered until the goods are unpacked at the buyer's premises in this country.

One solution used by companies that import much material is to have a full-time employee reside in or near the foreign country with which they are doing business. An inspector living in Japan can cover suppliers in Japan and also travel to China and Korea to check material for a fraction of what it would cost in time and expense from the U.S. Most companies don't import frequently enough to warrant the cost of an offshore full-time inspector.

Another solution is to hire one of the firms that specialize in offering inspection services. For a fee they provide people who do the inspections for many companies wherever and whenever those companies need their service. There must be very clear, accurate, and precise specifications including any necessary drawings in order for the inspector to evaluate the material properly. Not all buying companies have this type of documentation but it is necessary unless the buyer is willing to accept the subjective opinion of the inspector.

You can still buy without making inspections prior to shipment, but there is some risk in being compensated if the material is unsatisfactory. Companies minimize the risk by learning as much about the foreign supplier as they can. They also obtain samples of the supplier's product prior to placing an order and samples of the ordered material before each shipment. After approval of the samples, the foreign bank is notified that material is acceptable for shipment and authorization for payment is given.

What You Need to Know About ISO

The Geneva, Switzerland-based organization with 91 member nations developed a series of quality management and quality assurance standards referred to as ISO-9000-9004. Although the initials ISO do not actually stand for International Standards Organization, that is what they amount to and that is what is commonly believed. Businesses meeting the ISO standards are ISO-approved. Approval comes only through an elaborate auditing process performed by ISO-approved auditors. There is a large expense for a supplier to obtain approval. Each physical location of a company must go through the approval process. The fee includes the costs of the auditor's time and any necessary travel to each site as well as the costs of training employees in order to meet the standards.

Many manufacturing companies in the U.S. want to obtain ISO-approved status for several reasons. Improved quality can reduce actual operating costs and increase customer satisfaction. A major reason for wanting ISO approval is that companies in Europe in particular and also

Japan are requiring suppliers to have ISO approval before awarding business. Many major U.S. companies are now also requiring the same, particularly in the automotive and high-tech industries. Although service businesses can and do obtain the award, not many do so at present.

HOW ISO AFFECTS PURCHASING OPERATIONS

There are two important ways that ISO affects buyers and purchasing managers. First, if your company is ISO-approved and your company wants to sell to customers that require ISO status, you also need to buy from ISO-approved suppliers. This is a portion of the ISO total quality concept.

The second way in which ISO affects purchasing concerns your own company's approval. If you are only making application and have not yet been approved, your purchasing operation will need to be sure it is doing certain things that ISO requires. Basically, it requires good purchasing policies and procedures that are documented in writing and that actual activity corresponds to those written policies and procedures. The auditors will check to see that you are abiding by these requirements. If your company has already been approved, periodic audits will be made to see that you are continuing to operate as indicated by the manuals or that the manuals have been revised to correspond to any changes in actual practices.

THE IMPORTANCE OF ISO FOR THE BUYER

If your company is selling to ISO-approved customers, or if your company is exporting, it is best to find and use ISO-approved suppliers. If you have critical specifications for the health care, electronic, or other high-tech industries, you may get a higher degree of reliable quality, on average, if your suppliers are ISO-approved. Otherwise, you may simply be paying a higher cost for items that can be obtained from a non-approved source. Items from companies that simply do not have the resources to invest in obtaining approval may produce quality as good as if not better than those who obtained approval. As long as your supplier meets your own requirements (you know what you need in terms of quality, you test samples, and do systematic inspections) you probably have no reason to require suppliers to be ISO-approved.

Maintaining Adequate Quality Records

A good formal quality control or quality assurance function will keep records of rejections or discrepancies. In a manufacturing environment such a department may spend most of its time monitoring quality in its own production department and all but ignore quality from suppliers. However, about half of the product costs in a manufacturing organization may be for purchasing material and supplies. An adequately staffed and knowledgeable QC function will realize this and pay equal attention to purchased material. The records kept by QC are valuable to purchasing only if buyers are notified as the problems occur and if periodic reports are submitted to purchasing. Formerly, purchasing routinely received a hard copy of inspection reports or monthly QC reports. Today, the records may be fed into the computer and available online, but the information has no value unless the buyer is alerted to new instances of rejections or problems.

Purchasing departments may either keep a hard copy of quality reports or the information from inspectors, or the QC department may be merged with purchasing software to produce reports that initiate corrective action by purchasing. Buyers may need to take immediate measures to solve a particular rejection or problem or if no action is required at once, accumulate the supplier's quality performance record to discuss long-term remedies or negotiate settlements.

Solving Quality Problems with the Supplier

It is best to prevent as many quality problems as possible before they occur by giving complete descriptions and specifications for the product. Proper emphasis on the importance of quality before and as the order is given is essential. Nevertheless, there will always be some shipments that do not match the requirements. The objective is zero defects, but, in practice, this is rarely achieved and the cost of assuring a low rate of rejections is prohibitive for most products or applications. In 1979, the quality guru Philip B. Crosby, wrote a book entitled *Quality Is Free*. The author contended that the cost of correcting and controlling errors exceeds the cost of making sure processes are done right the first time. While the idea has merit, few businesses seem to know how to eliminate all errors.

Buyers are called upon to correct errors when they happen. They typically call the supplier to inform him that a shipment has been received with shortages or with the incorrect material or with incorrect specifications. Other problems include incorrect invoices and material received damaged. Many of these problems are easily solved. The supplier readily accepts responsibility and credits the buyer's account or sends a new, correct shipment of goods. There are always some problems that are more difficult.

It may not be easy to know for certain where the error happened or who is responsible. Goods are sometimes damaged in transit and the primary supplier will claim the carrier caused the problem. The carrier might retort that the goods were damaged before shipment or that the packaging was inadequate and the fault lies with the supplier.

In another situation the supplier may insist that the proper goods were received and the error happened in the buyer's facilities or was caused by the buying company's personnel.

It is up to the buyer to sort out who has the correct story. In all probability no one really knows who was to blame. However, someone must pay the cost of correcting the error.

Good negotiating skill and diplomacy are required to settle the matter without completely alienating one or more of the parties involved. In rare cases, the buyer must take a tough stand and insist that the supplier make amends, but compromise is usually the best approach.

If good quality records are kept, it is clear which suppliers have quality problems and which rarely, if ever, make mistakes. The buyer should use the Pareto principle to concentrate on improving the few suppliers that account for most of the errors. Others to be concerned about are those that are financially weak or are having labor problems. They may begin to take short cuts to save costs or employees may not care what they produce for the company. When the buyer knows there are potential problems from a supplier, he or she should look around for alternate sources to have them ready if needed. Increased inspection and sample submission might be helpful in discovering errors or preventing long-term problems.

Suppliers are often helpful and quick to solve individual quality problems but ignore getting to the root of the problem. A buyer can waste considerable time solving separate one-time problems without ever determining the underlying cause. It may take much longer initially to learn what the cause is and institute corrective actions, but in the long run the total time and effort will be reduced.

Summary

Quality depends on what you need and what you are willing to pay for. The quality of proprietary products is easier to measure because you provide your own specifications. Quality begins before the order is placed. You must learn the supplier's capabilities ahead of time and communicate your requirements effectively. On-time delivery, accurate counts, and correct invoices in addition to product acceptance are included in a complete evaluation of a supplier's performance. Product precision requirements vary depending on the buyer's industry. Material needs to be checked or inspected upon receipt, but also may be checked during the manufacturing process. Testing samples determines if goods are acceptable. Some goods require destructive testing of samples. There are many types of tools used to check specifications, and during a visit to a potential supplier the buyer should ask to see what tools are on hand and in use. Inspection and checking of material purchased from international suppliers and made at distant foreign locations is expensive. Outside inspection companies may be used provided the buyer can supply good specification documents or engineering drawings. Samples from international suppliers prior to shipment may be sufficient if the seller is strong financially and there are exceptionally good relations between the buying and selling companies.

ISO affects purchasing in several ways. ISO-approved suppliers meet certain standards that should provide better quality although their products may be higher in price. Purchasing must have good policy and procedure manuals and actual activities must correspond to what is required by those documents in order for a company to become ISO-approved.

Records must be kept of rejections or any type of poor quality experience in order to measure supplier performance objectively and to determine which suppliers need most improvement. Buyers should try to determine who is responsible for errors and negotiate for solutions. It is not enough to get individual errors corrected. Learning the cause is the first step in eliminating future similar problems.

Chapter 10

Methods
of Cost
Minimization

Purchasing for business used to be primarily concerned about bargaining for a lower price. In recent years the emphasis has shifted to a consideration of the total costs of obtaining the proper kind of goods when they are needed. Price is only one element of all types of costs. Meeting quality requirements, the scheduled delivery date, and minimizing the risk of purchase are other "costs."

Nevertheless price may reflect these other costs. For instance, it is more risky to place an order with a new unknown business than with a well-established business that feels justified in asking a higher price. New businesses charge less because there is a risk cost of placing an order with them. Another example is cost of better quality: obviously, it is going to cost you more for a heavier gauge of steel than for a lighter gauge. If you need the heavier gauge you don't mind paying for it. Otherwise you are wasting money.

The required delivery date is most important. Companies will sometimes pay more for quick delivery. It may not be worth a very low price if the supplier can not meet the delivery date you want.

Even though all factors are important in evaluating a buyer's performance, some are difficult to measure. Price seems to be the easiest indicator to measure. For that reason alone, the buyer should place heavy emphasis on obtaining the lowest price possible, providing the specifications are met and delivery is made when the material is needed. Price should not be the primary motivation in lowering costs; the proper objective is to maximize profits for the organization, and in most cases paying as little as possible for the right material certainly helps achieve that objective.

Why in most cases and not in all? The reason is that sometimes it is better to pay more to get a different product that accomplishes the job better and costs less in the long run. For example, say you are buying a coating or paint, one which is $10 dollars a gallon and another which is $20 a gallon. If you know that the $20-a-gallon paint will last three times as long as the $10-a-gallon paint, you would be foolish to buy the cheaper one because in the long-run it will cost more. For a proper evaluation you will also need to consider the cost of labor to apply the paint and how often repainting will be necessary. Also you will need to consider the pigment solids in the paint to determine how many gallons will be required of each.

A buyer's job is a lot more complex and more interesting than would first appear. It is not just placing an order. It is not only negotiating for the first-time buy. It involves analysis, calculation, constant evaluation, and a continual effort to minimize the costs of acquisition and possession of every type of product and service.

Reducing MRO Expenses

Maintenance, repair, and operating expenses are incurred by any type of business organization. They include office supplies, janitorial supplies, and repairs for the office, warehouse, or factory. While raw material, components, and assemblies for resale get most of the attention in manufacturing organizations, MRO items should not be neglected because substantial savings can be achieved.

HOW TO REDUCE OFFICE SUPPLY EXPENSES

Some companies operate with little or no office supply expense. Others spend enormous amounts. The difference might be that some companies have many more office workers, which is generally true. The more office workers, the more the expense. However, if you compare expenses in terms of dollars spent per office worker, then every company should be about the same regardless of the number of office personnel. A rule of thumb is about $1000 per year per office or clerical employee.

When you measure according to this formula, there can still be big differences between one company and another even in the same industry. In part that may be because some companies control their expenses while others do not. Here are some suggestions to help you get those expenses down and keep them down.

STANDARDIZE PRODUCTS

Where possible, establish standardized company supplies. Choose economical products that most users will find acceptable. Some companies have their own internal catalogs that they distribute to employees which list the items that are usually ordered or that are kept in stock. For example, you might restrict the choice to three or four pens instead of allowing employees to select from the myriad choice in the office supply catalog. The supplier catalog we have shows 131 different types not including color choices.

If employees can choose an item that is in the store room or one that requires waiting several days for a special order, they will usually pick the item that is in stock. If some insist on expensive products that must be special ordered, let them know that not only will they have to wait a few days, but they may also exceed the budget. Advise them how much they exceeded the budget when they do.

CONTROL FORMS DESIGN AND USAGE

Establish a forms design and forms control function. It keeps forms cost low by reducing printing expense, saving form preparation time, and eliminating unnecessary paperwork. Order economical quantities but avoid large quantities if there is a chance the forms will be revised. Try to plan revisions so that the supply of old forms will be used up just about the time the new form arrives.

STOCK SUPPLIES SECURELY

Have a centrally located storage area for office supplies. Keep the area locked and have one person responsible for controlling access, receiving and distributing stock, taking physical inventory, and maintaining records.

ELIMINATE SECONDARY STORAGE AREAS

Encourage people to take only what they are going to use within a few weeks. In addition to inventory in the stock room, departments often keep their own. Then individual employees keep extra supplies for themselves in their desk drawers. All these extra supplies can expand inventory to two or three times what is necessary. Some organizations periodically collect and return them to one central location.

CONTROL STOCKING AND USAGE INTERNALLY

Don't let salespeople call on every office employee to see if they need any supplies. The offer to do this sounds better than it is. The salesperson claims he or she will eliminate the need for storage and improve communication and employee satisfaction. In fact, the salesperson, whether deliberately or not, will influence employees to order expensive items which they don't need.

USE A SYSTEMS CONTRACT

Obtain bids based on annual estimated usage from office suppliers periodically. Try to obtain bids from three or more suppliers. Award contracts for your total requirements based on the total annual cost of all items rather than on the cost of individual items.

BUDGET VARIOUS TYPES OF SUPPLIES

Establish a reasonable and generous budget for each department and charge actual requisitions or inventory withdrawals to those departments. Notify them during the year if their usage indicates a budget overrun. Although budgeting and other controls involve a cost in themselves, the savings are usually worth it. Nevertheless, look at the results carefully. If they don't reduce your cost, eliminate them one by one so you can measure what that control achieved. Most of the budgeting and record keeping can be done easily by using the computer and as a by-product of order fulfillment.

UNDERSTAND THE USAGE TO DETERMINE THE CHANNEL

You can buy many commodities, raw material, components, and even finished goods from distributors, middlemen, or the manufacturer, depending on the amount you need at any one time or for an extended length of time. For example, steel may be purchased from a so-called "warehouse," or "service center," or it may be obtained directly from a mill where the price is usually lower. However, those businesses normally won't sell to you if you buy in low quantities. Furthermore, they usually will not stock the material for an extended period, and, depending on the type of product and industry, they may not produce the product to the schedule you want.

Since you generally obtain a lower price from the manufacturer, it pays to keep an eye on your volume and find out what volume is necessary or will interest the manufacturer. Don't assume that the prices are the same for everyone, or that one manufacturer will have the same policy as its competitor regarding the necessary volume.

PAY ATTENTION TO INTERNAL COSTS

Buyers are most concerned about negotiating with the most competitive suppliers to obtain material and services at the lowest costs. But they sometime lose sight of internal costs that may erode any savings obtained elsewhere. Internal costs, which include labor and administrative expenses, sometimes exceed the cost of the purchased items. Here are some ways that internal costs can be excessive.

1. The specifications produced by engineers or users may call for products or services that are higher priced than other equally satisfactory products.

2. Low quantities are requested by users even though the items are used continually and must be constantly reordered. This means paying a higher price than necessary because you lose quantity discounts or higher quantity price breaks. In addition it wastes time and effort processing orders for the same item multiple times. This happens because requestors have not planned their requirements and therefore cannot forecast their usage, or because they believe, in error, that ordering a higher quantity for inventory will always increase costs. This only increases costs if there is no compensating price reduction or reduction in other costs. It is frequently up to the buyer to determine if an item is going to be used on a continual basis. Even when this is the case, she may need to obtain approval to order a larger quantity. Keep in mind that the purchase agreement may not call for the total quantity to be delivered or paid for at one time.

Controlling the Cost of Capital Equipment

Capital equipment items are those products that are durable and long-lasting. They normally are relatively high-priced per unit compared with other items that are either consumable or used in production processes. Furniture, computers, machinery, and certain tooling are examples of capital equipment categories.

Capital items may be strictly controlled by some organizations or completely neglected by others. Sometimes the policies and procedures for ordering capital equipment are inadequate to minimize cost of the products. For example, prices may be obtained far in advance of the actual purchase in order to get budget approval for the product. Such prices may be obtained quickly without much negotiating effort or competitive comparison. They may be based on a particular set of specifications that are not necessarily the best for the purpose intended. Then when it is time to make the actual purchase, the buyer is almost forced to use those specifications and, consequently, the supplier who submitted the information. Buyers and purchasing managers should educate management why such a procedure can be very costly. The budgeting process should be separate from the shopping, negotiating, and supplier selection process.

DETERMINING THE TYPE AND COSTS OF CAPITAL TOOLING

The word "tooling" is often misleading. Buyers may purchase hand tools, but tooling usually refers to machine tools or the items necessary to produce other products. For example, metal plates may be purchased for the production of printed forms. Cutting dies may be purchased for the production of various sizes of corrugated containers. Stamping dies may be purchased to produce metal stampings. Molds and patterns are used for castings. Other types of dies are needed for metal forgings and extrusions. Another type of die is needed for plastic injection molding. All of these items are expensive, ranging in price from hundreds to many thousands of dollars. It would not be unusual to pay $300,000 for a certain type or size of die.

The buyer of such tooling has various decisions to make regarding these purchases. In most cases engineers or manufacturing personnel either specify or assist in these decisions. In any case, because of the large expenditures involved, buyers should learn how these decisions are made and be able to either make the best decision if necessary or to recommend an alternative purchase.

The cost of the tooling will vary because of its durability, complexity, accuracy and size. A less durable tool may do the job and may be the desired choice if only a few pieces are to be made. A tool with closer tolerances may be required to produce precision parts. A larger die with more cavities will produce more finished parts in less time but will cost more. If higher quantities are needed, the higher tooling cost is worth the price; if not, it is wasted money. One large tool versus two smaller ones will mean that only one supplier can produce the product. On the other hand, buying two smaller tools instead of one large tool may require a greater investment. You need the input of marketing, finance, and purchasing management to make the best decision.

Controlling the Cost of Raw Material, Components for Production, and Finished Goods for Resale

Purchasing items for production or resale is similar to purchasing capital goods in that it may involve large expenditures. The main difference is that these items are usually ordered continuously. Note that we are referring to items that go into the product rather than items that are used to help make the product, which fall under the MRO category (Maintenance, Repair, and Operating Supplies). For example, oil to lubricate machinery used to make items for resale is an MRO item, whereas oil that is used in a mass-produced machine that will be resold is a production item.

Manufacturing companies give production items most attention. They want to keep the cost of these items as low as possible, because the final price to the customer depends on the total cost of all material and labor going into the product. The price to the final customer must include a markup and that price must be competitive if the company is going to stay in business for very long. Thus, while a buyer may be criticized for paying too much for an MRO item, questions will probably be more frequent and more intense when it is a production item. There are exceptions. Critics are more likely to see lower prices for an office supply item than they are for a certain type of bearing or gasket. However, the smart manager or executive knows that it is much more important to look at the component cost of items for resale rather than at items with small value and small internal usage.

Don't confuse items with small value to items with a low price. A high volume raw material item or component may only cost a fraction of a cent, but amount to many dollars in annual purchases. This is an important point.

You must look at the expenditure of purchases over time when evaluating the cost effect of production items. The automotive companies are concerned about the third decimal point when looking at the cost of a screw.

Take Preventative Action to Avoid Price Increases

You might be able to delay or eliminate a price increase altogether if you take action when you anticipate such an increase. Send a letter to the top sales executive indicating why you believe a price decrease is justified. If necessary, hold a meeting to discuss why a price reduction is called for. Your arguments may fall on deaf ears during a period of high inflation, but the supplier may reconsider any planned increases. Price increases announced by the steel industry were rescinded when many buyers objected to them across-the-board.

USE THE LEARNING CURVE

The learning curve shows that companies reduce their costs as they gain experience. The buyer can use this concept by telling the supplier that a portion of the savings from experience should result in a price reduction. The learning curve is simply a diagram of falling costs as a result of improvements in efficiency when workers have more experience. In other words, when workers begin to do a job they are slow and may not use the best techniques. As they become more experienced they are able to work faster and use methods that reduce labor or material. Even wasted material is reduced that may have been factored into the original price.

Break Out Component Costs

Suppliers like to give you a price of a finished product or assembly without furnishing the costs of the components. They dislike telling the buyer how many hours it takes to produce each component and what labor rates are to produce those components. Perhaps "dislike" is not the appropriate word; perhaps they just don't know. Although the salesperson may not know, hopefully his accounting people will. Otherwise how are fair prices established? The answer is that prices are not always based on what is fair or what the supplier's cost is. The price can be based on what the market will bear or on an inflated markup from the total estimated cost of the product. Even when suppliers believe they know their actual costs, frequently they may not. When that is the case they often charge excessive prices and become very profitable, at least temporarily until the competition takes their business through lower pricing policies. Of course, there are times when suppliers unknowingly price products below their costs because they didn't calculate their costs correctly. If this happens once in a while, it probably has no serious or lasting effect, but if it is across-the-board on many products or continues for very long, the company can go out of business.

Although it is nice to get a real bargain, it may not be in the buyer's interest to purchase material below true cost if the seller is unaware of the situation. The buying company will gain in the short run, but if purchases are continually made below cost, the supplier will be lost and it will be difficult if it is the only supplier that produces the material. If only a higher-priced supplier is available when the low-priced supplier goes out of business, then prices may go higher still when there is no further competition. It is only good business to get a low price for the products you buy, but you should allow and expect your suppliers to make a reasonable profit.

The buyer may get detailed cost information in other ways when a supplier fails to provide component costs. Although the cost obtained from other sources may not be the exact prices that the supplier is paying, they will usually be close enough to use in estimating the total assembly costs. Assume you are buying a hydraulic pump that is made up of a casting, nylon gaskets, some screws, lock washers, a few nuts, and a name plate. It is easy to go to the Thomas Register or some other directory and find out who supplies these components. Then you can simply call them and get the prices of various quantities. You must add the cost of freight and the cost of labor for assembly. Then you need to increase the total by a good estimate for overhead, administrative, and sales expense, say 50%.

Then add another 10% to 20% for profit, and you most likely will have the minimum price that the product could be sold for. You may also obtain various raw material or commodity prices from the financial pages of newspapers and from business magazines. Commodity price indexes and labor rates are available in the publications of the U.S. Department of Labor, Bureau of Labor Statistics or through their Internet site. You can use a price index to calculate the effect of price changes once you learn the base price at a point in time.

Armed with your best estimate you then can approach the seller and discuss why your total may be different from the price offered. This approach often enlightens the seller about true costs: it catches pricing mistakes; it tells the supplier that you are a professional buyer interested in doing business rather than in just placing orders. Your interest in discussing the details normally is not resented by suppliers who really want your business. More often they realize that you want to place an order with them, but first it must be an advantageous one.

Postpone Price Increases

It is better to pay the same amount later than to pay it now. "Time is money" is more than a cliche. You can put any dollars that you don't spend into an investment that pays interest or use it in other ways that will make more money for you. Therefore, when any supplier announces a price increase, you should try to postpone its effective date as long as possible.

In a clause about prices in a long-term agreement, the buyer should indicate that price increase changes are only to be made at certain intervals, such as at year end or for the model year, or every six months, and that they must be based on changes in actual costs paid by the supplier. The supplier should be required to furnish documented proof of increases paid in the form of invoices or the supplier's labor contract agreement showing amounts and effective dates.

Attempts at postponement should be made even if no long-term agreement exists and the relationship with the supplier is on an order-by-order basis. In no case should price changes apply to existing orders with a firm price. The buyer should first ask for 90 days (or until year-end if that is later). If the seller won't agree, the buyer should then try for a 60 days postponement.

Write Escalator Clauses with Care

It is common to include escalator clauses in long-term agreements which simply allow the supplier to change the price if his prices rise. The buyer should make sure that such clauses include a provision, discussed previously, that the supplier must document cost increases. The buyer should also try to negotiate that no amount for extra profit will be added to the change.

Not long ago purchasing people, as well as business people in general, took a high degree of inflation as normal and routine. The term "escalator clause" itself reflects that attitude. But the moving staircase also can go down and times change. There may yet be deflation someday, and the clause should be written so those suppliers must also reduce prices when their costs go down.

Buying Legal, Accounting, and Other Services

The advice on this subject is probably for the reader in a small company who has some general management responsibility, usually either general management or a non-purchasing department manager selects professional services and makes agreements with them without the advice or talents of purchasing professionals. While this is understandable in some respects, the fees that are paid can be exorbitant and the services provided inadequate. Accounting firms, law firms, or others should be thoroughly checked in the same way that any other supplier is investigated. It is interesting that executive search firms are hired at high cost to find purchasing executives without the slightest idea what purchasing does or what makes a good purchasing executive.

Fees from accounting firms and law firms are usually based on per-hour rates that can skyrocket if not controlled. Firms may charge the rate for senior partners but use a novice to perform the work. Firms with only a few people who may or may not be the best qualified can charge as much as the biggest and most respected in the business.

The solution is to discuss fees ahead of time. Prepare an itemized list of what will be charged for what. Put a limit on what will be done and on the maximum you are willing to spend. Any agreement with an open price term is like asking for an inflated charge. Make sure that bills are itemized and check out what was done. Have auditors sign in and sign out so you know when they are on the premises.

Don't be timid about questioning bills. If you think they are too high or incorrect, ask for a reduction. Bills from lawyers, accountants, engineers, and consultants are frequently reduced when questioned.

Consider Unusual Channels of Supply

What a deal you can get if you buy from a company that is going out of business! A company that is closing a plant or office sometimes wants to get rid of almost new equipment without having to move it. Businesses decide not to continue carrying a certain product and just want the space for other items. The inventory is brand new, but is up for sale at a fraction of its cost; they may even be willing to settle for less.

There is a risk, however, that one must guard against. Don't buy from someone who pulls up in a car or truck and tries to sell you brand new tools or other supplies at half price. The items may be stolen and there is a possibility the police could confiscate them. Anything you paid would simply be money lost. Also the goods may not be what they seem. They may be defective or mislabeled.

BUYING AT AUCTIONS

You can get a bargain when you buy at an auction but you have to know what you are doing. There are different types of auctions: in some there is no minimum bid; in others that are held with reserve, a successful bid must be a certain minimum to purchase the product. Auctions primarily feature used machinery, used office equipment, land and buildings, and used automobiles and trucks. Antique, collectibles, and estate sale auctions appeal to consumers rather than buyers for business. Events are announced in the business section of newspapers and through direct mail to potential buyers. Interested buyers may call various auction firms that are listed in the telephone book and elsewhere to be placed on the mailing list.

Procedures differ but potential buyers normally need to register at least a few hours in advance and show creditworthiness. Many potential buyers attend the offer event and bid against each other. Payment is usually required immediately and the buyer must arrange for pickup and transportation of the purchased product within a short time.

Buyers who attend auctions regularly have prearranged signals that indicate acceptance of price called out by the auctioneer. It might be scratching the nose or pulling on the ear or just shaking the head. In some cases auctioneers hand out numbered cards that are held up if the auctioneer wants to accept an offered price. Anyone attending must be careful not to make a motion that might be misinterpreted as acceptance of an offer. Once a buyer makes an offer, it cannot be withdrawn and the buyer is obligated to pay for the item. That is why potential buyers are usually given the opportunity to inspect the goods a day or two before the auction is held. When no other bids are being made the acceptance of the last bid is made by the auctioneer saying, "going once, going twice, sold" and simultaneously striking a gavel.

You can get great bargains at auctions, but also lemons. There is no warranty, and it is doubtful that you can obtain any compensation for poor products if they were not misrepresented by the auctioneer.

OBTAINING MATERIAL BY BARTERING

The oldest way of obtaining products or services is by exchanging things you have for other things that you need. Called bartering, it was used before the invention of money. Today there are firms to assist in using this function. Many companies tell the bartering company what they have to give and what products or services they need. The bartering company acts as a clearinghouse assigning a dollar value to the goods and matching complementary requirements where possible. All parties to transactions gain when an exchange is made without the use of any cash. The apparent savings in taxes are misleading because the government requires such transactions to be reported and taxable. The major advantages are that surplus material or inventory can be used to obtain useful products or services with little or no costs, and transactions can be accomplished without financing or drawing on cash.

BUYING USED EQUIPMENT FROM DEALERS AND NEW EQUIPMENT SUPPLIERS

Acquiring less costly used equipment rather than buying new can also conserve cash. Sometimes products can be obtained in practically new condition at substantially lower prices. Usual products are office furniture, computers, machine tools, and automobiles and trucks. Used equipment dealers usually specialize in certain products. Used, reconditioned, or remanufactured products can often be purchased from new equipment sellers as well. They, however, are not likely to offer used items unless the buyer first indicates an interest or unless the buyer seems unwilling to pay the asking price for new items.

Buyers should be particularly cautious about any items with moving parts to make sure they are in good working condition. Used equipment may have no warranty or one of very short duration. It may be difficult or impossible to obtain repair parts for older equipment, for equipment manufactured by companies no longer in business, or by foreign manufacturers.

BUYING FROM RETAIL OUTLETS

Retail outlets are a possible source for items needed in emergencies or in small quantities. Generally, prices will be much higher, but there are exceptions because some retailers make a special effort to obtain business customers. They may even have separate divisions that sell to business buyers.

Summary

Although price is a major consideration for business buyers, they should be more concerned about total costs, which include meeting quality needs, making the delivery schedule, and the amount of risk involved as well as the price. Expenses can be reduced by standardizing products. Good forms design and control will lower expenses and save time. Supplies should be stocked in a secure location and secondary storage areas minimized, if not eliminated. Control should be by employees only. The use of systems contracts reduces administrative and other costs. Supplies should be budgeted and controlled. The proper supply channel is necessary to obtain the lowest cost. Internal activities affect the purchase cost. Capital equipment budget limitations should be divorced from purchasing negotiations. Buying the proper tooling requires analysis and planning. Select raw material and production component items for negotiating efforts that have the highest total expenditures for a year without regard to unit cost.

Ask for price and other cost reductions before price increases are announced. Instruct the supplier to use the learning curve principle and provide component costs of purchased items. Postpone any announced price increases by sixty or ninety days or until the end of the year. Make sure that escalator clauses include cost reduction reporting from deflation as well as inflation.

Other supply channels include buying at auctions, bartering, used equipment dealers, and retail outlets. Although bargains may be obtained from these types of suppliers, the buyer must be cautious. There may be no warranties, and repair parts may be difficult if not impossible to obtain.

Chapter 11

Business
Functions
Related
to Buying

Many types of duties are involved in purchasing. A buyer must make certain to get sufficient information from a requestor to make the appropriate purchase. The information must be accurate and the purchase properly authorized.

One of the most important duties is to locate qualified suppliers, obtain cost information from each before any orders are given. The cost information from each supplier must be compared in order to select the lowest cost supplier.

The buyer must monitor the supplier to make certain that deliveries are made on time. Any discrepancies in quantity or quality must be resolved with the responsible party.

All of these duties and others are normal functions of the purchasing department; but there are others that may or may not be delegated to buyers or other individuals in purchasing. Some of those duties or responsibilities that are often included are value analysis, the sale of scrap or surplus material, controlling inventory, forecasting cost changes of various types, preparing budgets and objectives, and preparing various reports for management. In addition to inventory control, sometimes purchasing has full responsibility for all materials management functions such as traffic, warehousing, shipping, and receiving. Here is a closer look at each of these functions.

Using Value Analysis to Slash Costs

Sometimes called Value Engineering, Value Analysis is an under-utilized and frequently misunderstood method of substantially reducing business costs. It is a systemized method of reducing the cost of material or services. Purchasing people are often give the responsibility to lead a VA program since the material or services involved in the analysis are either purchased or may be purchased. Seldom do employees from other departments understand or appreciate the tremendous contribution that VA can provide. Buyers usually do, but they often fail to take full advantage of their unique knowledge and positions because of insufficient time to handle the extra work that VA may add.

However, very little time may be required if the program is properly managed. As little as one or two hours a month may be all that is necessary to have some type of VA program and some effort with VA is better than none.

The objective of VA is to reduce costs of products or services by choosing those that are either produced in-house or more frequently purchased from outside the organization. Although VA has been used chiefly by manufacturing companies, it can be used just as well by retailers or service businesses. The target items for analysis may be used internally or may be items that are sold to the organization and may be purchased services as well as tangible products.

The normal method used to conduct the analysis is to establish a committee made up of one individual from various departments within the organization such as accounting, sales, engineering, production (if it is a manufacturing company), quality control, and purchasing. This latter person is the logical choice as the leader or chairperson of the group.

To establish an agenda pick the appropriate items for analysis and establish meeting times. A convenient time may be in the evening after normal business hours.

The first major undertaking should be to determine the function of the product or service, a crucial step in the process.

Next comes the brainstorming session, during which the members of the committee are encouraged to suggest their ideas, however unorthodox, to accomplish the same function in as many different ways as possible. No idea should be rejected outright and none ridiculed.

People are selected from various departments to bring fresh ideas to the table. Often those too involved with the products fail to look beyond the obvious. Those uninformed about the product or service may suggest something that seems absurd, but upon closer scrutiny turns out to be brilliant.

Suggestions can involve eliminating a component or feature, changing the raw material, combining items or processes, changing packaging, adding a component or feature to reduce in-house labor, changing the shape, size, or other characteristic of the product.

Next is costing out the suggestions. This is where the buyer's effort is usually called for. The suggestions may involve new material or a different product entirely. The buyer must obtain prices and costs from suppliers who may be helpful in suggesting various ways of reducing costs; the buyer should encourage such suggestions and report them to the committee for consideration.

Final steps include eliminating the least favorable ideas and testing the best solutions. The results then must be reported to the departments affected and to general management. VA programs often fail because the reporting stage is given insufficient attention.

Sale of Scrap, Surplus, and Obsolete Material

The sale of unneeded purchased material is a responsibility often given to the purchasing department, which some purchasing people find hard to understand since it seems more like a sales function than a purchasing function. But the buyer may be able to get the supplier who originally sold the material to take it back or even have another supplier who deals with the same type of material be willing to buy it. In either case, the amount offered may be considerably less than the original purchase price. The amount received depends on the condition of the material, the length of time it has been in stock, and the buyer's negotiating ability.

There are other ways of disposing of the material. Lists of the material may be mailed to companies known to use it. Advertisements may be placed in trade magazines or newspapers. The buyer may contact used equipment dealers who may purchase the goods or accept it on consignment basis, although the latter is not a recommended solution.

If there is a great amount of equipment or material, for example, because of a plant or facility closing, an auction company is a good solution. It will do the advertising, mark the material, and handle the sale. Such companies earn their revenue in several different ways. An agreement may be based on a flat fee, on a percentage of the sales, or on some combination of each. The seller (buyer) can establish a minimum acceptable price for each item.

Another solution is to list items for sale on the Web. The American Purchasing Society will list surplus items for sale at no charge if you are a member. For further information contact the Society at 630 859-0250.

Maintaining the Proper Level of Inventory

Control of inventory is not easy. It depends to a large extent on the method used, on the products involved, the size of the organization, and the type of business. Keeping inventory to a minimum while satisfying customer needs is of major concern to general management. Many companies have failed, at least in part, because of poor inventory control. Many theories and methods are used in controlling inventory levels, about which much has been written, but here is a capsule look at some:

INVENTORY METHOD USED

There are two major and separate ways of looking at and controlling inventory. One is the way accounting looks at inventory; the other is the way users of the products look at inventory. Accountants are primarily concerned with the financial aspects of inventory control. All good managers should be concerned about inventory costs, but users and the managers of other departments tend to be more concerned about making sure there is enough material available to do their jobs and achieve their non-financial objectives. For example, if raw material in a manufacturing environment is not available to produce a finished product, the fact that inventory cost is low makes little difference.

Or the sales department of a distributor would not be consoled by low inventory costs if orders were continually delivered late to customers because of out-of-stock conditions.

One of the first concerns of business is to make certain material is available when and where needed. It is therefore necessary to closely monitor the quantity of goods available to meet those needs. If the job is done properly, the accountants will be satisfied because very little excess quantity will be on hand to cause unnecessary costs.

Financial control of inventory involves looking at the number of turns per time period, in particular the ratio of net sales in dollars to the inventory value in dollars which indicates inventory turnover and marketing efficiency. The higher the rate of movement of inventory, the better. A low figure indicates that some material may be unsaleable because of obsolescence or other reasons and must be written off as a loss for the organization.

Although buyers and purchasing managers may want to look at the total dollar figures, the value of individual items should be of most concern to determine what items to work on first. Concentrate on those that involve many dollars tied up in excess inventory. However, to determine the proper inventory level, the quantities on hand must be compared to the usage within a given time period.

Management of inventory may be done manually or by computer. Manual systems were always necessary before the use of the computer. They may still be acceptable to control a small number of items, or until the organization feels control of inventory is of paramount importance, but manual systems are often prone to error and labor intensive. This makes record keeping costly.

A manual system posts, that is records, the quantity of each item received, and the quantity used. Thus the balance should reflect what is on hand. Periodically, physical counts of the actual material are made to compare with the written record, or what is referred to as the book figures.

An even simpler manual system is based on the physical appearance of the material. A decision to reorder is triggered when the stock gets to a certain level. Some organizations use a marker to indicate when to reorder. For example, if the material is a stack of forms, a colored piece of paper is inserted at some point in the stack. When the pile is reduced to that level, a new order is placed for more forms.

Computer-controlled systems do the same thing as manual systems, only they do more. The information may be entered manually into the computer upon receipt, or usage of the goods, or entered from other documents. For example, generation of a purchase order may automatically include the quantities on order in the inventory records, although it will not show the material available until actually received. Likewise, customer orders may automatically deduct the quantities needed to fill those orders. Inventory control systems are frequently a module of accounting software.

The Type of Products Affects Control of Inventory

Products that are susceptible to theft are called pilferable items. Administrative procedures need not be different for this type of stock, but physical controls should be. Pilferable items may be in a special cage with a lock or even kept in a safe if small enough. Access to the storage area may be restricted to certain trusted personnel. Such an example would be gold salts that are used to manufacture PC boards.

Obsolete products that are kept in inventory inflate the total value on hand and distort the financial picture. The buyer should be careful not to order material that is expected to become outdated or that will be replaced. Buyers should communicate often with sales, marketing, and engineering to learn about products that may be discontinued or replaced. A routine procedure should be set in place to notify purchasing well in advance of any anticipated or planned change. A note of such planned changes should be made on the item's inventory record as well as on any buy card or other purchasing record so the buyer will be alerted not to order more than the minimum.

The cost of the product unit itself is more likely to be of concern for smaller companies than for big organizations. Large cash commitments may seriously strain working capital of the smaller concern. The buyer should make sure that the financial officer or appropriate manager is aware of such orders before they are placed. It is better to place more frequent orders for smaller quantities rather than delay payment to a supplier and have a poor credit report on the records.

If smaller orders cause a price increase, the buyer can perhaps negotiate a firm agreement for the larger quantity, but spread out delivery until needed and the time for payments at an appropriate time after each delivery. Such an arrangement provides the advantage of the lower price from a large quantity, keeps inventory at a minimum, and assures the ability to pay on time. The seller gains by making a big sale.

The physical size of the product is an important factor to consider before ordering. Every other variable may indicate that 2,500 pieces should be ordered, but that could be costly if there is only room for 1,500. It is not uncommon to see plants so overcrowded with material that stock gets misplaced, lost, or damaged. Crowded conditions cause inefficient operations; the need to move material to a public warehouse is costly.

EOQ (Economic Order Quantity) formulas are helpful in considering administrative and holding costs when calculating order size, but they do not take storage space or obsolescence into consideration, nor do they allow for price advantages offered for different quantities. If you are using such formulas, stop and think about these other factors before placing the order.

The usual formula is $EOQ = (2AS/pI)^{1/2}$

where A = the annual usage, S = the ordering cost, p = the unit delivered price, and I = the inventory carrying cost expressed as a decimal fraction of average inventory.

Companies use different inventory methods for different types of products. Expensive and high usage items are usually controlled by more sophisticated methods. There is often little control of low-value or seldom-purchased items which may be controlled by visual inspection of the stock level. Actual counts are frequently estimated. An example is the method of counting hardware or fasteners such as nuts, bolts, screws, and washers. A small sample is counted and then weighed. Then the entire lot is weighed and a simple calculation determines the total number of pieces in the lot. This is close enough and is less labor-intensive than counting many thousands or millions of pieces. The actual difference or margin of error between an exact count and this method is very small since it is common to lose some pieces just by moving stock around.

Organization Size Affects the Inventory System

Larger organizations can afford more specialists to concentrate on a particular function or duty. Control of inventory may be assigned to a separate department, especially in manufacturing organizations where inventory represents a major investment. Smaller organizations with leaner workforces frequently assign inventory control to the person handling the buying function. As long as there are relatively few items to control or sufficient time is given to performing proper buyer procedures, an adequate job may be done in both areas. This is more possible today because computers and good inexpensive software make inventory record-keeping simpler.

It is important to adequately staff both purchasing and inventory control. If the workload makes it difficult to do either job adequately, management should be alerted so that remedial action can be taken.

Inventory control involves keeping pilferable material secure, protecting perishable material, and providing enough space and shelving to store the material so that it is easily accessible and not misplaced.

The organization's structure affects who will be responsible for inventory. If purchasing is done from a central location, but material is stored in branch locations, some controls must be carried out at the local level. It is ill advised to hold purchasing totally responsible for material that is stored elsewhere. Quantities to order may be assigned to purchasing provided adequate information about physical counts is made available from the local level, and local employees are responsible for physical control.

The Type of Business Influences Inventory Methods

Inventory control is of major concern to manufacturing organizations for several reasons. First, inventory usually represents one of the largest expenditures that the company makes. Second, raw material must be available to keep the plant running; insufficient material causes lost time. Final product may not be produced quickly enough to satisfy customer requirements and sales may be lost. Inventory control for the manufacturing organization goes beyond purchased material from outside sources. It should include control of in-process goods, that is, goods that are partially manufactured. It also should include the control of finished goods placed in stock or ready to ship to customers.

Inventory control at retail companies is also important. Most of their items are for resale, and they can deteriorate on the shelf and become shopworn. They may become out of fashion and hard to sell.

Overstocks of such items are usually kept to a minimum by reducing prices and holding sales for consumers. A smaller number of items, such as light bulbs, paper towels, pens, pencils, and hundreds of other products, are for internal use and can be classified as MRO items, or maintenance, repair, and operating supplies. Control of these items is usually minimal in retailing except for the largest of organizations.

Service businesses have the smallest amount of inventory. By definition all of the material on hand falls into the MRO category. The larger service organizations, such as insurance companies, some banks, and other financial institutions with many branches, do maintain control over these items.

Discrepancies between the handwritten or computer records and the actual amount on hand may come about for the following reasons:

- Recording of incorrect quantities received. This may be due to an error by the person making the recording such as reversing the order of the numbers on the receiving document. For example, a 12 may be recorded as 21. Another possibility is that there may have been what is referred to as a hidden discrepancy: a box may have contained less than the amount shown on the outside.

- Lost stock because items may be placed in the wrong location. Sometimes similar stock is placed in the wrong bin. In this case two errors may be recorded. The bin containing the wrong stock may show a higher quantity than it should and the bin that the stock should have been placed in will indicate a lower quantity than should be available.

- Unreported used, damaged, or scrapped stock will result in the inventory records showing higher counts than they should.

Calculating Proper Inventory Levels

Under the JIT concept, material arrives "Just in Time" or not until needed, neither early nor late. Great in theory, and some companies plan and execute such a system successfully. But it is better suited to some types of businesses and organizations than others. It works best when sales forecasts can be made accurately and when there are standard products used on a continual basis for an extended period of time.

The use of JIT is probably not suited to a company that is small, works with informal procedures, or usually orders different material. If that is your situation, using older and more traditional approaches will most likely serve you better.

Maintaining proper inventory level is more difficult for new items because there is little data on which to base the calculations. Buyers need to base their order quantities on one or more available factors including a forecast of usage from users, from the sales department, and on experience with other similar items. The buyer should still look at the reasonableness of the figures and projected quantities and question any numbers that seem to contradict good judgment. It is easier to balance inventory for an item that has been purchased before because you have some direct experience and data with which to base future order quantities. To calculate the optimum inventory level for either a new or previously ordered material, you need to ask the following questions and use the data that is available.

1. What service level does management want? In other words, how many stockouts are acceptable? Remember, in order to have zero stockouts, an infinite amount of inventory would be necessary. Most companies are satisfied with 95% coverage.

2. What is the average usage per time period, say a month?

3. How much is presently on hand?

4. How much is presently on order or in transit?

5. Is usage seasonal? Is the rate of usage constant or does it fluctuate?

6. What is the sales or user forecast in the short-term as well as long-term?

7. What is the normal lead time from suppliers?

8. Are there any supplier interruptions anticipated within the time frame for reorder? Are labor disputes or labor contracts up for negotiation?

9. What is the normal transportation method and what is the normal time to transport the goods? Extra time must be allowed for overseas shipments and for goods to clear customs.

10. Are other suppliers available and able to deliver if the present supplier fails to deliver?

The answers to these questions provide the input to make your calculations. Initially, a certain quantity, referred to as "safety stock," is usually added to the calculated figure to cover problems such as those just described.

You can use a formal approach with formulas, but don't use any without thinking about the reasonableness of the quantity to be ordered. People make arithmetic errors and decimal points get misplaced. If you order 10,000 pieces when only 1,000 were needed, you may have great difficulty getting rid of the excess.

Providing Information for Accounting and Management

Another duty of purchasers is to provide information to other departments, such as accounting or marketing, which is used to help plan the business and make decisions necessary to keep the business healthy.

Financial people often request a forecast of expenditures to determine cash flow for the business. Accountants do not always get information about bills that will be received in the future from sources other than purchasing. Buyers can project when invoices will be received if the material arrives as scheduled. They also know what terms have been agreed upon. The accountant will compare his or her cash on hand plus any anticipated revenue with the bills that must be paid. If the comparison reveals a shortage of cash, plans can be made to obtain a loan. If there is more cash available than needed for those bills, then the accountant can either retire a loan or invest the surplus funds in other moneymaking opportunities.

Even if the accounting department has a system that uses purchase orders and delivery dates to provide such information, there are often contractual agreements that may not be shown in the system. For example, a buyer may have a long-term agreement to buy a certain amount of material within a year.

International purchases involving foreign currencies create still more uncertainty. Accountants may want to consider changes in currency rates that could have a major effect on cash flow.

Major anticipated price changes are of interest to accountants, marketers, and general management. Price changes affect cash flow, profits, and sales. The cost of products and changes in the cost of a product affect what prices an organization needs to charge to break even or make a profit.

CHECKING INVOICES

Matching invoices to purchase orders and receiving documents is now done mostly by computers, although small companies still match these manually. This should be an accounting function to insure proper financial control, although a few companies assign it to purchasing personnel. Even when accounting routinely performs it, buyers are asked to resolve discrepancies. If the wrong price is on the invoice, that is if it doesn't match the purchase order, or if the incorrect quantity is received, the buyer must contact the supplier to get the problem corrected one way or another.

Traffic Management Duties of Purchasing Personnel

Traffic departments determine the most economical carriers and the fastest routing for shipments. Large companies and many smaller ones have separate departments for this function. Some of those departments restrict their time to outbound shipments to the organization's customers.

Others, particularly in large organizations, also concern themselves with inbound material from suppliers.

Methods of shipment in order of their costs from lowest to highest include rail carload, less carload, truckload, less truck load or LTL, and air freight. Shipments may also be sent via United Parcel Service, by Parcel Post, or by other forms of the U.S. Mail. International shipments require ocean vessels. Rates of all carriers vary depending on weight, volume, distance, particular destination, and the type of products being shipped. It may be less expensive to take a longer route if you know how to organize this; buyers in general do not know how to do this. This is a job for the traffic specialist. But buyers can decide on a method of transportation based on how quickly items are needed. They can also compare various truck lines for their advice and competitive information.

You can obtain lower rates by using what are called pool cars for domestic shipments or cargotainers for ocean shipments. Full cars or ocean containers are made up of smaller shipments from many suppliers. The disadvantage is that the cars or containers do not leave as frequently as an individual shipment and, therefore, transit time is longer.

Transportation cost is an important component of total cost and must be considered when selecting suppliers. More distant suppliers may have a lower price, but any savings are obliterated by the cost of transportation, or the increase in leadtime makes it difficult to obtain material when needed. Nevertheless, with the speed of modern transportation, distance should not prevent buyers from checking the costs from suppliers wherever they may be.

Effective Warehousing and Receiving Makes Buying Easier

The warehousing function is part of materials management and sometimes reports to purchasing. Protection of inventory by proper storage minimizes the need to replace damaged goods and reduces inventory cost. Good warehousing provides security, lowers incidents of theft, reduces delays in filling orders, and eliminates lost material.

Receiving should check that incoming items match the documents and the purchase order, and must report mismatches promptly to the buyer, to the accounting department, and to the supplier. This reporting to all departments is immediate and automatic with proper programming if the data is entered on a computer terminal at the receiving dock. Prompt reporting, even if it is done manually, minimizes the need for buyers to follow-up with suppliers for needed stock that is already in the building.

Buyers Help Develop Suppliers

Supplier development is simply finding the right type of supplier, improving an existing supplier, or creating a new business. Existing suppliers may not be capable of producing or delivering what a business needs. Buyers and other company personnel may be involved in assisting suppliers to meet a company's needs through technical advice or support, through financial backing, or by supplying material for a supplier's use. Educating current suppliers by giving them a clear understanding of your company's objectives and requirements should be an ongoing process. Locating and educating interested new suppliers gives them an opportunity to obtain profitable business while also satisfying the purchaser's needs.

Outsourcing or Make-Buy Analysis

Recently outsourcing has become a popular way of reducing cost by downsizing the firm. It is the modern equivalent of one side of the traditional make-buy decision. The make-buy analysis looks at the factors that determine whether it is better to buy certain products or to produce them internally. More than financial considerations matter, although comparative costs are key. Another factor is the availability of capable and technically trained personnel either within the organization or at potential suppliers.

The need for prompt delivery may be important. For example, it is usually easier to get goods when you need them if you can establish the schedule within your own organization.

Having the machinery or tools necessary to produce the products may tilt the decision in favor of internal production. Available and unused equipment makes the decision easier than if a large investment were needed or if the equipment were needed to produce other items.

A decision may involve outsourcing products that have been produced internally. Suppliers may have all the machinery and tools needed to produce the products or may not. If they don't, these items may be acquired from the buyer at a bargain price. Tooling such as dies and molds can be transferred to the supplier for use, but ownership can still be retained by the buying company. Such tooling may not fit the supplier's equipment without modification, and the buyer will need to pay for the costs of making the necessary revisions.

Report Preparation

Most companies—except for the smallest—usually require reports about activities to provide information for making decisions. General managers set the tone of how the reports should be prepared, what types are needed, and how frequently they should be issued. Some require detailed and formal written papers; others short summaries or oral reports. The accounting function traditionally prepares many types of reports in addition to periodic financial statements. Purchasing people may or may not be required to issue written reports, but it is to their advantage to issue those that improve purchasing activities or help the business succeed. Following are some reports that buyers and purchasing managers prepare and use:

- *Activity Report.* Prepared periodically, usually monthly, it shows the major activity during the period. This would include major price increases or reductions, problems such as unresolved claims for damaged material, impending strikes that may interrupt supply, or other matters that affect the business.

- *Variance Reports.* Some compare budgets with actual performance and show the amount under- or over-budget for the period and year-to-date. These reports may be for expenses by category or for individual items that are sometimes listed by part number only.

- *Lead time Reports.* A highly useful report issued by Purchasing that shows current lead times for various types of material or services. This report helps requestors plan their needs so they will not run out of material.

- *Supplier Information Reports.* These help the buyer decide what is important and what to work on first, and help in evaluating supplier performance objectively.

- *Purchase Volume by Supplier.* This report shows the total dollars spent with each supplier in dollar volume-descending order. It allows the buyer to spend most time with those suppliers that account for the highest volume.

- *Purchase Volume by Buyer.* The purchasing manager uses this report to help evaluate workload among buyers. It should show the dollar volume that each buyer spends as well as the number of items that each buyer handles. It may also show the number of purchase orders issued by each buyer. It can be combined with a Purchasing Activity by Buyer report and also shows orders behind schedule and other information.

- *Supplier Performance.* One or more reports that indicate the number or percentages of late shipments, the number of rejections, and other indicators of supplier performance.

- *Follow-up and Expediting Activity.* This provides information on how deliveries are being made in comparison to schedules. It may show promised delivery dates by item for important material and shows what action has been taken by the buyer to assure delivery on time or expedite delivery.

Executives and managers may ask for reports to make informed decisions without considering the costs. Indicating at the top of a report how much time was involved in preparation helps to alert managers to the cost. Buyers should avoid long, wordy, and detailed reports that include routine matters. Exception reports that highlight problem areas and summary reports that give totals and percentages save time and provide useful information. Details may either be attached to the summary sheet or made available upon request.

Summary

Purchasing personnel normally have various duties not commonly recognized as buying responsibilities. They are sometimes involved in value analysis programs, the sale of scrap and obsolete material, and the control of inventory. Buyers help forecast cash requirements for accounting and price movements for accounting and marketing. Purchasing people help prepare budgets and work within approved budgets. Purchasing may or may not handle the traffic function, but buyers must be concerned about the cost of transportation and be sure that deliveries are made as quickly as possible. The warehousing and receiving function may be supervised by purchasing. In any case, when the function is done well the buyer has less work to do and material is available when needed. The buyer needs to develop good new sources or to replace or supplement present suppliers. Make-buy decisions determine if there are more advantages to produce certain items internally or to buy them from outside suppliers. Buyers and purchasing managers prepare many types of reports to inform management and users about purchasing activities. Some of these reports provide information to help management make decisions. The lead time report helps users plan their needs by knowing how far ahead of time they must request material to obtain delivery.

Selected Bibliography

Books

ACCOUNTING AND FINANCE

Dixon, Robert L. *The McGraw-Hill 36-Hour Accounting Course*, Second Edition, New York, NY: McGraw-Hill Book Company, 1982

Tracy, John A. *How to Read a Financial Report*, Third Edition, New York, John Wiley & Sons, 1989

LAW

Ambrose, Cunningham, Hancock, Rolitsky, and Victor *Legal Aspects of International Sourcing*, Chesterland, OH: Business Laws, Inc., 1986

Ellentuck, Elmer, Ed. *Purchasing and the Law, A Handbook of Cases for Purchasing Managers*, New York, NY: BRP Publications, Inc. 1992

Prentice Hall Editorial Staff *Lawyer's Desk Book*, Ninth Edition, Englewood Cliffs, NJ: Prentice-Hall, Inc., 1989

Ritterskamp, Jr., James J. *Purchasing Manager's Desk Book of Purchasing Law*, Englewood Cliffs, NJ: Prentice-Hall, Inc., 1987

Ritterskamp, Jr., James J. *1990 Supplement, Purchasing Manager's Desk Book of Purchasing Law*, Englewood Cliffs, NJ: Prentice-Hall, Inc., 1990

MATERIALS MANAGEMENT

Ammer, Dean S. *Materials Management and Purchasing*, 4th ed., Homewood, IL.: Richard D. Irwin, Inc., 1980

Hall, Robert W. with American Production & Inventory Control Society *Zero Inventories*, Homewood, IL: Dow Jones-Irwin, 1983

Janson, Robert L. *Handbook of Inventory Management*, Englewood Cliffs, NJ: Prentice-Hall, Inc., 1987

Mather, Hal *How To Really Manage Inventories*, New York, NY: McGraw-Hill Book Company, 1984

Orlicky, Joseph *Materials Requirements Planning*, New York, NY: McGraw-Hill Book Company, 1975

Ptak, Carol A. *MRP and Beyond*, Chicago, Richard D. Irwin, Inc., 1997

Silver, Edward A.; Pyke, David F.; and Peterson, Rein *Inventory Management and Production Planning and Scheduling*, Third Edition, New York: John Wiley & Sons, 1998.

NEGOTIATING

Fisher, Roger and Brown, Scott *Getting Together, Building Relationships As We Negotiate*, Boston, MA: Houghton Mifflin Company, 1988; Paperback New York, NY: Penguin Books, 1989

Fisher, Roger and Ury, William *Getting To Yes, Negotiating Agreement Without Giving In*, Boston, MA: Houghton Mifflin Company, 1981; Paperback New York, NY, Penguin Books, 1983

Cohen, Herb *You Can Negotiate Anything*, Secaucus, NJ: Lyle Stuart Inc., 1980

Fuller, George *The Negotiator's Handbook*, Englewood Cliffs, NJ: Prentice-Hall, Inc., 1991

Koch, H. William, Jr. *Negotiator's Factomatic*, Englewood Cliffs, NJ: Prentice-Hall, Inc., 1988

Leritz, Len *No-Fault Negotiating*, New York, NY: Warner Books, Inc., 1987

Mastenbroek, William *Negotiate*, First translation Oxford and New York, NY: Basil Blackwell Inc., 1989

Nierenberg, Gerard I. *Fundamentals of Negotiating*, New York, NY: Harper & Row Publishers, Inc., 1973 Available in paperback from Perennial Library Division of Harper & Row.

Raiffa, Howard *The Art & Science of Negotiation*, Cambridge MA and London, England: The Belknap Press of Harvard University Press, 1982

Schatzki, Michael with Wayne R. Coffey *Negotiation, The Art of Getting What You Want*, New York, NY: Signer, The New American Library, Inc., 1981

PRICES AND COSTS

Armed Services Pricing Manual, 2 volumes, Chicago, IL: Commerce Clearing House, Inc., 1987

Figgie, Harry E. Jr. *Cutting Costs, An Executive's Guide to Increased Profits*, Paperback edition, New York, NY: AMACOM Division, American Management Association, 1990

PURCHASING, GENERAL

Ashley, James M. *International Purchasing Handbook*, Paramus, N.J.: Prentice-Hall, 1998

Burt, David N. *Proactive Procurement, The Key To Increased Profits, Productivity, and Quality*, Englewood Cliffs, NJ: Prentice-Hall, Inc., 1984

Corey, E. Raymond *Procurement Management: Strategy, Organization, and Decision-Making*, Boston, MA: CBI Publishing Company, Inc., 1976

Federal Acquisition Regulation, Chicago, IL: Commerce Clearing House, Inc., 1987

Harding, Michael *Profitable Purchasing*, New York, NY: Industrial Press, 1990

Heinritz, Farrell, Giunipero, and Kolchin *Purchasing Principles and Applications*, Eighth Edition, Englewood Cliffs, NJ: Prentice-Hall, Inc. 1991

Hough, Harry E. and Ashley, James M. *Handbook of Buying and Purchasing Management*, Englewood Cliffs, N.J.: Prentice-Hall, Inc. 1992

Hough, Harry E. *Purchasing for Manufacturing*, New York: Industrial Press, 1996

Leenders, Fearon, and England *Purchasing and Materials Management*, Ninth Edition, Homewood, IL: Richard D. Irwin, Inc., 1989

Professional Purchasing Study Material and Certification Guidance Manual, Port Richey, FL: American Purchasing Society, 1990

Scheuing, Eberhard E. *Purchasing Management*, Englewood Cliffs, NJ: Prentice-Hall, Inc., 1989

Tyndall, Gopal, Partsch, and Kamauff *Supercharging Supply Chains*, New York: John Wiley & Sons, Inc., 1998

Woodside, Arch G. and Vyas Nyren *Industrial Purchasing Strategies*, Lexington, MA: Lexington Books Division of D. C. Heath and Company, 1987

QUALITY

Barra, Ralph *Putting Quality Circles To Work*, New York, NY: McGraw-Hill Book Company, 1983

Crosby, Philip B. *Quality Is Free, The Art of Making Quality Certain*, New York, NY: McGraw-Hill Book Company, 1979

Ingle, Sud *In Search of Perfection, How to Create/Maintain, Improve Quality*, Englewood Cliffs, NJ: Prentice-Hall, Inc., 1985

Peach, Robert W., Editor *The ISO 9000 Handbook*, Third Edition, New York: McGraw-Hill, 1997

Cassettes

Crosby, Philip B. *Quality Is Free, The Art of Making Quality Certain*, Fullerton, CA: McGraw-Hill, 1989

Crosby, Philip B. *Quality Without Tears, The Art of Hassle-Free Management*, Fullerton, CA: McGraw-Hill, 1989

Dawson, Roger *The Secrets of Power Negotiating*, Chicago, IL: Nightingale-Conant Corporation, 1990

Fisher, Roger and Ury, William *Getting To Yes, How To Negotiate Agreement Without Giving In*, Six Audiocassettes and a study guide, New York, NY: Simon & Schuster Audio Publishing Division, 1986

Hough, Harry E. *Negotiating for Purchasing*, Aurora, IL: American Purchasing Society, 1991

Hough, Harry E. *Purchasing and Accounting, Transactions Between The Departments*, Aurora, IL: American Purchasing Society, 1991

Hough, Harry E. *Purchasing and Engineering*, Aurora, IL: American Purchasing Society, 1991

Nierenberg, Gerard I. *The Art of Negotiation*, Holmes, PA: Sound Editions from Random House, 1987

Reck, Ross R. and Long, Brian G. *The Win Win Negotiator*, Chicago, IL: Nightingale-Conant Corporation, 1985

Warschaw, Tessa Albert *Negotiating To Win*, Fullerton, CA: TDM/McGraw-Hill, 1987

15 Things You Shouldn't Tell a Supplier

This list is intended as a reminder for buyers and a guide for non-purchasing people who may be involved in discussions with suppliers. While there are always exceptions to rules, the reasons behind these recommendations are logical. Experienced purchasing professionals have long avoided disclosing the information listed here. Not only does disclosure weaken a buyer's negotiating position, in some cases it is unethical to do so.

1. *Don't tell what you pay another supplier.*

   Giving the price you pay allows the supplier to target the price low enough to get the business, but not as low as it might be without such knowledge.

2. *Don't lie about what you pay another supplier or what another supplier has bid.*

   There is a possibility that the truth may be found out and the individuals and organization they represent could be subject to legal penalties. Of course, it is also unethical.

3. *Don't lie about terms or conditions given by another supplier.*

   There is a possibility that the truth may be found out and the individuals and organization they represent could be subject to legal penalties. Of course, it is also unethical.

4. *Avoid discussing problems you have with other suppliers.*

   New suppliers do not have to offer as much to get the business when they know that the existing supplier is performing poorly.

5. *Don't say you can't find another source.*

   A supplier does not have to offer as much to get the business if he knows you have no alternative.

6. *No need to say you are going to buy one time only.*

   A buyer should try to make it as interesting as possible for a supplier to want the business. The supplier will find it much more interesting if there might be other orders to come. You shouldn't lie, but why divulge the information that you may not place another order if you don't have to?

7. *Don't reveal your budget for any item.*

   Telling your budget allows the supplier to target the price low enough to get the business, but not as low as it might be without such knowledge.

8. *Never tell a potential supplier who you asked to bid.*

   It allows the supplier to target bids higher. Salespeople know who their toughest competition is.

9. *Avoid revealing that your company is in a weak or shaky financial condition.*

   The buyer should make it attractive to do business. A supplier who knows your finances are weak will probably want greater compensation for the additional risk of not getting paid. Don't provide such information unless you are in a desperate situation and it is a last resort to beg for help before declaring bankruptcy.

10. *Postpone revealing that your company is going to discontinue a product.*

    A supplier may not have much interest in the business if he knows more orders will not be coming. Don't divulge this information unless you have good reason to do so to negotiate a settlement of a contract, negotiate return of goods, or avoid being responsible for the supplier investing in your behalf.

11. *Don't reveal that you are receiving poor or worse quality from a competitor.*

    New suppliers do not have to offer as much to get the business when they know that the existing supplier is performing poorly.

12. *Don't reveal that you are receiving late shipments from a competitor.*

    For the same reason as in the previous recommendation. Also, revealing too many problems may make the buyer seem like a difficult customer that will be hard to satisfy.

13. *Don't repeat gossip or disparage another supplier or salesperson.*

    Most people realize if you talk about someone else, you may talk about them. They will be reluctant to deal openly with you. Also, the person you talk about may hear about what you said.

14. *Avoid telling potential suppliers who your present supplier is.*

    It allows the new supplier to target bids more accurately. Salespeople know who their toughest competition is.

15. *Avoid saying the product is needed immediately.*

    It weakens your bargaining position. Try to negotiate everything else first before you ask for an early delivery date.

12 Things You Should Tell a Supplier

These twelve items make it attractive for a supplier to do business with the buyer. They offer the supplier the type of business environment that most want. They see that doing business with the buyer is an opportunity for an ever-increasing amount of profitable business.

1. The company is growing.
2. The company is profitable.
3. The company always pays its bills on time.
4. The company has used good suppliers for years.
5. The company wants its suppliers to make a reasonable profit.
6. The company is more interested in minimizing the total cost than the lowest price.
7. Supplier suggestions are welcome.
8. The company is always receptive to buying better products.
9. Suppliers are measured objectively.
10. Management always wants to operate legally.
11. Management always wants to operate ethically.
12. The company rewards good performance.

Appendix C

How to Improve Communications

A manager thinks he is rewarding an employee by giving her what is considered to be a promotion to a more responsible buying assignment. The employee is unhappy because the job is not what she wanted. The manager is unhappy, sensing ingratitude.

In another situation, a supplier tries to impress the buyer by shipping the goods one week earlier than promised. The buyer is not pleased because the receiving department is overloaded with work and there is insufficient storage area in the warehouse.

Or take the ambitious and conscientious young buyer who is trying to make every effort to please the boss. Every possible source is shopped for a large quantity of safety gloves before the order is awarded. The selected source provides a high quality glove much lower in price than any of the competition. The buyer is very disappointed that the plant manager is unhappy with the purchase and wanted cheap cotton gloves that could be thrown away within a short time.

In each of these examples there is a failure of communications and the failure results in unnecessary cost to both the company and the employees involved. In the first example, the company suffers because the employee does not perform as well in the new job as in the former, more satisfying one. The employee would also do better in a job that was more personally desirable. In the second example, the supplier may lose future business because he fails to understand the needs of the purchaser. The buying company incurred added expense because of congestion and inefficiencies resulting from poor scheduling. Even if the stock is refused at the receiving dock, someone has to take the time to notify the supplier of the problem and some ill will is probable.

In the third example, the company is burdened with the cost of a higher quality product than necessary, and confidence in the purchasing department's ability to obtain what the user wants has been reduced.

In all three cases the parties involved were making assumptions about other people's needs and desires. They were looking at each situation from a subjective point of view rather than trying to work toward department and company goals objectively.

Today it is a cliche to say that we don't communicate. Most people agree, but believe they understand what it takes to communicate better. They believe it is a simple matter to correct the problem if they really put their minds to it. Not so. It takes effort and practice to communicate effectively. Training helps. Here are some things that you can do to help yourself and others communicate better both orally and in writing.

9 Things You Can Do to Communicate Better*

1. Avoid acronyms unless you are absolutely certain all your audience understands their meaning. If you must use them, explain what they mean when you use them the first time in a conversation or in writing. If someone else uses them and you are not sure what they mean, ask them what the letters stand for. However, don't press the issue. A lot of people don't know what the letters stand for even though they use them and understand the ideas they signify.

2. Avoid use of obscure or technical words unless you are sure your audience is familiar with them. People are not always impressed by words they don't understand. They may simply think you are trying to show off your knowledge of vocabulary.

3. Ask questions for clarification. Don't be afraid to show your ignorance. No one can know everything.

4. If you have the least doubt that someone is understanding what you are saying, say it again in a different way. Ask if you are making yourself clear.

5. Use examples to illustrate what you mean.

6. Use graphics, slides, drawings, and videos if appropriate to get your message across.

---

*Reprinted from Professional Purchasing, October 1990, ©American Purchasing Society, Inc.

7. Appeal to as many senses as is practical. If you want someone to buy a replacement item such as a refill for a pen, let them see and feel the old item. Describe the color, the size, and any other specification you can think of. Explain it orally and then put it in writing. The more complex the item, the more important every detail is. If you are the buyer, ask as many questions as you can about the item to be purchased as well as what it will be used for. The questions may sound silly at first, but many problems are avoided by someone asking what he thought was a silly question.

8. Listen with both ears and concentrate on what other people are saying rather than thinking about what you are going to say next. After they have finished speaking, you can pause long enough to think about what you want to say. If necessary, you can take a break to gather your thoughts.

9. Above all, try to understand other people's point of view. Never assume that what they want is what you would want.

21 Ways to Get a Price Reduction

1. *Ask for lower prices.*

   Rarely are prices reduced voluntarily. The most successful buyers ask for lower prices and frequently get them.

2. *Offer to pay cash.*

   If you have the funds available and the supplier needs to improve cash flow, an offer of cash payment upon delivery may be enough to motivate the supplier to give a lower price.

3. *Offer either a partial or full payment in advance.*

   Although advance payment is not always wise, if the supplier is reliable and the risk is small, an advance or partial payment may help get a price reduction.

4. *Offer to make a firm commitment to buy from the supplier for an extended period.*

   Suppliers often make price concessions for business they can count on in the future. Their selling expense is reduced and they can plan their workload and workforce better.

5. *Threaten to go into the market for competitive bids.*

   Sellers may give a lower price rather than have a buyer shop and negotiate with competitors. They prefer not to have the buyer possibly discover better products or more flexible suppliers.

6. *Offer to buy a larger quantity.*

   Higher quantities provide cost reductions through fewer setup expenses and other efficiencies. Such cost reductions normally result in lower prices.

7. *Threaten to change suppliers.*

   Although a strong-arm tactic, a diplomatically-worded suggestion that it may be necessary to change sources can influence a price reduction.

8. *Threaten to give some business to another supplier.*

   If a supplier has all of the business, he may not want to give another supplier the opportunity of getting in the door.

9. *Explain why a price reduction is justified.*

   Some salespeople will help convince their management why a price reduction is essential if they feel it is fair to do so.

10. *Explain why your company needs a reduction.*

    A supplier may reduce prices and profits rather than lose all of the business if the customer fails to survive.

11. *Obtain bids from other suppliers.*

    A buyer should continually use the bid system to quickly find out if prices from other sources are lower.

12. *Use the learning curve.*

    The cost of proprietary items purchased over time should go down. Cost is reduced by improved efficiency from experience.

13. *Explain why you may buy another product.*

    The supplier knows that once business is lost, it is difficult to get it back.

14. *Offer to store inventory on consignment.*

    Taking goods on consignment gives the supplier a double benefit of eliminating storage cost and providing some assurance of continual business.

15. *Offer to accept a later delivery schedule.*

    A supplier may be able to reduce cost by better scheduling.

16. *Offer to accept an earlier delivery schedule.*

    A supplier may be able to reduce cost by reducing inventory. Sometimes a supplier finds it advantageous to obtain sales revenue in a different time period.

17. *Allow the supplier to use your company's name or photo when advertising its product.*

    A testimonial or product endorsement can be very valuable from the proper person or organization.

18. *Invite suppliers to tour your facility.*

    Improved relations with key people and knowledge of your operation may help the supplier appreciate your business and the potential for more business.

19. *Show how price increases have exceeded indexes or decreases have not been given when indexes drop.*

    Suppliers often fail to realize how much they have increased prices or how unreasonable their prices are.

20. *Ask for suggestions to reduce the price.*

    The supplier may have a less costly product or other idea.

21. *Buy the supplier's raw material at a lower cost.*

    The buyer may be able to obtain a better price for raw material because of the organization's size or type of business.

Appendix F

How to Measure Purchasing Savings[*]

It is much easier for a buyer to obtain savings than it is to measure those savings accurately and report them in a believable way. Buyers and purchasing managers often overlook this fact. They then sometimes wonder why they are not appreciated when they have consistently reported large savings. They seldom realize that their reports may not be fully believed because the executive receiving the report chooses not to question the premises that the reports are based on.

Though there may be doubt of a report's validity, the executive may be too busy in other areas to delve into the details of the alleged saving. If the buyer has ever exaggerated an achievement or used a shaky premise for taking credit for a saving, the executive will tend to doubt the accuracy of all reported savings.

It is important to report the results of purchasing activity to be able to justify an adequate staff and to make sure that purchasing personnel are compensated in relation to their contribution. Reports that are poorly prepared or unbelievable, however, do more damage than good.

A proper savings report must be based on pre-defined criteria. Those criteria should be discussed with your company's executives so that they agree or can revise the definition to suit their standards. Here are some of the things you need to consider when you decide how you will define savings.

*Reprinted with permission from Professional Purchasing, December 1990, ©American Purchasing Society, Inc.

How long a period should be used to accumulate savings? The usual period is one year. Determine if the year should be the calendar or the fiscal year.

If the cost of a product or service is lowered and it is repeatedly purchased at the lower cost, how long should the savings be reported? Many companies only allow credit for the savings within the year it was first obtained. This is unfair if you obtain the savings near the end of the year. It also might be a negative incentive for the buyer. The buyer might postpone efforts to get a supplier to reduce cost until the new year when he will receive a full twelve months of benefit. It seems better to allow credit for twelve months after the date of the initial savings.

Must all savings be related to price? If the buyer pays the same amount for better quality goods or improved specifications that make the product last twice as long, who determines the value of the saving? If a buyer is not given credit for this type of saving, he might be inclined always to look for lower priced goods rather than for goods that are higher in quality and result in lower cost over the long run.

How should cost-avoidance be reported? Who will decide on the value and how will it be calculated? If inflation causes the average price of products to go up five percent, but purchased goods only go up three percent, should the buyer get credit for holding the price line? Should this be reported as a saving? Some companies use several categories of savings, one for price changes and one for cost-avoidance. Separating the two helps the accounting function forecast profits more accurately.

What is the starting point for measuring cost-avoidance? If a previous price actually paid is used, an unrealistic figure will be obtained when the previous purchase was made several years ago. Some companies allow the buyer to use the prices announced by the supplier even though those prices were never actually paid. For example, the supplier may announce an increase of 4%, but then rescind it. The buyer may have negotiated the revision or sometimes buyers from other companies may have been the actual cause for the change. Since there is no way to know for sure, a decision must be made on how this will be interpreted and reported.

Buyers frequently can get price increases postponed and they should be credited with those savings if they can be substantiated by some type of announcement or documentation. For example, let us say you spend

$5000 per month on a product. The supplier increases the price so that your cost will be 5% more and the new price will take effect in 30 days. Through your efforts and skill in negotiating you are able to get the supplier to postpone the increase for five months (which may be the end of the year). Therefore, you would be credited with four months of savings at $250 per month or a total of $1000 in cost-avoidance.

As you see, what may have seemed a simple process at the outset becomes rather complex with many variables to consider. Reported savings are approximate since actual savings are difficult to calculate accurately. Nevertheless, every effort should be made to be as close to the truth as possible. If everyone uses the same definitions within an organization, then the data will be accepted more readily.

12 Common Purchasing Myths*

Here are common purchasing myths that can defeat your efforts to obtain all the profits that a good purchasing operation should contribute.

Myth Number 1. You get what you pay for.

A popular misconception. Naturally goods that require tighter specifications or more costly material are going to cost more than goods with looser specifications and less expensive material. The more expensive material may last longer or provide additional advantages and therefore is worth paying a higher price, but the implication of the statement is that if the price is higher the goods are better-made or the goods have better quality built in. More often this is not the case.

The intelligent buyer compares products with different prices to see what the differences are. And those differences are not always easy to detect. If there are really no differences you are wasting your money by paying the higher price. This assumes of course that all other things are equal.

*Reprinted from Professional Purchasing, ©February 1990, American Purchasing Society, Inc.

Myth Number 2. Purchasing is a service function.

This implies that buyers should obtain whatever the requestor wants without question. It implies that the purchasing function is different from other business functions such as accounting or sales or manufacturing. Nothing could be further from the truth. Purchasing is one of the most important departments in a company. Purchasing performance may have more influence on a company's profit than any other department. If the purchasing operation fails to buy goods at the right cost, sales may be low because it is necessary to price the product too high. If purchasing obtains poor quality, sales may fall because of customer dissatisfaction. If purchasing cannot obtain delivery to meet schedules, sales may fall because customers cancel orders and buy elsewhere. If the purchase price is too high but the sales department prices the product to meet competition, profits may evaporate.

Of course purchasing must provide service to the requestor and obtain the products that are needed by the company, but so must the accounting department prepare reports and provide service to management. So must the engineers design products to satisfy the customer. So must manufacturing make products that satisfy the customer and meet the needs of the sales department. So the statement, on the face of it, is true, but the implications are not.

Myth Number 3. All buyers are honest.

It is up to the purchasing manager to make sure that purchasing activities are conducted honestly. It is up to the controller and general management to make sure that the purchasing department conducts business honestly. Although only a small percentage of people may be dishonest, you cannot assume that employees are completely honest regardless of their position in the company. And a high degree of integrity in purchasing is particularly important to make sure that the company's interests are insured. Furthermore, if non-professional purchasing people are involved in the purchase, the risks of improprieties and the consequence for the company are accentuated.

Myth Number 4. All buyers are dishonest.

Many organizations assume that there is a certain degree of dishonesty in everyone and therefore there is little point in trying too hard to control it unless the cost becomes unbearable. The truth is that poor integrity costs the company money and it does not take much in the purchasing area to make a company unprofitable. That is one reason why purchasing should only be done by purchasing department personnel. It makes control easier by restricting buying to the professionals.

Myth Number 5. Tougher buyers get better results.

It depends what you mean by tougher. Appearances can be deceiving, especially with negotiators. Talking tough may kill a business transaction. Winning a supplier over to your position by persuasion and convincing the supplier of the advantages of a good business relationship is far more effective than making threats or exhibiting a blustering overbearing demeanor.

Myth Number 6. All companies know their true cost.

Oh, if only it were true. Many buyers assume that if a company is in business to make a profit, it must know the cost of the product it sells. If you ask any of the salespeople or company executives, they will assure you they know what their costs are. Nevertheless many companies either overestimate or underestimate their costs.

As a buyer, you may not fare too badly on a given transaction if the seller underestimated the cost. However, it is always possible that the supplier will discover the incorrect cost calculation before the product is delivered or before it is billed. In such a case, the supplier may delay delivery and try to renegotiate the price. Or the supplier may substitute inferior material. If the error is not detected, eventually the supplier may go out of business and may cause you considerable trouble in obtaining product to meet your requirements.

More often the supplier estimates costs higher than they actually are. This may be done because all costs are not known when they are calculated and an extra amount is added to make certain that a profit is attained. Or it may be done because certain costs are difficult or impossible to calculate. The result often turns out to be that you pay more than necessary unless you understand how to overcome this common problem.

Myth Number 7. Buyers should be loyal to their suppliers.

This is a statement frequently made by salespeople trying to justify their high prices or their uncompetitive position. It is easy for a buyer to fall for this line and feel sorry for the supplier. Our economic system is based on competition. The most competitive seller is rewarded and the others are penalized.

That does not mean that you should be unfair. It does not mean that you are going to pounce on every mistake. It simply means you will consider all factors and award business on that basis.

Myth Number 8. Anybody can be a buyer without training.

Too often companies appoint untrained buyers without any previous purchasing experience or training. Then they allow them to stay in those positions for years without encouraging them to get any formal training. Little wonder that companies overpay for products, become unprofitable, and go out of business.

Myth Number 9. Good buyers are born, not made.

Nearly everyone has heard the old saying that someone is a born salesperson. Many believe the same thing about buyers. While it is true that certain personality traits help a person become a good buyer, buying and negotiating skills can be and are learned. Most everyone can become a better buyer by studying and applying the available knowledge.

Myth Number 10. Good suppliers deliver on schedule without penalty.

If you use your buying clout, you can usually improve on a supplier's quoted delivery time. It is astounding what you can accomplish if you apply enough pressure properly. Do this once or twice and you may escape without much consequence. Do it continually and ignore the supplier's normal lead time and you will end up paying more although you may never realize it.

Even the supplier may not realize that you have added to his costs by disrupting normal workflow and by making planning impossible. Thus the supplier becomes inefficient and costs are higher than necessary.

Myth Number 11. Good buyers need little time to obtain new products.

Many people within an organization feel that if they want something they should be able to get it almost immediately. Therefore, they often complain if they don't get fairly quick action. To avoid such complaints, buyers and purchasing managers alike will sacrifice good purchasing principles.

Good purchasing requires shopping and negotiating. Good negotiating takes time. Few non-purchasing people realize this. They know they can go out and buy what they want within a few hours. If you don't do the same, they feel you are not doing a good job. The opposite is usually true. If you buy a new product without checking the marketplace and without negotiating, you are probably paying too much.

Myth Number 12. Buying is not as important to the business as selling.

Management might deny that it feels this way while giving large bonuses to salespeople, holding sales meetings in exotic resorts, and providing various other "perqs" to the sales force while ignoring purchasing personnel. Many managements don't realize that increasing sales may not add to profits. If you are losing money on a product, increasing sales simply makes you lose more. On the other hand every dollar that purchasing saves goes directly into profit.

Smart business people don't accept the conventional wisdom. To get the most out of your purchasing operation you should not accept the statements that are made by others who have their own agendas and are serving their own interests. You should look after your company's interest first. Examine each statement carefully and look deeper to see if it is only a half-truth. Then use professional purchasing techniques to achieve all you can.

Appendix H

How Close to Suppliers is Too Close?*

There is a fine line between having a good relationship with a supplier and being too close. It is all too easy to slip over that line and find yourself in the uncomfortable position of feeling obligated to a supplier. Most seasoned purchasing professionals are aware of the dangers of becoming overly familiar with suppliers because they have unwittingly fallen into the situation once or twice in their careers. Sometimes, it has not been their fault. Sometimes, it is caused by other employees or company executives who promote close relationships without realizing the consequences for cost-effective purchasing.

Sales and marketing people are only too eager to encourage the closest possible relationship. They realize that the buyer will consciously or unconsciously favor them with business if there is any doubt about who is best-qualified. And they shouldn't be blamed for this attitude. If you are in a sales position, your job is to get orders and being friendly with buyers helps achieve that end. It hardly can be looked at as dishonest or unethical as long as no laws are broken and the accepted ethical standards are not violated.

However, the same standards may not apply to buyers. Those in purchasing must use stricter rules of conduct. If your buying decision is being

---

*Reprinted with permission from Professional Purchasing, October 1992, ©American Purchasing Society, Inc.

influenced or might be influenced by your relationship or activities with a supplier, then you have overstepped the bounds. For example, you might attend a party or convention with a supplier and find you have many things in common. You discuss your personal affairs and the salesperson tells you about his. You enjoy each other's company and sincerely like each other. At some point, you are more than likely to have this relationship influence your buying decisions for future transactions. Note that nothing has been said about who paid for anything. You don't have to receive gratuities to be unfairly prejudiced in making purchasing decisions.

Current purchasing opinion favors the partnering concept, that is, the close working together of buyer and seller. It involves openly sharing information, exchanging ideas, and each party properly benefiting from each other's contribution. We can't argue with this concept as long as it is held within certain bounds. If buyers close their eyes and shut their ears to what the competition is offering or what they might offer, then the relationship is too close.

Even though it is detrimental to be too close to a supplier, it is advantageous to get to know your supplier well. Business people in other countries may understand this better than most Americans. It is difficult to do business in Japan, for example, until the suppliers get to know you. The better they know you the more likely you will get the most profitable agreements.

Getting to know your supplier without becoming too close is helpful in a number of ways. Knowing your supplier or your potential supplier helps you determine if it is the most appropriate source at a given time or for a given product. For example, a supplier may handle a certain product line that makes it extremely busy during certain times of the year because of the seasonal nature of the business of its primary customers. Getting to know your supplier lets you know if it is the most cost-efficient source for the volume of business you want to place. Getting to know the supplier's key people allows you to properly assess their capabilities and tells you if you can trust them and to what extent you can depend upon them.

The more you know about a supplier the better you are able to negotiate. You can offer what the supplier wants or needs in return for concessions that you would like. For example, if you know the supplier is having a cash flow problem, you could offer a down payment in return for a five-percent price reduction. If you know the supplier has open production time during the first three months of the year, you can have the supplier produce your requirements for the year at a lower cost and hold them until you need them.

Knowing the various employees that work for your supplier and how they relate to each other helps you know who to contact about various problems. It helps you to know how you might get those problems solved quickly.

You should know the salesperson sufficiently well so that you can determine if your messages are being passed along quickly to others who will take the action you want. It sometimes is necessary to even ask for a different sales representative to call on you if you want to continue to do business with a certain supplier.

You get to know your supplier in various ways. They include the qualifying supplier investigation, the interviews with salespeople, by observation such as physical inspection of the supplier's facilities, by the experiences you have with performance on orders you place, and by small talk and asking the right questions.

The Hidden Meaning Behind Questions*

Suppose a salesperson asks a buyer if he or she has the final authority to decide on who gets the order. What do you think is the reason behind that question? Most buyers would suspect that the salesperson isn't going to waste much time on them if they don't have the authority to decide who gets the order. If the buyer indicates that someone else makes the final decision or if several other people will decide, the next question will be to ask the names of those people.

Everyone realizes questions are used to obtain information. Questions are also used to give information. When someone asks a question about a certain topic, the subject of the question shows interest in that topic. It may reveal that the answer is very important.

Suppose a supplier asks, "Do you realize we haven't had a price increase in three years?" You are being told that you are about to receive a price increase. You are simply being prepared for the increase to come. This type of question is what we call a rhetorical question. It is really a statement in disguise. No answer is wanted or expected. Take another example. A supplier may say, "You can't expect me to keep the prices the same year after year, can you?" Or, "Do you want us to lower our quality standards to keep the price down?"

---

*Reprinted with permission from Professional Purchasing, November 1992, ©American Purchasing Society, Inc.

Following are some questions that sellers often ask to get information and what they are probably thinking when they ask them:

- Who makes the decision on which product to buy? I don't want to waste my time selling to the wrong person or miss the sale because I have not contacted the person with authority to choose my product.

- Who are you buying from now?

- Who else is bidding on this order? I know who my most serious competition is and what prices and terms they usually give. If the buyer tells me who she is buying from or who I am bidding against, I can bid just low enough to get the business without cutting my profit more than I have to.

- What is your budget for this item? I don't want to bid more than is in the buyer's budget and there is no sense in bidding less than the budget. I want to price my product as high as I can without losing the business.

- How long have you worked here? I need to know how secure the buyer is and if her opinion is well-regarded. If the buyer is new to the company, she will have to prove herself and maybe get cost reductions quickly. Or she may be inexperienced and does not know the market very well. If she hasn't shopped very much maybe I can ask a little more for my product.

- Who do you report to? If I know how high the buyer is in the organization, I will know approximately how much authority he has and how much his opinions will be respected. Also I might have to go over this buyer's head to sell my product.

- Do you like to go to ball games? Maybe I can offer tickets to a ball game and influence the buyer's decision to buy from me.

- Can you get away from the office for golf? Does this buyer have the freedom to do what she wants or is she being watched every moment?

- How much of this product do you buy in a year? If there is enough volume, I can justify cutting the price to my boss. If the volume is very low, I don't want to waste too much time with this customer.

- Is our bid in the ballpark?

- How much do I have to come down to get the business?

- What are you paying for the product now? If I know how close I am to my competitors, I may be able to adjust my bid to beat them. I don't want to reduce my price any more than I need to. Even if I don't get this order, I will have ammunition to bid against competitors with other customers.

- If I reduce my price by 15%, can I have the order now? If I leave without the order, the buyer will have time to analyze my bid and shop elsewhere. Another salesperson may offer something better or have greater influence on the buyer.

How you handle these questions is important to the success of any negotiation. Sometimes you want to answer frankly and provide all the information that the seller wants. Other times you want to avoid giving a direct answer or give only a partial answer. Take a lesson from the winning politicians. Notice how they get around answering the questions without usually seeming to be belligerent or annoyed by the questions. Don't feel compelled to immediately answer every question posed. You can always say, "Well, before I answer that, let's talk about so and so." Sometimes, you might answer a question with a question. For example, when the seller asks, "How much do I have to come down to get the business?" You might answer, "What percent can you reduce your price and still make a fair profit?" Another technique is to be somewhat vague with your answers. For example when the salesperson asks, "Who makes the decision on which product to buy?" you might answer, "It depends on the product and the bid we receive. Sometimes I make the decision alone, other times many people are involved."

A question is sometimes a device to give unpleasant or threatening information. Here are a few examples that a salesperson might use and what he might be thinking.

- Do you know that Mr. Jones, our president, is very friendly with Mr. Brown, the president of your company? This will make sure I am given special consideration because the buyer will not risk the possibility of having his decision questioned by Mr. Brown.

- I know you give some business to our competitor XYZ Company. Do you know that it is closing one of its plants? The buyer will be nervous about giving more orders to XYZ because he won't be sure he can get delivery when he needs it. He will realize that XYZ is in poor financial shape and will look favorably on giving me more business.

Think a few moments before answering a seller's questions. Try to understand the motives behind the questions. As you build relationships with suppliers, you can be more relaxed because they will know more about you and your company and you will know more about them. Nevertheless, always be aware that questions are not always what they seem.

Sellers are not the only ones who find the use of questions a powerful tool in conducting business. Questions are just as important, if not more so, for buyers. Here are some questions that buyers often ask and the reasons why.

Questions that Buyers Ask Suppliers

- How long have you been in business? Most companies fail within the first few years of being in business. If you have a choice between a company that has been in business for a long time versus a new company and everything else is equal, it is prudent to go with the older company.

- Do you have full authority to make a contract and make decisions about terms and conditions of an order? If you are going to negotiate and get agreement, you must obtain agreement from an authorized agent. The salesperson who does not have the authority to make concessions will only be a messenger. Not only is it doubtful your message will be delivered, but if it is, negotiations will take much longer.

- How much do you pay your secretaries? What is the hourly rate of your plant employees? Average wages for various geographical areas and various industries are published by the U.S. Department of

Labor. If the supplier is paying much higher than the average, chances are total cost will be higher and this may be reflected in uncompetitive pricing. If wages are much lower than the average, you should be concerned with checking quality level very carefully. If you find the quality level meets your needs, there may be room to negotiate lower costs.

- Is your company unionized? Unionized companies usually pay higher wages and therefore have higher costs. There may also be more risk for work stoppages and possibly delay in shipping your order.

- When will the union contract expire? The buyer should be prepared to protect supply when a union contract is close to expiration. There may be a strike. Also the new contract may result in higher wages which will be passed along to customers. Those price increases may happen slightly before the contract expiration date if the company is anticipating the need to pay wage hikes or may come soon after the settlement. A wise buyer will shop around for alternate sources. Then he or she will be prepared to go to a new source if the new cost is uncompetitive or at least be prepared to negotiate to keep costs within proper bounds.

- What is your normal lead time? How fast can you deliver in an emergency? Salespeople will often answer these questions with a question of their own, such as, how fast do you need it? Or they will give you a vague answer. Insist on a specific time. However, keep in mind that the lead time that is quoted is often fictitious even though the sales management believes what they are telling you. Only experience with the supplier will give you a lead time figure you can depend on.

- What types of equipment do you have? What are speeds of the machines? How many parts will they produce in an hour? How long does it take for setup? All of these questions are important if you want to judge the supplier's ability to meet your quantity and delivery time requirement. Some suppliers fail to calculate what they have the ability to really do and will bite off more than they can chew. If you fail to do the arithmetic yourself, you may find that you can't get stock when you need it.

- How do you ship? Which carrier do you use? Do you have any objection if we pick up our orders and make delivery in our own trucks? Some suppliers have good cost controls in the work they do themselves but their purchase cost for goods and services is higher than it should be. In addition, they may mark up to you any goods and services they must pay for. Buyers should ask to see actual freight bills and consider obtaining their own transportation for purchased items. It may even be less expensive to make your own pick-ups and deliveries if the volume is sufficient. A thorough cost analysis must be made before a final decision.

- Do you do any business with our competitors? Which ones? How much business do you get from each? The salesperson may think you simply want to know if his company is capable of producing your type of product. If he is sharp, he may be suspicious that you are fishing for information about your competition. He may be partially right about the latter, but what you really are trying to find out is how secure your own product information is. You also might be concerned that your order may be delayed and the orders of your competitor given priority.

There are many other questions buyers ask. The number depends on the importance of the sourcing decision. Both buyers and sellers use questions to get and give information. Every buyer should try to develop the art of questioning.

Make a list of the questions you want to ask before you meet with suppliers. It is a good idea to have a standard list of questions to routinely ask potential suppliers and special lists prepared as you need them to negotiate major agreements. Use the sample buyers' questions as a guide to the type of questions you might want to ask. Go over the list and anticipate possible answers and any follow up questions you should ask in response. Proper preparation saves time by avoiding extra meetings and neglecting to cover important topics.

A supplier has the right to refuse to answer a particular question and the buyer has the right to refuse to give business to that supplier. Sometimes a salesperson is reluctant to give out certain information such as financial figures about his company. Simply explain why you need the information to make an intelligent buying decision. Often this is sufficient to get the information.

Putting the questions in the right order is important. Build up to sensitive questions. Once a salesperson has divulged a certain amount of information, additional information often flows freely. Don't spring your sensitive question out of the blue. Wait for the right time. Questions with easy answers might be asked almost any time. Those that are critical but might hurt a relationship if asked too early or at the wrong time should be postponed. Build your case and throw in the bombshell when the supplier can do nothing more but answer candidly or give in to your request.

When a salesperson avoids answering a critical question you can try re-phrasing the question. If you still get no satisfactory reply, re-phrase it again or ask why you are not getting a straight answer.

Silence is another useful tool to get or give information when you negotiate. When a salesperson hesitates before answering, above all, don't interrupt. Don't say anything. The silence becomes almost unbearable very quickly. If, when the answer is given it sounds implausible, keep quiet for a few moments. Give him a chance to revise his answer or squirm a little. And finally, don't forget to ask "why" a lot.

Tips for Buyers

The following tips for buyers appeared in various issues of Professional Purchasing and are reprinted here with permission of the American Purchasing Society, Inc.

Take a Notebook Computer When Visiting Suppliers

When you visit a supplier take along a notebook computer stuffed with data about the supplier. Make sure the data includes a price history of your purchases, open orders, inventory status on the items you buy from the supplier, and other information that will help you negotiate. A record of rejections and delivery schedule performance is helpful.

When Can Orders Be Cancelled?

A buyer submitted the following information. "Our scheduling department is always making changes. No sooner do we place an order than they want the quantity increased. Then a week later they come back and say, cancel the order. Usually, the supplier accepts these cancellations, but I now have a supplier who says we can't cancel and if we don't pay, he will sue us. Can he do that? When can we cancel and when can't we?"

Fortunately most business transactions are completed without resorting to legal help. Buyers find that one way to keep out of trouble is to establish long term relationships with suppliers and to treat suppliers fairly. There is a point where constantly changing schedules becomes a burden on a supplier. The supplier may then raise prices to you to offset the problems your business causes or may simply insist that you live up to your contract.

Yes, you can change schedules and yes, you can cancel orders, often without penalty. However, a supplier who has incurred a cost or done some work on your order has the right to recoup those expenses plus any profit lost by selling to you rather than to someone else. Generally, you can cancel any order if no work has been done and the supplier has no expense. The supplier who has ordered material or done any work has a right to be reimbursed for any investment. You can usually cancel orders for shelf items without penalty if they can be readily sold to another customer.

Correcting Billing Errors

Another buyer relates the following. "Our accounting department always sends incorrect invoices to purchasing. The accountants insist that the buyer contact the supplier to make the supplier send in a revised invoice or that the buyer issue a revised purchase order. Purchasing feels that accounting should simply return the incorrect invoices directly to the supplier with a note stating that the invoice does not match the purchase order and ask them to send in a correct invoice or contact the buyer if there is a dispute. What is the correct method?"

The buyer's position is correct in principle. However, accounts payable people often take the stand that they do not wish to argue with suppliers. They therefore try to avoid all contacts with suppliers as much as possible. For the sake of peace, the buyer might find it better to mail a standard form letter to the supplier and return the incorrect invoice directly from purchasing.

Suppliers should understand from the start that correct invoicing is part of total quality, and the measurement of their performance includes correct billing. Purchase orders and invoices should agree. A supplier should question the price or other terms on a purchase order before sending an invoice that does not agree. However, payment of extremely small differences in price may be more economical than spending time on correcting the invoice.

Appendix K

Sample Job Description*

MRO Buyer

Reports to and supervised by: Purchasing Manager

MAJOR RESPONSIBILITIES:

The MRO Buyer is responsible to buy all maintenance, repair, and operating supplies for the organization upon receipt of properly authorized requisitions from users or other authorized employees. The MRO Buyer is responsible to obtain goods and services to satisfy reasonable user needs promptly and make purchases in accordance with the approved purchasing policy and procedure manual.

All purchases should be made at the lowest cost where cost is interpreted to include both external and internal costs of material, labor, shipping, financing, packaging, scheduling, and the risks of doing business.

The MRO Buyer is responsible to know and keep up-to-date on the legal requirements of business contracts and to use such knowledge to protect the interest of the organization.

---

*Reprinted with permission from the American Purchasing Society's Sample Job Descriptions included in the *Purchasing Policy and Procedure Manual,* ©1994.

As time permits, the MRO Buyer may be called upon to assist the Purchasing Manager or other buyers to place orders for capital equipment or other items needed by the organization. In such cases, the Purchasing Manager will approve all purchases before commitments are made to suppliers.

AUTHORITY AND LIMITATIONS OF AUTHORITY:

The MRO Buyer may place orders for repair or emergency items directly with appropriate suppliers and sign purchase orders for those items without further approval providing good purchasing practices are used and the value of the orders does not exceed $1000. Other categories of items or orders exceeding $1000 must be placed with approved sources only unless the orders are signed by the Purchasing Manager.

DUTIES OF THE MRO BUYER:

1. The MRO Buyer should check requisitions for completeness and clarity. Missing or unclear information should be obtained from the user.

2. Items should be shopped for the lowest cost to meet delivery requirements wherever possible.

3. The MRO Buyer should negotiate with suppliers to obtain the best offer available within time constraints of the requirements. In order to provide time to maximize negotiating efforts and reduce the need for rush transactions, negotiating should be conducted in advance of actual needs for products wherever practical.

4. The MRO Buyer should develop blanket agreements or systems contracts to minimize administrative and other costs.

5. Orders should be placed with suppliers either orally or in writing, but all orders should be documented by confirming written purchase orders or properly prepared contract confirmations.

6. The MRO Buyer should analyze purchases to determine if the lowest cost methods are being used and the lowest cost products are being purchased for MRO items. The analysis should also check to determine if the most economical quantities are being purchased. The results of the analysis should be submitted to the Purchasing Manager in the form of a written report.

7. The MRO Buyer should keep adequate records of all transactions and records required by the policy and procedure manual.

Managing Time

- Prioritize your negotiating efforts. Spend most of the time negotiating on the highest expenditures. Make a list of the suppliers you deal with in descending order of annual purchases. Concentrate your efforts where you spend the most money. Do the same thing for product categories.

- Computerize as many tasks as possible. Proper use of the computer saves time and helps you do a better buying and purchasing management job as well.

- Use blanket orders, long-term contracts, and systems contracts to eliminate shopping and negotiating for every transaction.

- Make sure requisitions, purchase orders, and other forms used by purchasing are designed for efficiency. Provide instructions how to fill out forms properly and clearly (the back of the form can be used). Eliminate unneeded copies.

- Control the time spent in discussions with suppliers. Discourage "courtesy calls."

- If possible, avoid attending in-house meetings unless there is an agenda and a specific purpose. Encourage those at any meeting you attend to stick to the agenda.

What to Do if a Supplier is Failing or Going Out of Business[*]

Various problems may be encountered when a supplier goes out of business. Supply for manufacturing may be interrupted. Repair parts for office equipment or plant machinery may become unavailable. The ability to enforce warranty provisions on purchased equipment is jeopardized. It may become difficult to obtain the buyer's inventory or tools already paid for but stored at the supplier's facilities.

It is better to prevent these problems by selecting new suppliers carefully and monitoring their financial condition periodically. However, even these precautions aren't always enough. Companies still go out of business unexpectedly because of catastrophes such as fire, flood, accident, or the death of the owner.

Even though a company may not go out of business completely, they may decide to stop producing a certain product or product line. A company may be sold to new owners who no longer are interested in selling a particular product.

The best way to minimize problems is to be prepared for the unexpected and to take action immediately when you hear about a company failure or impending failure.

---

*Reprinted with permission from "Buyers Checklist Number 11," ©1998, American Purchasing Society, Inc.

What to Do Before Supplier Failure

1. Keep accurate and complete records of open orders.

2. Keep accurate records of warranties still in force.

3. Maintain records of frequently needed repair items or proprietary supplies needed for various types of equipment.

4. Keep careful records of paid-for inventory held by suppliers. Obtain on-hand counts periodically from the supplier. Physically check the quantities on hand periodically.

5. Keep careful records of buyer-owned tooling in the supplier's possession. Have it periodically checked physically to see that it is clearly marked as owned by the buyer. Keep track of where and how it is stored.

6. Obtain names, home addresses, and telephone numbers of supplier's skilled technical people in case of need.

7. Periodically check the supplier's financial condition and ask the supplier to keep you informed of any changes in ownership.

What to Do After Supplier Failure

1. Quickly determine which orders will not be completed and if and when the material must be delivered by any source of supply.

2. Find out if needed inventory, supplies, or repair items can be obtained from one or more other sources of supply.

3. Check all items under warranty and file claims and/or take legal action to possibly recoup damages from the bankruptcy court.

4. Find out if a supply of frequently-needed repair or supply items can be purchased and stocked for future needs before the doors of the failing company are completely closed.

5. Get all buyer's inventory delivered to buyer's location. If necessary obtain a *writ of replevin* from the court to obtain buyer's property.

6. Get all of buyer's tooling delivered to new supplier or buyer's facility. Obtain a *writ of replevin* if required.

7. Investigate the need and possibility of hiring former skilled and technical people from the failed company.

Questions to Ask Candidates for a Buyer's Job

Ideally a buyer should have knowledge of purchasing law, have good mathematical skills, and be able to communicate well both orally and in writing. The person should have knowledge of accounting and finance and have some training in engineering, or at least engineering drawing. Knowledge of applied psychology and economics is very important. Above all, the person should have the highest of ethical standards. While it is a rare person who has a background in all of these areas, the closer a person can come the better. In addition, an individual must have a personality that adapts to the rigors of a high- pressure position and is able to make some tough decisions. The person should be assertive without being rude or undiplomatic. Here are some easy sample questions that will give interviewers a start in assessing a candidate's potential.

1. The price of a product is $50 and you reduced the price to $45. What percentage did you save? Answer: 10%.

2. If the price of a product is $45 and the supplier wants to increase the price to $50, but you convinced the supplier to keep the price the same, what percentage did you save? Answer: 11.1%

3. What makes a contract? Answer: Capable parties, an offer, an acceptance, and consideration.

4. What is meant by the phrase "the buyer's right to cover"? Answer: If a supplier fails to deliver according to contract, the buyer may purchase elsewhere and regain any difference in cost from the original seller.

5. If you received a request from an employee to purchase a pen, what would you do first? Answer: Make sure the purchase was properly authorized. Find out from the requestor what type of pen and what color.

6. Suppose you are giving a large order for a major product to a new supplier that requires a high expenditure for tooling with a long lead time. How would you make sure the supplier is going to be in business for the duration of the order and until the product is shipped? Answer: Get a D & B report; ask for financial statements for three years; check the current ratio, the sales and profitability trend of the company for the past three years; and check out references.

7. If you are asked to buy a piece of steel that is six feet long plus or minus 0.125", what is the shortest or longest length that is acceptable? Answer: No shorter than 5' 11.875" or longer than 6' 0.125".

8. If you are asked to buy floor tile for a room that is 12 feet by 12 feet, how many square feet must you buy? Answer: 144.

9. If someone asks you to buy 38 pencils, and the pencils required only come in packages of a dozen each, how many pencils will you buy? Answer: 48

10. Five different suppliers give you prices of $2.00, $3.00, $5.00, $5.00, and $5.00. What is the mean? Answer: $4.

11. What would you do if a supplier showed appreciation for the business you gave him by giving you a Christmas gift of a few shares of stock in his company? Answer: Return the shares, report the instance to your boss, and look for a different supplier.

12. Prepare a letter in proper business form indicating the reasons why you want or are qualified for a job as a buyer. Answer: The letter should be in proper business form with correct spelling and grammar.

Articles 1 & 2 of the Uniform Commercial Code

Title
An Act

To be known as the Uniform Commercial Code, Relating to Certain Commercial Transactions in or regarding Personal Property and Contracts and other Documents concerning them, including Sales, Commercial Paper, Bank Deposits and Collections, Letters of Credit, Bulk Transfers, Warehouse Receipts, Bills of Lading, other Documents of Title, Investment Securities, and Secured Transactions, including certain Sales of Accounts, Chattel Paper, and Contract Rights; Providing for Public Notice to Third Parties in Certain Circumstances; Regulating Procedure, Evidence and Damages in Certain Court Actions Involving such Transactions, Contracts or Documents; to Make Uniform the Law with Respect Thereto; and Repealing Inconsistent Legislation.

Article 1/General Provisions

PART 1/SHORT TITLE, CONSTRUCTION, APPLICATION AND SUBJECT MATTER OF THE ACT

Section 1–101. Short Title

This Act shall be known and may be cited as Uniform Commercial Code.

Section 1–102. Purposes; Rules of Construction; Variation by Agreement

(1) This Act shall be liberally construed and applied to promote its underlying purposes and policies.

(2) Underlying purposes and policies of this Act are

(a) to simplify, clarify and modernize the law governing commercial transactions;

(b) to permit the continued expansion of commercial practices through custom, usage and agreement of the parties;

(c) to make uniform the law among the various jurisdictions.

(3) The effect of provisions of this Act may be varied by agreement, except as otherwise provided in this Act and except that the obligations of good faith, diligence, reasonableness and care prescribed by this Act may not be disclaimed by agreement, but the parties may by agreement determine the standards by which the performance of such obligations is to be measured if such standards are not manifestly unreasonable.

(4) The presence in certain provisions of this Act of the words "unless otherwise agreed" or words of similar import does not imply that the effect of other provisions may not be varied by agreement under subsection (3).

(5) In this Act unless the context otherwise requires

(a) words in the singular number include the plural, and in the plural include the singular;

(b) words of the masculine gender include the feminine and the neuter, and when the sense so indicates, words of the neuter gender may refer to any gender.

Section 1–103. Supplementary General Principles of Law Applicable

Unless displaced by the particular provisions of this Act, the principles of law and equity, including the law merchant and the law relative to capacity to contract, principal and agent, estoppel, fraud, misrepresentation, duress, coercion, mistake, bankruptcy, or other validating or invalidating cause shall supplement its provisions.

Section 1–104. Construction Against Implicit Repeal

This Act being a general act intended as a unified coverage of its subject matter, no part of it shall be deemed to be impliedly repealed by subsequent legislation if such construction can reasonably be avoided.

Section 1–105. Territorial Application of the Act; Parties' Power to Choose Applicable Law

(1) Except as provided hereafter in this section, when a transaction bears a reasonable relation to this state and also to another state or nation, the parties may agree that the law either of this state or of such other state or nation shall govern their rights and duties. Failing such agreement, this Act applies to transactions bearing an appropriate relation to this state.

(2) Where one of the following provisions of this Act specifies the applicable law, that provision governs and a contrary agreement is effective only to the extent permitted by the law (including the conflict of laws rules) so specified:

> Rights of creditors against sold goods. Section 2–402.
>
> Applicability of the Article on Bank Deposits and Collections. Section 4–102.
>
> Bulk transfers subject to the Article on Bulk Transfers. Section 6–102.
>
> Applicability of the Article on investment Securities. Section 8–106.
>
> Perfection provisions of the Article on Secured Transactions. Section 9–103.

Section 1–106. Remedies to Be Liberally Administered

(1) The remedies provided by this Act shall be liberally administered to the end that the aggrieved party may be put in as good a position as if the other party had fully performed, but neither consequential or special nor penal damages may be had except as specifically provided in this Act or by other rule of law.

(2) Any right or obligation declared by this Act is enforceable by action unless the provision declaring it specifies a different and limited effect.

Section 1–107. Waiver or Renunciation of Claim or Right After Breach

Any claim or right arising out of an alleged breach can be discharged in whole or in part without consideration by a written waiver or renunciation signed and delivered by the aggrieved party.

Section 1–108. Severability

If any provision or clause of this Act or application thereof to any person or circumstances is held invalid, such invalidity shall not affect other provisions or applications of the Act which can be given effect without the invalid provision or application, and to this end the provisions of this Act are declared to be severable.

Section 1–109. Section Captions

Section captions are part of this Act.

PART 2/GENERAL DEFINITIONS AND PRINCIPLES OF INTERPRETATION

Section 1–201. General Definitions

Subject to additional definitions contained in the subsequent Articles of this Act which are applicable to specific Articles or Parts thereof, and unless the context otherwise requires, in this Act:

(1) "Action" in the sense of a judicial proceeding includes recoupment, counter-claim, set-off, suit in equity and any other proceedings in which rights are determined.

(2) "Aggrieved party" means a party entitled to resort to a remedy

(3) "Agreement" means the bargain of the parties in fact as found in their language or by implication from other circumstances including course of dealing or usage of trade or course of performance as provided in this Act (Sections 1–205 and 2–208). Whether an agreement has legal consequences is determined by the provisions of this Act, if applicable; otherwise by the law of contracts (Section 1–103). (Compare "Contract.")

(4) "Bank" means any person engaged in the business of banking.

(5) Bearer" means the person in possession of an Instrument, document of title, or security payable to bearer or indorsed in blank.

(6) "Bill of lading" means a document evidencing the receipt of goods for shipment issued by a person engaged in the business of transporting or forwarding goods, and includes an airbill. "Airbill" means a document serving for air transportation as a bill of lading does for marine or rail transportation, and includes an air consignment note or air waybill.

(7) "Branch" includes a separately incorporated foreign branch of a bank.

(8) "Burden of establishing" a fact means the burden of persuading the triers of fact that the existence of the fact is more probable than its nonexistence.

(9) "Buyer in ordinary course of business" means a person who in good faith and without knowledge that the sale to him is in violation of the ownership rights or security interest of a third party in the goods buys in ordinary course from a person in the business of selling goods of that kind but does not include a pawnbroker. All persons who sell minerals or the like (including oil and gas) at wellhead or minehead shall be deemed to be persons in the business of selling goods of that kind. "Buying" may be for cash or by exchange of other property or on secured or unsecured credit and includes receiving goods or documents of title under a preexisting contract for sale but does not include a transfer in bulk or as security for or in total or partial satisfaction of a money debt.

(10) "Conspicuous": A term or clause is conspicuous when it is so written that a reasonable person against whom it is to operate ought to have noticed it. A printed heading in capitals (as: *non-negotiable bill of lading*) is conspicuous. Language in the body of a form is "conspicuous" if it is in larger or other contrasting type or color. But in a telegram any stated term is "conspicuous." Whether a term or clause is 'conspicuous" or not is for decision by the court.

(11) "Contract" means the total legal obligation which results from the parties' agreement as affected by this Act and any other applicable rules of law. (Compare "Agreement")

(12) "Creditor" includes a general creditor, a secured creditor, a lien creditor and any representative of creditors, including an assignee for the benefit of creditors, a trustee in bankruptcy, a receiver in equity and an executor or administrator of an insolvent debtor's or assignor's estate.

(13) "Defendant' includes a person in the position of defendant in a cross-action or counterclaim.

(14) "Delivery" with respect to instruments, documents of title, chattel paper or securities means voluntary transfer of possession.

(15) Document of title" includes bill of lading, dock warrant, dock receipt, warehouse receipt or order for the delivery of goods, and also any other document which in the regular course of business or financing is treated as adequately evidencing that the person in possession of it is entitled to receive, hold and dispose of the document and the goods it covers. To be a document of title a document must purport to be issued by or addressed to a bailee and purport to cover goods in the bailee's possession which are either identified or are fungible portions of an identified mass.

(16) "Fault" means wrongful act, omission or breach.

(17) "Fungible" with respect to goods or securities means goods or securities of which any unit is, by nature or usage of trade, the equivalent of any other like unit. Goods which are not fungible shall be deemed fungible for the purposes of this Act to the extent that under a particular agreement or document unlike units are treated as equivalents.

(18) "Genuine" means free of forgery or counterfeiting.

(19) "Good faith" means honesty in fact in the conduct or transaction concerned.

(20) "Holder" means a person who is in possession of a document of title or an instrument or an investment security drawn, issued or indorsed to him or to his order or to bearer or in blank.

(21) To "honor" is to pay or to accept and pay, or where a credit so engages, to purchase or discount a draft complying with the terms of the credit.

(22) "Insolvency proceedings" includes any assignment for the benefit of creditors or other proceedings intended to liquidate or rehabilitate the estate of the person involved.

(23) A person is "insolvent" who either has ceased to pay his debts in the ordinary course of business or cannot pay his debts as they become due or is insolvent within the meaning of the federal bankruptcy law.

(24) "Money" means a medium of exchange authorized or adopted by a domestic or foreign government as a part of its currency.

(25) A person has "notice" of a fact when

(a) he has actual knowledge of it; or

(b) she has received a notice or notification of it; or

(c) from all the facts and circumstances known to him at the time in question he has reason to know that it exists.

A person "knows" or has "knowledge" of a fact when he has actual knowledge of it. "Discover" or "learn" or a word or phrase of similar import refers to knowledge rather than to reason to know. The time and circumstances under which a notice or notification may cease to be effective are not determined by this Act.

(26) A person "notifies" or "gives" a notice or notification to another by taking such steps as may be reasonably required to inform the other in ordinary course whether or not such other actually comes to know of it. A person "receives" a notice or notification when

(a) it comes to his attention; or

(b) it is duly delivered at the place of business through which the contract was made or at any other place held out by him as the place for receipt of such communications.

(27) Notice, knowledge or a notice of notification received by an organization is effective for a particular transaction from the time when it is brought to the attention of the individual conducting that transaction, and in any event from the time when it would have been brought to his attention if the organization had exercised due diligence. An organization exercises due diligence if it maintains reasonable routines for communicating significant information to the person conducting the transaction and there is reasonable compliance with the routines. Due diligence does not require an individual acting for the organization to communicate information unless such communication is part of his regular duties or

unless he has reason to know of the transaction and that the transaction would be materially affected by the information.

(28) "Organization" includes a corporation, government or governmental subdivision or agency, business trust, estate, trust, partnership or association, two or more persons having a joint or common interest, or any other legal or commercial entity.

(29) "Party," as distinct from "third party," means a person who has engaged in a transaction or made an agreement within this Act.

(30) "Person" includes an individual or an organization (see Section 1–102).

(31) "Presumption" or "presumed" means that the trier of fact must find the existence of the fact presumed unless and until evidence is introduced which would support a finding of its nonexistence.

(32) "Purchase" includes taking by sale, discount, negotiation, mortgage, pledge, lien, issue or re-issue, gift or any other voluntary transaction creating an interest in property.

(33) "Purchaser" means a person who takes by purchase.

(34) "Remedy" means any remedial right to which an aggrieved party is entitled with or without resort to a tribunal.

(35) "Representative" includes an agent, an officer of a corporation or association, and a trustee, executor or administrator of an estate, or any other person empowered to act for another.

(36) "Rights" includes remedies.

(37) "Security interest" means an interest in personal property or fixtures which secures payment or performance of an obligation. The retention or reservation of title by a seller of goods notwithstanding shipment or delivery to the buyer (Section 2–401) is limited in effect to a reservation of a "security interest." The term also includes any interest of a buyer of accounts or chattel paper which is subject to Article 9. The special property interest of a buyer of goods on identification of such goods to a contract for sale under Section 2–401 is not a "security interest," but a buyer may also acquire a "security interest" by complying with Article 9. Unless a lease or consignment is intended as security, reservation of title thereunder is not a "security interest" but a consignment is in any event

subject to the provisions on consignment sales (Section 2–326). Whether a lease is intended as security is to be determined by the facts of each case; however, (a) the inclusion of an option to purchase does not of itself make the lease one intended for security, and (b) an agreement that upon compliance with the terms of the lease the lessee shall become or has the option to become the owner of the property for no additional consideration or for a nominal consideration does make the lease one intended for security.

(38) "Send" in connection with any writing or notice means to deposit in the mail or deliver for transmission by any other usual means of communication with postage or cost of transmission provided for and properly addressed and in the case of an instrument to an address specified thereon or otherwise agreed, or if there be none to any address reasonable under the circumstances. The receipt of any writing or notice within the time at which it would have arrived if properly sent has the effect of a proper sending.

(39) "Signed" includes any symbol executed or adopted by a party with present intention to authenticate a writing.

(40) "Surety" includes guarantor.

(41) "Telegram" includes a message transmitted by radio, teletype, cable, any mechanical method of transmission, or the like.

(42) "Term" means that portion of an agreement which relates to a particular matter.

(43) "Unauthorized" signature or indorsement means one made without actual, implied or apparent authority and includes a forgery.

(44) "Value." Except as otherwise provided with respect to negotiable instruments and bank collections (Sections 3–303, 4–208 and 4–209) a person gives "value" for rights if he acquires them.

    (a) in return for a binding commitment to extend credit or for the extension of immediately available credit whether or not drawn upon and whether or not a charge-back is provided for in the event of difficulties in collection; or

    (b) as security for or in total or partial satisfaction of a preexisting claim;

or

    (c) by accepting delivery pursuant to a preexisting contract for purchase; or

    (d) generally, in return for any consideration sufficient to support a simple contract.

(45) "Warehouse receipt" means a receipt issued by a person engaged in the business of storing goods for hire.

(46) "Written" or "writing" includes printing, typewriting or any other intentional reduction to tangible form.

Section 1–202. Prima Facie Evidence by Third Party Documents

A document in due form purporting to be a bill of lading, policy or certificate of insurance, official weigher's or inspector's certificate, consular invoice, or any other document authorized or required by the contract to be issued by a third party shall be prima fade evidence of its own authenticity and genuineness and of the facts stated in the document by the third party.

Section 1–203. Obligation of Good Faith

Every contract or duty within this Act imposes an obligation of good faith in its performance or enforcement.

Section 1–204. Time; Reasonable Time; "Seasonably"

(1) Whenever this Act requires any action to be taken within a reasonable time, any time which is not manifestly unreasonable may be fixed by agreement.

(2) What is a reasonable time for taking any action depends on the nature, purpose and circumstances of such action.

(3) An action is taken "seasonably" when it is taken at or within the time agreed or, if no time is agreed, at or within a reasonable time.

Section 1–205. Course of Dealing and Usage of Trade

(1) A course of dealing is a sequence of previous conduct between the parties to a particular transaction which is fairly to be regarded as estab-

lishing a common basis of understanding for interpreting their expressions and other conduct.

(2) A usage of trade is any practice or method of dealing having such regularity of observance in a place, vocation or trade as to justify an expectation that it will be observed with respect to the transaction in question. The existence and scope of such usage are to be proved as facts. If it is established that such a usage is embodied in a written trade code or similar writing the interpretation of the writing is for the court.

(3) A course of dealing between parties and any usage of trade in the vocation or trade in which they are engaged or of which they are or should be aware give particular meaning to and supplement or qualify terms of an agreement.

(4) The express terms of an agreement and an applicable course of dealing or usage of trade shall be construed wherever reasonable as consistent with each other; but when such construction is unreasonable, express terms control both course of dealing and usage of trade and course of dealing controls usage of trade.

(5) An applicable usage of trade in the place where any part of performance is to occur shall be used in interpreting the agreement as to that part of the performance.

(6) Evidence of a relevant usage of trade offered by one party is not admissible unless and until he has given the other party such notice as the court finds sufficient to prevent unfair surprise to the latter.

Section 1–206. Statute of Frauds for Kinds of Personal Property Not Otherwise Covered

(1) Except in the cases described in subsection (2) of this section, a contract for the sale of personal property is not enforceable byway of action or defense beyond five thousand dollars in amount or value of remedy unless there is some writing which indicates that a contract for sale has been made between the parties at a defined or stated price, reasonably identifies the subject matter, and is signed by the party against whom enforcement is sought or by his authorized agent.

(2) Subsection (1) of this section does not apply to contracts for the sale of goods (Section 2–201) nor of securities (Section 8–319) nor to security agreements (Section 9–203).

Section 1–207. Performance or Acceptance Under Reservation of Rights

A party who with explicit reservation of rights performs or promises performance or assents to performance in a manner demanded or offered by the other party does not thereby prejudice the rights reserved. Such words as "without prejudice," "under protest" or the like are sufficient.

Section 1–208. Option to Accelerate at Will

A term providing that one party or his successor in interest may accelerate payment or performance or require collateral or additional collateral "at will" or "when he deems himself insecure" or in words of similar import shall be construed to mean that he shall have power to do so only if he in good faith believes that the prospect of payment or performance is impaired. The burden of establishing lack of good faith is on the party against whom the power has been exercised.

Section 1–209. Subordinated Obligations

An obligation may be issued as subordinated to payment of another obligation of the person obligated, or a creditor may subordinate his right to payment of an obligation by agreement with either the person obligated or another creditor of the person obligated. Such a subordination does not create a security interest as against either the common debtor or a subordinated creditor. This section shall be construed as declaring the law as it existed prior to the enactment of this section and not as modifying it.

Article 2/Sales

PART 1 /SHORT TITLE, GENERAL CONSTRUCTION AND SUBJECT MATTER

Section 2–101. Short Title

This Article shall be known and may be cited as Uniform Commercial Code–Sales.

Section 2–102. Scope; Certain Security and Other Transactions Excluded From This Article

Unless the context otherwise requires, this Article applies to transactions in goods; it does not apply to any transaction which although in the form of an unconditional contract to sell or present sale is intended to operate only as a security transaction nor does this Article impair or repeat any statute regulating sales to consumers, farmers or other specified classes of buyers.

Section 2–103. Definitions and Index of Definitions

(1) In this Article, unless the context otherwise requires,

   (a) "Buyer" means a person who buys or contracts to buy goods.

   (b) "Good faith" in the case of a merchant means honesty in fact and the observance of reasonable commercial standards of fair dealing in the trade.

   (c) "Receipt" of goods means taking physical possession of them:

   (d) "Seller" means a person who sells or contracts to sell goods.

(2) Other definitions applying to this Article or to specified Parts thereof, and the sections in which they appear are:

"Acceptance." Section 2–606.

"Banker's credit." Section 2–325.

"Between merchants." Section 2–104.

"Cancellation." Section 2–106(4).

"Commercial unit." Section 2–105.

"Confirmed credit." Section 2–325.

"Conforming to contract." Section 2–106.

"Contract for sale." Section 2–106.

"Cover." Section 2–712.

"Entrusting." Section 2–403.

"Financing agency." Section 2–104.

"Future goods." Section 2–105.

"Future goods." Section 2–105.

"Goods." Section 2–105.

"Identification." Section 2–501.

"Installment contract." Section 2–612.

"Letter of Credit." Section 2–325.

"Lot." Section 2–105.

"Merchant." Section 2–104.

"Overseas." Section 2–323.

"Person in position of seller." Section 2–707.

"Present sale." Section 2–106.

"Sale." Section 2–106.

"Sale on approval." Section 2–326.

"Sale or return." Section 2–326.

"Termination." Section 2–106.

(3) The following definitions in other Articles apply to this Article:

"Check." Section 3–104.

"Consignee." Section 7–102.

"Consignor." Section 7–102.

"Consumer goods." Section 9–109.

"Dishonor." Section 3–507.

"Draft." Section 3–104.

(4) In addition Article 1 contains general definitions and principles of construction and interpretation applicable throughout this Article.

Section 2–104. Definitions: "Merchant"; "Between Merchants"; "Financing Agency"

(1) "Merchant" means a person who deals in goods of the kind or otherwise by his occupation holds himself out as having knowledge or skill peculiar to the practices or goods involved in the transaction or to whom such knowledge or skill may be attributed by his employment of

an agent or broker or other intermediary who by his occupation holds himself out as having such knowledge or skill.

(2) "Financing agency" means a bank, finance company or other person who in the ordinary course of business makes advances against goods or documents of title or who by arrangement with either the seller or the buyer intervenes in ordinary course to make or collect payment due or claimed under the contract for sale, as by purchasing or paying the seller's draft or making advances against it or by merely taking it for collection whether or not documents of title accompany the draft. "Financing agency" includes also a bank or other person who similarly intervenes between persons who are in the position of seller and buyer in respect to the goods (Section 2–707).

(3) "Between merchants" means in any transaction with respect to which both parties are chargeable with the knowledge or skill of merchants.

Section 2–105. Definitions: Transferability; "Goods"; "Future" Goods; "Lot"; "Commercial Unit"

(1) "Goods" means all things (including specially manufactured goods which are movable at the time of identification to the contract for sale other than the money in which the price is to be paid, investment securities (Article 8) and things in action. "Goods" also includes the unborn young of animals and growing crops and other identified things attached to realty as described in the section on goods to be severed from realty (Section 2–107).

(2) Goods must be both existing and identified before any interest in them can pass. Goods which are not both existing and identified are "future" goods. A purported present sale of future goods or of any interest therein operates as a contract to sell.

(3) There may be a sale of a part interest in existing identified goods.

(4) An undivided share in an identified bulk of fungible goods is sufficiently identified to be sold although the quantity of the bulk is not determined. Any agreed proportion of such a bulk or any quantity thereof agreed upon by number, weight or other measure may to the extent of the

seller's interest in the bulk be sold to the buyer who then becomes an Owner in common.

(5) "Lot" means a parcel or a single article which is the subject matter of a separate sale or delivery, whether or not it is sufficient to perform the contract.

(6) "Commercial unit" means such a unit of goods as by commercial usage is a single whole for purposes of sale and division of which materially impairs its character or value on the market or in use. A commercial unit may be a single article (as a machine) or a set of articles (as a suite of furniture or an assortment of sizes) or a quantity (as a bale, gross, or carload) or any other unit treated in use or in the relevant market as a single whole.

Section 2–106. Definitions: "Contract"; "Agreement"; "Contract for Sale"; "Sale"; "Present Sale"; "Conforming" to Contract; Termination"; "Cancellation"

(1) In this Article unless the context otherwise requires, "contract" and "agreement" are limited to those relating to the present or future sale of goods. "Contract for sale" includes both a present sale of goods and a contract to sell goods at a future time. A "sale" consists in the passing of title from the seller to the buyer for a price (Section 2–401) A 'present sale" means a sale which is accomplished by the making of the contract.

(2) Goods or conduct, including any part of a performance, are "conforming" or conform to the contract when they are in accordance with the obligations under the contract.

(3) "Termination" occurs when either party pursuant to a power created by agreement or law puts an end to the contract otherwise than for its breach. On "termination" all obligations which are still executory on both sides are discharged but any right based on prior breach or performance survives.

(4) "Cancellation" occurs when either party puts an end to the contract for breach by the other and its effect is the same as that of "termination" except that the canceling party also retains any remedy for breach of the whole contract or any unperformed balance.

Section 2–107. Goods to Be Severed From Realty: Recording

(1) A contract for the sale of minerals or the like (including oil and gas) or a structure or its materials to be removed from realty is a contract for the sale of goods within this Article if they are to be severed by the seller, but until severance a purported present sale thereof which is not effective as a transfer of an interest in land is effective only as a contract to sell.

(2) A contract for the sale apart from the land of growing crops or other things attached to realty and capable of severance without material harm thereto but not described in subsection (1) or of timber to be cut is a contract for the sale of goods within this Article whether the subject matter is to be severed by the buyer or by the seller even though it forms part of the realty at the time of contracting, and the parties can by identification effect a present sale before severance.

(3) The provisions of this section are subject to any third party rights provided by the law relating to realty records, and the contract for sale may be executed and recorded as a document transferring an interest in land and shall then constitute notice to third parties of the buyer's rights under the contract for sale.

PART 2/FORM, FORMATION AND READJUSTMENT OF CONTRACT

Section 2–201. Formal Requirements; Statute of Frauds

(1) Except as otherwise provided in this section, a contract for the sale of goods for the price of $500 or more is not enforceable by way of action or defense unless there is some writing sufficient to indicate that a contract for sale has been made between the parties and signed by the party against whom enforcement is sought or by his authorized agent or broker. A writing is not insufficient because it omits or incorrectly states a term agreed upon but the contract is not enforceable under this paragraph beyond the quantity of goods shown in such writing.

(2) Between merchants, if within a reasonable time a writing in confirmation of the contract and sufficient against the sender is received and the party receiving it has reason to know its contents, it satisfies the requirements of subsection (1) against such party unless written notice of objection to its content is given within 10 days after it is received.

(3) A contract which does not satisfy the requirements of subsection (1) but which is valid in other respects is enforceable.

    (a) if the goods are to be specially manufactured for the buyer and are not suitable for sale to others in the ordinary course of the seller's business and the seller, before notice of repudiation is received and under circumstances which reasonably indicate that the goods are for the buyer, has made either a substantial beginning of their manufacture or commitments for their procurement; or

    (b) if the party against whom enforcement is sought admits in his pleading, testimony or otherwise in court that a contract for sale was made, but the contract is not enforceable under this provision beyond the quantity of goods admitted; or

    (c) with respect to goods for which payment has been made and accepted or which have been received and accepted (Sec. 2–606).

Section 2–202. Final Written Expression: Parol or Extrinsic Evidence

Terms with respect to which the confirmatory memoranda of the parties agree or which are otherwise set forth in a writing intended by the parties as a final expression of their agreement with respect to such terms as are included therein may not be contradicted by evidence of any prior agreement or of a contemporaneous oral agreement but may be explained or supplemented

    (a) by course of dealing or usage of trade (Section 1–205) or by course of performance (Section 2–208); and

    (b) by evidence of consistent additional terms unless the court finds the writing to have been intended also as a complete and exclusive statement of the terms of the agreement.

Section 2–203. Seals Inoperative

The affixing of a seal to a writing evidencing a contract for sale or an offer to buy or sell goods does not constitute the writing a sealed instrument and the law with respect to sealed instruments does not apply to such a contract or offer.

Section 2–204. Formation in General

(1) A contract for sale of goods may be made in any manner sufficient to show agreement, including conduct by both parties which recognizes the existence of such a contract.

(2) An agreement sufficient to constitute a contract for sale may be found even though the moment of its making is undetermined

(3) Even though one or more terms are left open a contract for sale does not fail for indefiniteness if the parties have intended to make a contract and there is a reasonably certain basis for giving an appropriate remedy.

Section 2–205. Firm Offers

An offer by a merchant to buy or sell goods in a signed writing which by its terms gives assurance that it will be held open is not revocable, for lack of consideration, during the time stated or if no time is stated for a reasonable time, but in no event may such period of irrevocability exceed three months; but any such term of assurance on a form supplied by the offeree must be separately signed by the offeror.

Section 2–206. Offer and Acceptance in Formation of Contract

(1) Unless otherwise unambiguously indicated by the language or circumstances

    (a) an offer to make a contract shall be construed as inviting acceptance in any manner and by any medium reasonable in the circumstances;

    (b) an order or other offer to buy goods for prompt or current shipment shall be construed as inviting acceptance either by a prompt promise to ship or by the prompt or current shipment of conforming or non-conforming goods, but such a shipment of non-conforming goods does not constitute an acceptance if the seller seasonably notifies the buyer that the shipment is offered only as an accommodation to the buyer.

(2) Where the beginning of a requested performance is a reasonable mode of acceptance, an offeror who is not notified of acceptance within a reasonable time may treat the offer as having lapsed before acceptance.

Section 2–207. Additional Terms in Acceptance or Confirmation

(1) A definite and seasonable expression of acceptance or a written confirmation which is sent within a reasonable time operates as an acceptance even though it states terms additional to or different from those offered or agreed upon, unless acceptance is expressly made conditional on assent to the additional or different terms.

(2) The additional terms are to be construed as proposals for addition to the contract. Between merchants such terms become part of the contract unless:

    (a) the offer expressly limits acceptance to the terms of the offer;

    (b) they materially alter it; or

    (c) notification of objection to them has already been given or is given within a reasonable time after notice of them is received.

(3) Conduct by both parties which recognizes the existence of a contract is sufficient to establish a contract for sale although the writings of the parties do not otherwise establish a contract. In such case the terms of the particular contract consist of those terms on which the writings of the parties agree, together with any supplementary terms incorporated under any other provisions of this Act.

Section 2–208. Course of Performance or Practical Construction

(1) Where the contract for sale involves repeated occasions for performance by either party with knowledge of the nature of the performance and opportunity for objection to it by the other, any course of performance accepted or acquiesced in without objection shall be relevant to determine the meaning of the agreement.

(2) The express terms of the agreement and any such course of performance, as well as any course of dealing and usage of trade, shall be construed whenever reasonable as consistent with each other; but when such construction is unreasonable, express terms shall control course of performance and course of performance shall control both course of dealing and usage of trade (Section 1–205).

(3) Subject to the provisions of the next section on modification and waiver, such course of performance shall be relevant to show a waiver or modification of any term inconsistent with such course of performance.

Section 2–209. Modification, Rescission and Waiver

(1) An agreement modifying a contract within this Article needs no consideration to be binding.

(2) A signed agreement which excludes modification or rescission except by a signed writing cannot be otherwise modified or rescinded, but except as between merchants such a requirement on a form supplied by the merchant must be separately signed by the other party.

(3) The requirements of the statute of frauds section of this Article (Section 2–201) must be satisfied if the contract as modified is within its provisions.

(4) Although an attempt at modification or rescission does not satisfy the requirements of subsection (2) or (3) it can operate as a waiver.

(5) A party who has made a waiver affecting an executory portion of the contract may retract the waiver by reasonable notification received by the other party that strict performance will be required of any term waived, unless the retraction would be unjust in view of a material change of position in reliance on the waiver.

Section 2–210. Delegation of Performance; Assignment of Rights

(1) A party may perform his duty through a delegate unless otherwise agreed or unless the other party has a substantial interest in having his original promisor perform or control the acts required by the contract. No delegation of performance relieves the party delegating of any duty to perform or any liability for breach.

(2) Unless otherwise agreed, all rights of either seller or buyer can be assigned except where the assignment would materially change the duty of the other party, or increase materially the burden or risk imposed on him by his contract, or impair materially his chance of obtaining return performance. A right to damages for breach of the whole contract or a

right arising out of the assignor's due performance of his entire obligation can be assigned despite agreement otherwise.

(3) Unless the circumstances indicate the contrary, a prohibition of assignment of the "contract" is to be construed as barring only the delegation to the assignee of the assignor's performance.

(4) An assignment of "the contract" or of "all my rights under the contract" or an assignment in similar general terms is an assignment of rights and, unless the language or the circumstances (as in an assignment for security) indicate the contrary, it is a delegation of performance of the duties of the assignor, and its acceptance by the assignee constitutes a promise by him to perform those duties. This promise is enforceable by either the assignor or the other party to the original contract.

(5) The other party may treat any assignment which delegates performance as creating reasonable grounds for insecurity and may without prejudice to his rights against the assignor demand assurances from the assignee (Section 2–609).

PART 3/GENERAL OBLIGATION AND CONSTRUCTION OF CONTRACT

Section 2–301. General Obligations of Parties

The obligation of the seller is to transfer and deliver and that of the buyer is to accept and pay in accordance with the contract.

Section 2–302. Unconscionable Contract or Clause

(1) If the court as a matter of law finds the contract or any clause of the contract to have been unconscionable at the time it was made, the court may refuse to enforce the contract, or it may enforce the remainder of the contract without the unconscionable clause, or it may so limit the application of any unconscionable clause as to avoid any unconscionable result.

(2) When it is claimed or appears to the court that the contract or any clause thereof may be unconscionable, the parties shall be afforded a reasonable opportunity to present evidence as to its commercial setting, purpose and effect to aid the court in making the determination.

Section 2–303. Allocation or Division of Risks

Where this Article allocates a risk or a burden as between the parties "unless otherwise agreed," the agreement may not only shift the allocation but may also divide the risk or burden.

Section 2–304. Price Payable in Money, Goods, Realty, or Otherwise

(1) The price can be made payable in money or otherwise. If it is payable in whole or in part in goods each party is a seller of the goods which he is to transfer.

(2) Even though all or part of the price is payable in an interest in realty the transfer of the goods and the seller's obligations with reference to them are subject to this Article, but not the transfer of the interest in realty or the transferor's obligations in connection therewith.

Section 2–305. Open Price Term

(1) The parties, if they so intend, can conclude a contract for sale even though the price is not settled. In such a case, the price is a reasonable price at the time for delivery if

      (a) nothing is said as to price; or

      (b) the price is left to be agreed by the parties and they fail to agree; or

      (c) the price is to be fixed in terms of some agreed market or other standard as set or recorded by a third person or agency and it is not so set or recorded.

(2) A price to be fixed by the seller or by the buyer means a price for him to fix in good faith.

(3) When a price left to be fixed otherwise than by agreement of the parties fails to be fixed through fault of one party, the other may at his option treat the contract as cancelled or himself fix a reasonable price.

(4) Where, however, the parties intend not to be bound unless the price be fixed or agreed and it is not fixed or agreed, there is no contract. In such a case, the buyer must return any goods already received or if unable so to do must pay their reasonable value at the time of delivery and the seller must return any portion of the price paid on account.

Section 2–306. Output, Requirements and Exclusive Dealings

(1) A term which measures the quantity by the output of the seller or the requirements of the buyer means such actual output or requirements as may occur in good faith, except that no quantity unreasonably disproportionate to any stated estimate or in the absence of a stated estimate to any normal or otherwise comparable prior output or requirements may be tendered or demanded.

(2) A lawful agreement by either the seller or the buyer for exclusive dealing in the kind of goods concerned imposes, unless otherwise agreed, an obligation by the seller to use best efforts to supply the goods and by the buyer to use best efforts to promote their sale.

Section 2–307. Delivery in Single Lot or Several Lots

Unless otherwise agreed all goods called for by a contract for sale must be tendered in a single delivery and payment is due only on such tender; but where the circumstances give either party the right to make or demand delivery in lots, the price if it can be apportioned may be demanded for each lot.

Section 2–308. Absence of Specified Place for Delivery.

Unless otherwise agreed

(a) the place for delivery of goods is the seller's place of business or, if he has none, his residence; but

(b) in a contract for sale of identified goods which to the knowledge of the parties at the time of contracting are in some other place, that place is the place for their delivery; and

(c) documents of title may be delivered through customary banking channels.

Section 2–309. Absence of Specific Time Provisions; Notice of Termination

(1) The time for shipment or delivery or any other action under a contract if not provided in this Article or agreed upon shall be a reasonable time.

(2) Where the contract provides for successive performances but is indefinite in duration, it is valid for a reasonable time; but unless otherwise agreed may be terminated at any time by either party.

(3) Termination of a contract by one party, except on the happening of an agreed event, requires that reasonable notification be received by the other party and an agreement dispensing with notification is invalid if its operation would be unconscionable.

Section 2–310. Open Time for Payment or Running of Credit; Authority to Ship Under Reservation

Unless otherwise agreed

    (a) payment is due at the time and place at which the buyer is to receive the goods even though the place of shipment is the place of delivery; and

    (b) if the seller is authorized to send the goods, he may ship them under reservation, and may tender the documents of title, but the buyer may inspect the goods after their arrival before payment is due unless such inspection is inconsistent with the terms of the contract (Section 2–513); and

    (c) if delivery is authorized and made by way of documents of title otherwise than by subsection (b), then payment is due at the time and place at which the buyer is to receive the documents regardless of where the goods are to be received; and

    (d) where the seller is required or authorized to ship the goods on credit, the credit period runs from the time of shipment but post-dating the invoice or delaying its dispatch will correspondingly delay the starting of the credit period.

Section 2–311. Options and Cooperation Respecting Performance

(1) An agreement for sale which is otherwise sufficiently definite (subsection (3) of Section 2–204) to be a contract is not made invalid by the fact that it leaves particulars of performance to be specified by one of the parties. Any such specification must be made in good faith and within limits set by commercial reasonableness.

(2) Unless otherwise agreed, specifications relating to assortment of the goods are at the buyer's option and, except as otherwise provided in subsections (1) (c) and (3) of Section 2–319, specifications or arrangements relating to shipment are at the seller's option.

(3) Where such specification would materially affect the other party's performance but is not seasonably made or where one party's cooperation is necessary to the agreed performance of the other but is not seasonably forthcoming, the other party in addition to all other remedies

  (a) is excused for any resulting delay in his own performance; and

  (b) may also either proceed to perform in any reasonable manner or after the time for a material part of his own performance treat the failure to specify or to cooperate as a breach by failure to deliver or accept the goods.

Section 2–312. Warranty of Title and Against Infringement; Buyer's Obligation Against Infringement

(1) Subject to subsection (2), there is in a contract for sale a warranty by the seller that

  (a) the title conveyed shall be good, and its transfer rightful; and

  (b) the goods shall be delivered free from any security interest or other lien or encumbrance of which the buyer at the time of contracting has no knowledge.

(2) A warranty under subsection (1) will be excluded or modified only by specific language or by circumstances which give the buyer reason to know that the person selling does not claim title in himself or that he is purporting to sell only such right or title as he or a third person may have.

(3) Unless otherwise agreed a seller who is a merchant regularly dealing in goods of the kind warrants that the goods shall be delivered free of the rightful claim of any third person by way of infringement or the like but a buyer who furnishes specifications to the seller must hold the seller harmless against any such claim which arises out of compliance with the specifications.

Section 2–313. Express Warranties by Affirmation, Promise, Description, Sample

(1) Express warranties by the seller are created as follows:

  (a) Any affirmation of fact or promise made by the seller to the buyer which relates to the goods and becomes part of the basis of the bargain creates an express warranty that the goods shall conform to the affirmation or promise.

(b) Any description of the goods which is made part of the basis of the bargain creates an express warranty that the goods shall conform to the description.

(c) Any sample or model which is made part of the basis of the bargain creates an express warranty that the whole of the goods shall conform to the sample or model.

(2) It is not necessary to the creation of an express warranty that the seller use formal words such as "warrant" or "guarantee" or that he have a specific intention to make a warranty, but an affirmation merely of the value of the goods or a statement purporting to be merely the seller's opinion or commendation of the goods does not create a warranty.

Section 2–314. Implied Warranty: Merchantability; Usage of Trade

(1) Unless excluded or modified (Section 2–316), a warranty that the goods shall be merchantable is implied in a contract for their sale if the seller is a merchant with respect to goods of that kind. Under this section, the serving for value of food or drink to be consumed either on the premises or elsewhere is a sale.

(2) Goods to be merchantable must be at least such as

(a) pass without objection in the trade under the contract description; and

(b) in the case of fungible goods, are of fair average quality within the description; and

(c) are fit for the ordinary purposes for which such goods are used; and

(d) run, within the variations permitted by the agreement, of even kind, quality and quantity within each unit and among all units involved; and

(e) are adequately contained, packaged, and labeled as the agreement may require; and

(f) conform to the promises or affirmations of fact made on the container or label if any.

(3) Unless excluded or modified (Section 2–316), other implied warranties may arise from course of dealing or usage of trade.

Section 2–315. Implied Warranty: Fitness for Particular Purpose

Where the seller at the time of contracting has reason to know any particular purpose for which the goods are required and that the buyer is relying on the seller's skill or judgment to select or furnish suitable goods, there is unless excluded or modified under the next section an implied warranty that the goods shall be fit for such purpose.

Section 2–316. Exclusion or Modification of Warranties

(1) Words or conduct relevant to the creation of an express warranty and words or conduct tending to negate or limit warranty shall be construed wherever reasonable as consistent with each other; but, subject to the provisions of this Article on parol or extrinsic evidence (Section 2–202), negation or limitation is inoperative to the extent that such construction is unreasonable.

(2) Subject to subsection (3), to exclude or modify the implied warranty of merchantability or any part of it, the language must mention merchantability and in case of a writing must be conspicuous, and to exclude or modify any implied warranty of fitness the exclusion must be by a writing and conspicuous. Language to exclude all implied warranties of fitness is sufficient if it states, for example, that "There are no warranties which extend beyond the description on the face hereof."

(3) Notwithstanding subsection (2)

(a) unless the circumstances indicate otherwise, all implied warranties are excluded by expressions like "as is," "with all faults" or other language which in common understanding calls the buyer's attention to the exclusion of warranties and makes plain that there is no implied warranty; and

(b) when the buyer before entering into the contract has examined the goods or the sample or model as fully as he desired or has refused to examine the goods, there is no implied warranty with regard to defects which an examination ought in the circumstances to have revealed to him; and

(c) an implied warranty can also be excluded or modified by course of dealing or course of performance or usage of trade.

(4) Remedies for breach of warranty can be limited in accordance with the provisions of this Article on liquidation or limitation of damages and on contractual modification of remedy (Sections 2–718 and 2–719).

Section 2–317. Cumulation and Conflict of Warranties Express or Implied

Warranties whether express or implied shall be construed as consistent with each other and as cumulative, but if such construction is unreasonable the intention of the parties shall determine which warranty is dominant. In ascertaining that intention the following rules apply:

(a) Exact or technical specifications displace an inconsistent sample or model or general language of description.

(b) A sample from an existing bulk displaces inconsistent general language of description.

(c) Express warranties displace inconsistent implied warranties other than an implied warranty of fitness for a particular purpose.

Section 2–318. Third Party Beneficiaries of Warranties Express or Implied

Note: *If this Act is introduced in the Congress of the United States this section should be omitted. (States to select one alternative.)*

Alternative A

A seller's warranty whether express or implied extends to any natural person who is in the family or household of his buyer or who is a guest in his home if it is reasonable to expect that such person may use, consume or be affected by the goods and who is injured in person by breach of the warranty. A seller may not exclude or limit the operation of this section.

Alternative B

A seller's warranty whether express or implied extends to any natural person who may reasonably be expected to use, consume or be affected by the goods and who is injured in person by breach of the warranty. A seller may not exclude or limit the operation of this section.

Alternative C

A seller's warranty whether express or implied extends to any person who may reasonably be expected to use, consume or be affected by the goods and who is injured by breach of the warranty. A seller may not exclude or limit the operation of this section with respect to injury to the person of an individual to whom the warranty extends.

Section 2–319. F.O.B. and F.A.S. Terms

(1) Unless otherwise agreed, the term F.O.B. (which means "free on board") at a named place, even though used only in connection with the stated price, is a delivery term under which

- (a) when the term is F.O.B. the place of shipment, the seller must at that place ship the goods in the manner provided in this Article (Section 2–504) and bear the expense and risk of putting them into the possession of the carrier; or

- (b) when the term is F.O.B. the place of destination, the seller must at his own expense and risk transport the goods to that place and there tender delivery of them in the manner provided in this Article (Section 2–503);

- (c) when under either (a) or (b) the term is also F.O.B. vessel, car or other vehicle, the seller must in addition at his own expense and risk load the goods on board. If the term is F.O.B. vessel, the buyer must name the vessel and, in an appropriate case, the seller must comply with the provisions of this Article on the form of bill of lading (Section 2–323).

(2) Unless otherwise agreed, the term F.A.S. vessel (which means "free alongside") at a named port, even though used only in connection with the stated price, is a delivery term under which the seller must

- (a) at his own expense and risk deliver the goods alongside the vessel in the manner usual in that port or on a dock designated and provided by the buyer; and

- (b) obtain and tender a receipt for the goods in exchange for which the carrier is under a duty to issue a bill of lading.

(3) Unless otherwise agreed in any case falling within subsection (1) (a) or (c) or subsection (2) the buyer must seasonably give any needed instructions for making delivery, including, when the term is F.A.S. or F.O.B., the loading berth of the vessel and, in an appropriate case, its name and sailing date. The seller may treat the failure of needed instructions as a failure of cooperation under this Article (Section 2–311). He may also at his option move the goods in any reasonable manner preparatory to delivery or shipment.

(4) Under the term F.O.B. vessel or F.A.S., unless otherwise agreed, the buyer must make payment against tender of the required documents and the seller may not tender nor the buyer demand delivery of the goods in substitution for the documents.

Section 2–320. C.I.F. and C. & F. Terms

(1) The term C.I.F. means that the price includes in a lump sum the cost of the goods and the insurance and freight to the named destination. The term C. & F. or C.F. means that the price so includes cost and freight to the named destination.

(2) Unless otherwise agreed and even though used only in connection with the stated price and destination, the term C.I.F. destination or its equivalent requires the seller at his own expense and risk to

    (a) put the goods into the possession of a carrier at the port for shipment and obtain a negotiable bill or bills of lading covering the entire transportation to the named destination; and

    (b) load the goods and obtain a receipt from the carrier (which may be contained in the bill of lading) showing that the freight has been paid or provided for; and

    (c) obtain a policy or certificate of insurance, including any war risk insurance, of a kind and on terms then current at the port of shipment in the usual amount, in the currency of the contract, shown to cover the same goods covered by the bill of lading and providing for payment of loss to the order of the buyer or for the account of whom it may concern; but the seller may add to the price the amount of the premium for any such war risk insurance; and

(d) prepare an invoice of the goods and procure any other documents required to effect shipment or to comply with the contract; and

(e) forward and tender with commercial promptness all the documents in due form and with any indorsement necessary to perfect the buyer's rights.

(3) Unless otherwise agreed, the term C. & F. or its equivalent has the same effect and imposes upon the seller the same obligations and risks as a C.I.F. term except the obligation as to insurance.

(4) Under the term C.I.F. or C. & F., unless otherwise agreed the buyer must make payment against tender of the required documents and the seller may not tender nor the buyer demand delivery of the goods in substitution for the documents.

Section 2–321. C.I.F. or C. & F.: "Net Landed Weights"; "Payment on Arrival"; Warranty of Condition on Arrival

Under a contract containing a term C.I.F. or C. & F.

(1) Where the price is based on or is to be adjusted according to "net landed weights," "delivered weights," "out turn" quantity or quality or the like, unless otherwise agreed the seller must reasonably estimate the price. The payment due on tender of the documents called for by the contract is the amount so estimated, but after final adjustment of the price a settlement must be made with commercial promptness.

(2) An agreement described in subsection (1) or any warranty of quality or condition of the goods on arrival places upon the seller the risk of ordinary deterioration, shrinkage and the like in transportation but has no effect on the place or time of identification to the contract for sale or delivery or on the passing of the risk of 1oss.

(3) Unless otherwise agreed, where the contract provides for payment on or after arrival of the goods the seller must before payment allow such preliminary inspection as is feasible; but if the goods are lost, delivery of the documents and payment are due when the goods should have arrived.

Section 2–322. Delivery "Ex-Ship"

(1) Unless otherwise agreed, a term for delivery of goods "ex-ship" (which means from the carrying vessel) or in equivalent language is not restricted to a particular ship and requires delivery from a ship which has reached a place at the named port of destination where goods of the kind are usually discharged.

(2) Under such a term, unless otherwise agreed

    (a) the seller must discharge all liens arising out of the carriage and furnish the buyer with a direction which puts the carrier under a duty to deliver the goods; and

    (b) the risk of loss does not pass to the buyer until the goods leave the ship's tackle or are otherwise properly unloaded.

Section 2–323. Form of Bill of Lading Required in Overseas Shipment; "Overseas"

(1) Where the contract contemplates overseas shipment and contains a term C.I.F. or C. & F. or F.O.B. vessel, the seller unless otherwise agreed must obtain a negotiable bill of lading stating that the goods have been loaded on board or, in the case of a term C.I.F. or C. & F., received for shipment.

(2) Where in a case within subsection (1) a bill of lading has been issued in a set of parts, unless otherwise agreed, if the documents are not to be sent from abroad the buyer may demand tender of the full set; otherwise only one part of the bill of lading need be tendered. Even if the agreement expressly requires a full set.

    (a) due tender of a single part is acceptable within the provisions of this Article on cure of improper delivery (subsection (1) of Section 2–508); and

    (b) even though the full set is demanded, if the documents are sent from abroad the person tendering an incomplete set may nevertheless require payment upon furnishing an indemnity which the buyer in good faith deems adequate.

(3) A shipment by water or by air or a contract contemplating such shipment is "overseas" insofar as by usage of trade or agreement it is sub-

ject to the commercial, financing or shipping practices characteristic of international deep water commerce.

Section 2–324. "No Arrival, No Sale" Term

Under a term "no arrival, no sale" or terms of like meaning, unless otherwise agreed,

    (a) the seller must properly ship conforming goods and if they arrive by any means he must tender them on arrival, but he assumes no obligation that the goods will arrive unless he has caused the non-arrival; and

    (b) where without fault of the seller the goods are in part lost or have so deteriorated as no longer to conform to the contract or arrive after the contract time, the buyer may proceed as if there had been casualty to identified goods (Section 2–613).

Section 2–325. "Letter of Credit" Term; "Confirmed Credit"

(1) Failure of the buyer seasonably to furnish an agreed letter of credit is a breach of the contract for sale.

(2) The delivery to seller of a proper letter of credit suspends the buyer's obligation to pay. If the letter of credit is dishonored, the seller may on seasonable notification to the buyer require payment directly from him.

(3) Unless otherwise agreed, the term "letter of credit" or "banker's credit" in a contract for sale means an irrevocable credit issued by a financing agency of good repute and, where the shipment is overseas, of good international repute. The term "confirmed credit" means that the credit must also carry the direct obligation of such an agency which does business in the seller's financial market.

Section 2–326. Sale on Approval and Sale or Return; Consignment Sales and Rights of Creditors

(1) Unless otherwise agreed, if delivered goods may be returned by the buyer even though they conform to the contract, the transaction is

    (a) a "sale on approval" if the goods are delivered primarily for use, and

(b) a "sale or return" if the goods are delivered primarily for resale.

(2) Except as provided in subsection (3), goods held on approval are not subject to the claims of the buyer's creditors until acceptance; goods held on sale or return are subject to such claims while in the buyer's possession.

(3) Where goods are delivered to a person for sale and such person maintains a place of business at which he deals in goods of the kind involved, under a name other than the name of the person making delivery, then with respect to claims of creditors of the person conducting the business the goods are deemed to be on sale or return. The provisions of this subsection are applicable even though an agreement purports to reserve title to the person making delivery until payment or resale or uses such words as "on consignment or "on memorandum." However, this subsection is not applicable if the person making delivery

(a) complies with an applicable law providing for a consignor's interest or the like to be evidenced by a sign, or

(b) establishes that the person conducting the business is generally known by his creditors to be substantially engaged in selling the goods of others, or

(c) complies with the filing provisions of the Article on Secured Transactions (Article 9).

(4) Any "or return" term of a contract for sale is to be treated as a separate contract for sale within the statute of frauds section of this Article (Section 2–201) and as contradicting the sale aspect of the contract within the provisions of this Article on parol or extrinsic evidence (Section 2–202).

Section 2–327. Special Incidents of Sale on Approval and Sale or Return

(1) Under a sale on approval, unless otherwise agreed

(a) although the goods are identified to the contract, the risk of loss and the title do not pass to the buyer until acceptance; and

(b) use of the goods consistent with the purpose of trial is not acceptance but failure seasonably to notify the seller of election to return the goods is acceptance, and if the goods conform to the contract acceptance of any part is acceptance of the whole; and

(c) after due notification of election to return, the return is at the seller's risk and expense but a merchant buyer must follow any reasonable instructions.

(2) Under a sale or return, unless otherwise agreed

(a) the option to return extends to the whole or any commercial unit of the goods while in substantially their original condition, but must be exercised seasonably; and

(b) the return is at the buyer's risk and expense.

Section 2–328. Sale by Auction.

(1) In a sale by auction, if goods are put up in lots each lot is the subject of a separate sale.

(2) A sale by auction is complete when the auctioneer so announces by the fall of the hammer or in other customary manner. Where a bid is made while the hammer is falling in acceptance of a prior bid, the auctioneer may in his discretion reopen the bidding or declare the goods sold under the bid on which the hammer was falling.

(3) Such a sale is with reserve unless the goods are in explicit terms put up without reserve. In an auction with reserve, the auctioneer may withdraw the goods at any time until he announces completion of the sale. In an auction without reserve, after the auctioneer calls for bids on an article or lot, that article or lot cannot be withdrawn unless no bid is made within a reasonable time. In either case a bidder may retract his bid until his auctioneer's announcement of completion of the sale, but a bidder's retraction does not revive any previous bid.

(4) If the auctioneer knowingly receives a bid on the seller's behalf or the seller makes or procures such a bid, and notice has not been given that liberty for such bidding is reserved, the buyer may at his option avoid the sale or take the goods at the price of the last good faith bid prior to the completion of the sale. This subsection shall not apply to any bid at a forced sale.

PART 4/TITLE, CREDITORS AND GOOD FAITH PURCHASERS

Section 2–401. Passing of Title; Reservation for Security; Limited Application of This Section

Each provision of this Article with regard to the rights, obligations and remedies of the seller, the buyer, purchasers or other third parties applies irrespective of title to the goods except where the provision refers to such title. Insofar as situations are not covered by the other provisions of this Article and matters concerning title become material the following rules apply:

(1) Title to goods cannot pass under a contract for sale prior to their identification to the contract (Section 2–501), and unless otherwise explicitly agreed the buyer acquires by their identification a special property as limited by this Act. Any retention or reservation by the seller of the title (property) in goods shipped or delivered to the buyer is limited in effect to a reservation of a security interest. Subject to these provisions and to the provisions of the Article on Secured Transactions (Article 9), title to goods passes from the seller to the buyer in any manner and on any conditions explicitly agreed on by the parties.

(2) Unless otherwise explicitly agreed, title passes to the buyer at the time and place at which the seller completes his performance with reference to the physical delivery of the goods, despite any reservation of security interest and even though a document of title is to be delivered at a different time or place; and in particular and despite any reservation of a security interest by the bill of lading

    (a) if the contract requires or authorizes the seller to send the goods to the buyer but does not require him to deliver them at destination, title passes to the buyer at the time and place of shipment; but

    (b) If the contract requires delivery at destination, title passes on tender there.

(3) Unless otherwise explicitly agreed, where delivery is to be made without moving the goods,

    (a) if the seller is to deliver a document of title, title passes at the time when and the place where he delivers such documents; or

(b) if the goods are at the time of contracting already identified and no documents are to be delivered, title passes at the time and place of contracting.

(4) A rejection or other refusal by the buyer to receive or retain the goods, whether or not justified, or a justified revocation of acceptance revests title to the goods in the seller. Such revesting occurs by operation of law and is not a "sale."

Section 2–402. Rights of Seller's Creditors Against Sold Goods

(1) Except as provided in subsections (2) and (3), rights of unsecured creditors of the seller with respect to goods which have been identified to a contract for sale are subject to the buyer's rights to recover the goods under this Article (Sections 2–502 and 2–716).

(2) A creditor of the seller may treat a sale or an identification of goods to a contract for sale as void if as against him a retention of possession by the seller is fraudulent under any rule of law of the state where the goods are situated, except that retention of possession in good faith and current course of trade by a merchant-seller for a commercially reasonable time after a sale or identification is not fraudulent.

(3) Nothing in this Article shall be deemed to impair the rights of creditors of the seller
  (a) under the provisions of the Article on Secured Transactions (Article 9); or
  (b) where identification to the contract or delivery is made not in current course of trade but in satisfaction of or as security for a preexisting claim for money, security or the like and is made under circumstances which under any rule of law of the state where the goods are situated would apart from this Article constitute the transaction a fraudulent transfer or voidable preference.

Section 2–403. Power to Transfer; Good Faith Purchase of Goods; "Entrusting"

(1) A purchaser of goods acquires all title which his transferor had or had power to transfer except that a purchaser of a limited interest

acquires rights only to the extent of the interest purchased. A person with voidable title has power to transfer a good title to a good faith purchaser for value. When goods have been delivered under a transaction of purchase, the purchaser has such power even though

    (a) the transferor was deceived as to the identity of the purchaser, or

    (b) the delivery was in exchange for a check which is later dishonored, or

    (c) it was agreed that the transaction was to be a "cash sale" or

    (d) the delivery was procured through fraud punishable as larcenous under the criminal law.

(2) Any entrusting of possession of goods to a merchant who deals in goods of that kind gives him power to transfer all rights of the entruster to a buyer in ordinary course of business.

(3) "Entrusting" includes any delivery and any acquiescence in retention of possession regardless of any condition expressed between the parties to the delivery or acquiescence and regardless of whether the procurement of the entrusting or the possessor's disposition of the goods have been such as to be larcenous under the criminal law.

(4) The rights of other purchasers of goods and of lien creditors are governed by the Articles on Secured Transactions (Article 9), Bulk Transfers (Article 6) and Documents of Title (Article7).

PART 5/PERFORMANCE

Section 2–501. Insurable Interest in Goods; Manner of Identification of Goods

(1) The buyer obtains a special property and an insurable interest in goods by identification of existing goods as goods to which the contract refers even though the goods so identified are non-conforming and he has an option to return or reject them. Such identification can be made at any time and in any manner explicitly agreed to by the parties. In the absence of explicit agreement, identification occurs

   (a) when the contract is made, if it is for the sale of goods already existing and identified;

   (b) if the contract is for the sale of future goods other than those described in paragraph (c), when goods are shipped, marked or otherwise designated by the seller as goods to which the contract refers;

   (c) when the crops are planted or otherwise become growing crops or the young are conceived, if the contract is for the sale of unborn young to be born within twelve months after contracting or for the sale of crops to be harvested within twelve months or the next normal harvest season after contracting whichever is longer.

(2) The seller retains an insurable interest in goods so long as title to or any security interest in the goods remains in him; and where the identification is by the seller alone, he may until default or insolvency or notification to the buyer that the identification is final substitute other goods for those identified.

(3) Nothing in this section impairs any insurable interest recognized under any other statute or rule of law.

Section 2–502. Buyer's Right to Goods on Seller's Insolvency

(1) Subject to subsection (2), and even though the goods have not been shipped, a buyer who has paid a part or all of the price of goods in which he has a special property under the provisions of the immediately preceding section may, on making and keeping good a tender of any unpaid portion of their price, recover them from the seller if the seller becomes insolvent within ten days after receipt of the first installment on their price.

(2) If the identification creating his special property has been made by the buyer, he acquires the right to recover the goods only if they conform to the contract for sale.

Section 2–503. Manner of Seller's Tender of Delivery

(1) Tender of delivery requires that the seller put and hold conforming goods at the buyer's disposition and give the buyer any notification

reasonably necessary to enable him to take delivery. The manner, time and place for tender are determined by the agreement and this Article, and in particular

    (a) tender must be at a reasonable hour, and, if it is of goods, they must be kept available for the period reasonably necessary to enable the buyer to take possession; but

    (b) unless otherwise agreed, the buyer must furnish facilities reasonably suited to the receipt of the goods.

(2) Where the case is within the next section respecting shipment, tender requires that the seller comply with its provisions.

(3) Where the seller is required to deliver at a particular destination, tender requires that he comply with subsection (1) and also, in any appropriate case, tender documents as described in subsections (4) and (5) of this section.

(4) Where goods are in the possession of a bailee and are to be delivered without being moved

    (a) tender requires that the seller either tender a negotiable document of title covering such goods or procure acknowledgement by the bailee of the buyer's right to possession of the goods; but

    (b) tender to the buyer of a nonnegotiable document of title or of a written direction to the bailee to deliver is sufficient tender unless the buyer seasonably objects, and receipt by the bailee of notification of the buyer's rights fixes those rights as against the bailee and all third persons; but risk of loss of the goods and of any failure by the bailee to honor the non-negotiable document of title or to obey the direction remains on the seller until the buyer has had a reasonable time to present the document or direction, and a refusal by the bailee to honor the document or to obey the direction defeats the tender.

(5) Where the contract requires the seller to deliver documents

    (a) he must tender all such documents in correct form, except as provided in this Article with respect to bills of lading in a set (subsection (2) of Section 2–323); and

(b) tender through customary banking channels is sufficient and dishonor of a draft accompanying the documents constitutes nonacceptance or rejection.

Section 2–504. Shipment by Seller

Where the seller is required or authorized to send the goods to the buyer and the contract does not require him to deliver them at a particular destination, then, unless otherwise agreed, he must

(a) put the goods in the possession of such a carrier and make such a contract for their transportation as may be reasonable having regard to the nature of the goods and other circumstances of the case; and

(b) obtain and promptly deliver or tender in due form any document necessary to enable the buyer to obtain possession of the goods or otherwise required by the agreement or by usage of trade; and

(c) promptly notify the buyer of the shipment.

Failure to notify the buyer under paragraph (c) or to make a proper contract under paragraph (a) is a ground for rejection only if material delay or loss ensues.

Section 2–505. Seller's Shipment Under Reservation

(1) Where the seller has identified goods to the contract by or before shipment:

(a) his procurement of a negotiable bill of lading to his own order or otherwise reserves in him a security interest in the goods. His procurement of the bill to the order of a financing agency or of the buyer indicates in addition only the seller's expectation of transferring that interest to the person named.

(b) a nonnegotiable bill of lading to himself or his nominee reserves possession of the goods as security but except in a case of conditional delivery (subsection (2) of Section 2–507) a nonnegotiable bill of lading naming the buyer as consignee reserves no security interest even though the seller retains possession of the bill of lading.

(2) When shipment by the seller with reservation of a security interest is in violation of the contract for sale it constitutes an improper contract for transportation within the preceding section but impairs neither the rights given to the buyer by shipment and identification of the goods to the contract nor the seller's powers as a holder of a negotiable document.

Section 2–506. Rights of Financing Agency

(1) A financing agency by paying or purchasing for value a draft which relates to a shipment of goods acquires to the extent of the payment or purchase, and in addition to its own rights under the draft and any document of title securing it, any rights of the shipper in the goods, including the right to stop delivery and the shipper's right to have the draft honored by the buyer.

(2) The right to reimbursement of a financing agency which has in good faith honored or purchased the draft under commitment to or authority from the buyer is not impaired by subsequent discovery of defects with reference to any relevant document which was apparently regular on its face.

Section 2–507. Effect of Seller's Tender; Delivery on Condition

(1) Tender of delivery is a condition to the buyer's duty to accept the goods and, unless otherwise agreed, to his duty to pay for them. Tender entitles the seller to acceptance of the goods and to payment according to the contract.

(2) Where payment is due and demanded on the delivery to the buyer of goods or documents of title, his right as against the seller to retain or dispose of them is conditional upon his making the payment due.

Section 2–508. Cure by Seller of Improper Tender or Delivery; Replacement

(1) Where any tender or delivery by the seller is rejected because non-conforming and the time for performance has not yet expired, the seller may seasonably notify the buyer of his intention to cure and may then within the contract time make a conforming delivery.

(2) Where the buyer rejects a non-conforming tender which the seller had reasonable grounds to believe would be acceptable with or without

money allowance, the seller may if he seasonably notifies the buyer have a further reasonable time to substitute a conforming tender.

Section 2–509. Risk of Loss in the Absence of Breach

(1) Where the contract requires or authorizes the seller to ship the goods by carrier

    (a) if it does not require him to deliver them at a particular destination, the risk of loss passes to the buyer when the goods are duly delivered to the carrier even though the shipment is under reservation (Section 2–505); but

    (b) if it does require him to deliver them at a particular destination and the goods are there duly tendered while in the possession of the carrier, the risk of loss passes to the buyer when the goods are there duly so tendered as to enable the buyer to take delivery.

(2) Where the goods are held by a bailee to be delivered without being moved, the risk of loss passes to the buyer

    (a) on his receipt of a negotiable document of title covering the goods; or

    (b) on acknowledgment by the bailee of the buyer's right to possession of the goods; or

    (c) after his receipt of a nonnegotiable document of title or other written direction to deliver, as provided in subsection (4) (b) of Section 2–503.

(3) In any case not with subsection (1) or (2), the risk of loss passes to the buyer on his receipt of the goods if the seller is a merchant; otherwise the risk passes to the buyer on tender of delivery.

(4) The provisions of this section are subject to contrary agreement of the parties and to the provisions of this Article on sale on approval (Section 2–327) and on effect of breach on risk of loss (Section 2–510).

Section 2–510. Effect of Breach on Risk of Loss

(1) Where a tender or delivery of goods so fails to conform to the contract as to give a right of rejection, the risk of their loss remains on the seller until cure or acceptance

(2) Where the buyer rightfully revokes acceptance, he may to the extent of any deficiency in his effective insurance coverage treat the risk of loss as having rested on the seller from the beginning.

(3) Where the buyer, as to conforming goods already identified to the contract for sale, repudiates or is otherwise in breach before risk of their loss has passed to him, the seller may to the extent of any deficiency in his effective insurance coverage treat the risk of loss as resting on the buyer for a commercially reasonable time.

Section 2–511. Tender of Payment by Buyer; Payment by Check

(1) Unless otherwise agreed, tender of payment is a condition to the seller's duty to tender and complete any delivery.

(2) Tender of payment is sufficient when made by any means or in any manner current in the ordinary course of business unless the seller demands payment in legal tender and gives any extension of time reasonably necessary to procure it

(3) Subject to the provisions of this Act on the effect of an instrument on an obligation (Section 3–802), payment by check is conditional and is defeated as between the parties by dishonor of the check on due presentment.

Section 2–512. Payment by Buyer Before Inspection

(1) Where the contract requires payment before inspection, non-conformity of the goods does not excuse the buyer from so making payment unless

> (a) the non-conformity appears without inspection; or
>
> (b) despite tender of the required documents, the circumstances would justify injunction against honor under the provisions of this Act (Section 5–114).

(2) Payment pursuant to subsection (1) does not constitute an acceptance of goods or impair the buyer's right to inspect or any of his remedies.

Section 2–513. Buyer's Right to Inspection of Goods

(1) Unless otherwise agreed and subject to subdivision (3), where goods are tendered or delivered or identified to the contract for sale, the buyer has a right before payment or acceptance to inspect them at any

reasonable place and time and in any reasonable manner. When the seller is required or authorized to send the goods to the buyer, the inspection may be after their arrival.

(2) Expenses of inspection must be borne by the buyer but it may be recovered from the seller if the goods do not conform and are rejected.

(3) Unless otherwise agreed and subject to the provisions of this Article on C.I.F. contracts (subdivision (3) of Section 2–321), the buyer is not entitled to inspect the goods before payment of the price when the contract provides

    (a) for delivery "C.O.D." or on other like terms; or

    (b) for payment against documents of title, except where such payment is due only after the goods are to become available for inspection.

(4) A place or method of inspection fixed by the parties is presumed to be exclusive but, unless otherwise expressly agreed, it does not postpone identification or shift the place for delivery or for passing the risk of loss. If compliance becomes impossible, inspection shall be as provided in this section unless the place or method fixed was clearly intended as an indispensable condition, failure of which avoids the contract.

Section 2–514. When Documents Deliverable on Acceptance; When on Payment

Unless otherwise agreed, documents against which a draft is drawn are to be delivered to the drawee on acceptance of the draft if it is payable more than three days after presentment; otherwise, only on payment.

Section 2–515. Preserving Evidence of Goods in Dispute

In furtherance of the adjustment of any claim or dispute

    (a) either party on reasonable notification to the other, and for the purpose of ascertaining the facts and preserving evidence, has the right to inspect, test and sample the goods including such of them as may be in the possession or control of the other; and

(b) the parties may agree to a third party inspection or survey to determine the conformity or condition of the goods and may agree that the findings shall be binding upon them in any subsequent litigation or adjustment.

PART 6/BREACH, REPUDIATION AND EXCUSE

Section 2–601. Buyer's Rights on Improper Delivery

Subject to the provisions of this Article on breach in installment contracts (Section 2–612) and unless otherwise agreed under the sections on contractual limitations of remedy (Sections 2–718 and 2–719), if the goods or the tender of delivery fail in any respect to conform to the contract, the buyer may

(a) reject the whole; or

(b) accept the whole; or

(c) accept any commercial unit or units and reject the rest.

Section 2–602. Manner and Effect of Rightful Rejection

(1) Rejection of goods must be within a reasonable time after their delivery or tender. It is ineffective unless the buyer seasonably notifies the seller.

(2) Subject to the provisions of the two following sections on rejected goods (Sections 2–603 and 2–604),

(a) after rejection any exercise of ownership by the buyer with respect to any commercial unit is wrongful as against the seller; and

(b) If the buyer has before rejection taken physical possession of goods in which he does not have a security interest under the provisions of this Article (subsection (3) of Section 2–711), he is under a duty after rejection to hold them with reasonable care at the seller's disposition for a time sufficient to permit the seller to remove them; but

(c) the buyer has no further obligations with regard to goods rightfully rejected.

(3) The seller's rights with respect to goods wrongfully rejected are governed by the provisions of this Article on Seller's remedies in general (Section 2–703).

Section 2–603. Merchant Buyer's Duties as to Rightfully Rejected Goods

(1) Subject to any security interest in the buyer (subsection (3) of Section 2–711), when the seller has no agent or place of business at the market of rejection, a merchant buyer is under a duty after rejection of goods in his possession or control to follow any reasonable instructions received from the seller with respect to the goods and in the absence of such instructions to make reasonable efforts to sell them for the seller's account if they are perishable or threaten to decline in value speedily. Instructions are not reasonable if on demand indemnity for expenses is not forthcoming.

(2) When the buyer sells goods under subsection (1), he is entitled to reimbursement from the seller or out of the proceeds for reasonable expenses of caring for and selling them, and if the expenses include no selling commission then to such commission as is usual in the trade or, if there is none, to a reasonable sum not exceeding ten percent on the gross proceeds.

(3) In complying with this section, the buyer is held only to good faith and good faith conduct hereunder is neither acceptance nor conversion nor the basis of an action for damages.

Section 2–604. Buyer's Options as to Salvage of Rightfully Rejected Goods

Subject to the provisions of the immediately preceding section on perishables, if the seller gives no instructions within a reasonable time after notification of rejection the buyer may store the rejected goods for the seller's account or reship them to him or resell them for the seller's account with reimbursement as provided in the preceding section. Such action is not acceptance or conversion.

Section 2–605. Waiver of Buyer's Objections by Failure to Particularize

(1) The buyer's failure to state in connection with rejection a particular defect which is ascertainable by reasonable inspection precludes him from relying on the unstated defect to justify rejection or to establish breach

(a) where the seller could have cured it if stated seasonably; or

(b) between merchants when the seller has after rejection made a request in writing for a full and final written statement of all defects on which the buyer proposes to rely.

(2) Payment against documents made without reservation of rights precludes recovery of the payment for defects apparent on the face of the documents.

Section 2–606. What Constitutes Acceptance of Goods

(1) Acceptance of goods occurs when the buyer

(a) after a reasonable opportunity to inspect the goods signifies to the seller that the goods are conforming or that he will take or retain them in spite of their non-conformity; or

(b) fails to make an effective rejection (subsection (1) of Section 2–602), but such acceptance does not occur until the buyer has had a reasonable opportunity to inspect them; or

(c) does any act inconsistent with the seller's ownership; but if such act is wrongful as against the seller it is an acceptance only if ratified by him.

(2) Acceptance of a part of any commercial unit is acceptance of that entire unit.

Section 2–607. Effect of Acceptance; Notice of Breach; Burden of Establishing Breach After Acceptance; Notice of Claim or Litigation to Person Answerable Over

(1) The buyer must pay at the contract rate for any goods accepted.

(2) Acceptance of goods by the buyer precludes rejection of the goods accepted and if made with knowledge of a non-conformity cannot be revoked because of it unless the acceptance was on the reasonable assumption that the non-conformity would be seasonably cured but acceptance does not of itself impair any other remedy provided by this Article for non-conformity.

(3) Where a tender has been accepted

(a) the buyer must within a reasonable time after he discovers or should have discovered any breach notify the seller of breach or be barred from any remedy; and

(b) if the claim is one for infringement or the like (subsection (3) of Section 2–312) and the buyer is sued as a result of such a breach, he must so notify the seller within a reasonable time after he receives notice of the litigation or be barred from any remedy over for liability established by the litigation.

(4) The burden is on the buyer to establish any breach with respect to the goods accepted.

(5) Where the buyer is sued for breach of a warranty or other obligation for which his seller is answerable over

(a) he may give his seller written notice of the litigation. If the notice states that the seller may come in and defend and that if the seller does not do so he will be bound in any action against him by his buyer by any determination of fact common to the two litigations, then unless the seller after seasonable receipt of the notice does come in and defend he is so bound.

(b) if the claim is one for infringement or the like (subsection (3) of Section 2–312), the original seller may demand in writing that his buyer turn over to him control of the litigation including settlement or else be barred from any remedy over and if he also agrees to bear all expense and to satisfy any adverse judgment, then unless the buyer after seasonable receipt of the demand does turn over control the buyer is so barred.

(6) The provisions of subsections (3), (4) and (5) apply to any obligation of a buyer to hold the seller harmless against infringement or the like (subsection (3) of Section 2–312).

Section 2–608. Revocation of Acceptance in Whole or in Part

(1) The buyer may revoke his acceptance of a lot or commercial unit whose non-conformity substantially impairs its value to him if he has accepted it

(a) on the reasonable assumption that its non-conformity would be cured and it has not been seasonably cured; or

(b) without discovery of such non-conformity if his acceptance was reasonably induced either by the difficulty of discovery before acceptance or by the seller's assurances.

(2) Revocation of acceptance must occur within a reasonable time after the buyer discovers or should have discovered the ground for it and before any substantial change in condition of the goods which is not caused by their own defects. It is not effective until the buyer notifies the seller of it.

(3) A buyer who so revokes has the same rights and duties with regard to the goods involved as if he had rejected them.

Section 2–609. Right to Adequate Assurance of Performance

(1) A contract for sale imposes an obligation on each party that the other's expectation of receiving due performance will not be impaired. When reasonable grounds for insecurity arise with respect to the performance of either party, the other may in writing demand adequate assurance of due performance and until he receives such assurance may, if commercially reasonable, suspend any performance for which he has not already received the agreed return.

(2) Between merchants, the reasonableness of grounds for insecurity and the adequacy of any assurance offered shall be determined according to commercial standards.

(3) Acceptance of any improper delivery or payment does not prejudice the aggrieved party's right to demand adequate assurance of future performance.

(4) After receipt of a justified demand, failure to provide within a reasonable time, not exceeding thirty days, such assurance of due performance as is adequate under the circumstances of the particular case is a repudiation of the contract.

Section 2–610. Anticipatory Repudiation

When either party repudiates the contract with respect to a performance not yet due, the loss of which will substantially impair the value of the contract to the other, the aggrieved party may

(a) for a commercially reasonable time await performance by the repudiating party; or

(b) resort to any remedy for breach (Section 2–703 or Section 2–711), even though he has notified the repudiating party that he would await the latter's performance and has urged retraction; and

(c) in either case suspend his own performance or proceed in accordance with the provisions of this Article on the seller's right to identify goods to the contract notwithstanding breach or to salvage unfinished goods (Section 2–704).

Section 2–611. Retraction of Anticipatory Repudiation

(1) Until the repudiating party's next performance is due, he can retract his repudiation unless the aggrieved party has since the repudiation cancelled or materially changed his position or otherwise indicated that he considers the repudiation final.

(2) Retraction may be by any method which clearly indicates to the aggrieved party that the repudiating party intends to perform, but must include any assurance justifiably demanded under the provisions of this Article (Section 2–609).

(3) Retraction reinstates the repudiating party's rights under the contract with due excuse and allowance to the aggrieved party for any delay occasioned by the repudiation.

Section 2–612. "Installment Contract"; Breach

(1) An "installment contract" is one which requires or authorizes the delivery of goods in separate lots to be separately accepted, even though the contract contains a clause "each delivery is a separate contract" or its equivalent.

(2) The buyer may reject any installment which is non-conforming if the non-conformity substantially impairs the value of that installment and cannot be cured or if the non-conformity is a defect in the required documents; but if the non-conformity does not fall within subsection (3) and

the seller gives adequate assurance of its cure, the buyer must accept that installment.

(3) Whenever non-conformity or default with respect to one or more installments substantially impairs the value of the whole contract, there is a breach of the whole. But the aggrieved party reinstates the contract if he accepts a non-conforming installment without seasonably notifying of cancellation or if he brings an action with respect only to past installments or demands performance as to future installments.

Section 2–613. Casualty to Identified Goods

Where the contract requires for its performance goods identified when the contract is made, and the goods suffer casualty without fault of either party before the risk of loss passes to the buyer, or in a proper case under a "no arrival, no sale" term (Section 2–324) then

(a) if the loss is total the contract is avoided; and

(b) if the loss is partial or the goods have so deteriorated as no longer to conform to the contract the buyer may nevertheless demand inspection and at his option either treat the contract as avoided or accept the goods with due allowance from the contract price for the deterioration or the deficiency in quantity but without further right against the seller.

Section 2–614. Substituted Performance

(1) Where without fault of either party the agreed berthing, loading, or unloading facilities fail or an agreed type of carrier becomes unavailable or the agreed manner of delivery otherwise becomes commercially impracticable but a commercially reasonable substitute is available, such substitute performance must be tendered and accepted.

(2) If the agreed means or manner of payment fails because of domestic or foreign governmental regulation, the seller may withhold or stop delivery unless the buyer provides a means or manner of payment which is commercially a substantial equivalent. If delivery has already been taken, payment by the means or in the manner provided by the regulation discharges the buyer's obligation unless the regulation is discriminatory, oppressive or predatory.

Section 2–615. Excuse by Failure of Presupposed Conditions

Except so far as a seller may have assumed a greater obligation and subject to the preceding section on substituted performance:

(a) Delay in delivery or nondelivery in whole or in part by a seller who complies with paragraphs (b) and (c) is not a breach of his duty under a contract for sale if performance as agreed has been made impracticable by the occurrence of a contingency the nonoccurrence of which was a basic assumption on which the contract was made or by compliance in good faith with any applicable foreign or domestic governmental regulation or order whether or not it later proves to be invalid.

(b) Where the causes mentioned in paragraph (a) affect only a part of the seller's capacity to perform, he must allocate production and deliveries among his customers but may at his option include regular customers not then under contract as well as his own requirements for further manufacture. He may so allocate in any manner which is fair and reasonable.

(c) The seller must notify the buyer seasonally that there will be delay or nondelivery and, when allocation is required under paragraph (b), of the estimated quota thus made available for the buyer.

Section 2–616. Procedure on Notice Claiming Excuse

(1) Where the buyer receives notification of a material or indefinite delay or an allocation justified under the preceding section he may by written notification to the seller as to any delivery concerned, and where the prospective deficiency substantially impairs the value of the whole contract under the provisions of this Article relating to breach of installment contracts (Section 2–612), then also as to the whole,

(a) terminate and thereby discharge any unexecuted portion of the contract; or

(b) modify the contract by agreeing to take his available quota in substitution.

(2) If, after receipt of such notification from the seller, the buyer fails so to modify the contract within a reasonable time not exceeding thirty days, the contract lapses with respect to any deliveries affected.

(3) The provisions of this section may not be negated by agreement except insofar as the seller has assumed a greater obligation under the preceding section.

PART 7/REMEDIES

Section 2–701. Remedies for Breach of Collateral Contracts Not Impaired

Remedies for breach of any obligation or promise collateral or ancillary to a contract for sale are not impaired by the provisions of this Article.

Section 2–702. Seller's Remedies on Discovery of Buyer's Insolvency

(1) Where the seller discovers the buyer to be insolvent, he may refuse delivery except for cash including payment for all goods theretofore delivered under the contract, and stop delivery under this Article (Section 2–705).

(2) Where the seller discovers that the buyer has received goods on credit while insolvent, he may reclaim the goods upon demand made within ten days after the receipt, but if misrepresentation of solvency has been made to the particular seller in writing within three months before delivery the ten day limitation does not apply. Except as provided in this subsection, the seller may not base a right to reclaim goods on the buyer's fraudulent or innocent misrepresentation of solvency or of intent to pay.

(3) The seller's right to reclaim under subsection (2) is subject to the rights of a buyer in ordinary course or other good faith purchaser under this Article (Section 2–403). Successful reclamation of goods excludes all other remedies with respect to them.

Section 2–703. Seller's Remedies in General

Where the buyer wrongfully rejects or revokes acceptance of goods or fails to make a payment due on or before delivery or repudiates with respect to a part or the whole, then with respect to any goods directly affected and, if the breach is of the whole contract (Section 2–612), then also with respect to the whole undelivered balance, the aggrieved seller may

(a) withhold delivery of such goods;

(b) stop delivery by any bailee as hereafter provided (Section 2–705);

(c) proceed under the next section respecting goods still unidentified to the contract;

(d) resell and recover damages as hereafter provided (Section2–706);

(e) recover damages for nonacceptance (Section 2–708) or in a proper case the price (Section 2-709);

(f) cancel.

Section 2–704. Seller's Right to Identify Goods to the Contract Notwithstanding Breach or to Salvage Unfinished Goods

(1) An aggrieved seller under the preceding section may

(a) identify to the contract conforming goods not already identified if at the time he learned of the breach they are in his possession or control;

(b) treat as the subject of resale goods which have demonstrably been intended for the particular contract even though those goods are unfinished.

(2) Where the goods are unfinished an aggrieved seller may, in the exercise of reasonable commercial judgment for the purposes of avoiding loss and of effective realization, either complete the manufacture and wholly identify the goods to the contract or cease manufacture and resell for scrap or salvage value or proceed in any other reasonable manner.

Section 2–705. Seller's Stoppage of Delivery in Transit or Otherwise

(1) The seller may stop delivery of goods in the possession of a carrier or other bailee when he discovers the buyer to be insolvent (Section 2–702) and may stop delivery of carload, truckload, planeload or larger shipments of express or freight when the buyer repudiates or fails to make

a payment due before delivery or if for any other reason the seller has a right to withhold or reclaim the goods.

(2) As against such buyer, the seller may stop delivery until

(a) receipt of the goods by the buyer; or

(b) acknowledgment to the buyer by any bailee of the goods except a carrier that the bailee holds the goods for the buyer; or

(c) such acknowledgment to the buyer by a carrier by reshipment or as warehouseman; or

(d) negotiation to the buyer of any negotiable document of title covering the goods.

(3) (a) To stop delivery the seller must so notify as to enable the bailee by reasonable diligence to prevent delivery of the goods.

(b) After such notification the bailee must hold and deliver the goods according to the directions of the seller, but the seller is liable to the bailee for any ensuing charges or damages.

(c) If a negotiable document of title has been issued for goods, the bailee is not obliged to obey a notification to stop until surrender of the document.

(d) A carrier who has issued a non-negotiable bill of lading is not obliged to obey a notification to stop received from a person other than the consignor.

Section 2–706. Seller's Resale Including Contract for Resale

(1) Under the conditions stated in Section 2–703 on seller's remedies, the seller may resell the goods concerned or the undelivered balance thereof. Where the resale is made in good faith and in a commercially reasonable manner, the seller may recover the difference between the resale price and the contract price together with any incidental damages allowed under the provisions of this Article (Section 2–710), but less expenses saved in consequence of the buyer's breach.

(2) Except as otherwise provided in subsection (3) or unless otherwise agreed, resale may be at public or private sale including sale by way of one or more contracts to sell or of identification to an existing contract

of the seller. Sale may be as a unit or in parcels and at any time and place and on any terms but every aspect of the sale including the method, manner, time, place and terms must be commercially reasonable. The resale must be reasonably identified as referring to the broken contract, but it is not necessary that the goods be in existence or that any or all of them have been identified to the contract before the breach.

(3) Where the resale is at private sale, the seller must give the buyer reasonable notification of his intention to resell.

(4) Where the resale is at public sale

(a) only identified goods can be sold except where there is a recognized market for a public sale of futures in goods of the kind; and

(b) it must be made at a usual place or market for public sale if one is reasonably available and except in the case of goods which are perishable or threaten to decline in value speedily the seller must give the buyer reasonable notice of the time and place of the resale; and

(c) if the goods are not to be within the view of those attending the sale, the notification of sale must state the place where the goods are located and provide for their reasonable inspection by prospective bidders; and

(d) the seller may buy.

(5) A purchaser who buys in good faith at a resale takes the goods free of any rights of the original buyer even though the seller fails to comply with one or more of the requirements of this section.

(6) The seller is not accountable to the buyer for any profit made on any resale. A person in the position of a seller (Section 2–707) or a buyer who has rightfully rejected or justifiably revoked acceptance must account for any excess over the amount of his security interest, as hereinafter defined (subsection (3) of Section 2–711).

Section 2–707. "Person in the Position of a Seller"

(1) A "person in the position of a seller" includes, as against a principal, an agent who has paid or become responsible for the price of goods

on behalf of his principal or anyone who otherwise holds a security interest or other right in goods similar to that of a seller.

(2) A person in the position of a seller may as provided in this Article withhold or stop delivery (Section 2–705) and resell (Section 2–706) and recover incidental damages (Section 2–710).

Section 2–708. Seller's Damages for Non-acceptance or Repudiation

(1) Subject to subsection (2) and to the provisions of this Article with respect to proof of market price (Section 2–723), the measure of damages for non acceptance or repudiation by the buyer is the difference between the market price at the time and place for tender and the unpaid contract price together with any incidental damages provided in this Article (Section 2–710), but less expenses saved in consequence of the buyer's breach.

(2) If the measure of damages provided in subsection (1) is inadequate to put the seller in as good a position as performance would have done, then the measure of damages is the profit (including reasonable overhead) which the seller would have made from full performance by the buyer, together with any incidental damages provided in this Article (Section 2–710), due allowance for costs reasonably incurred and due credit for payments or proceeds of resale.

Section 2–709. Action for the Price

(1) When the buyer fails to pay the price as it becomes due, the seller may recover, together with any incidental damages under the next section, the price

    (a) of goods accepted or of conforming goods lost or damaged within a commercially reasonable time after risk of their loss has passed to the buyer; and

    (b) of goods identified to the contract if the seller is unable after reasonable effort to resell them at a reasonable price or the circumstances reasonably indicate that such effort will be unavailing.

(2) Where the seller sues for the price, he must hold for the buyer any goods which have been identified to the contract and are still in his control except that if resale becomes possible he may resell them at any time

prior to the collection of the judgment. The net proceeds of any such resale must be credited to the buyer and payment of the judgment entitles him to any goods not resold.

(3) After the buyer has wrongfully rejected or revoked acceptance of the goods or has failed to make a payment due or has repudiated (Section 2–610), a seller who is held not entitled to the price under this section shall nevertheless be awarded damages for non-acceptance under the preceding section.

Section 2–710. Seller's Incidental Damages

Incidental damages to an aggrieved seller include any commercially reasonable charges, expenses or commissions incurred in stopping delivery, the transportation, care and custody of goods after the buyer's breach, in connection with return or resale of the goods or otherwise resulting from the breach.

Section 2–711. Buyer's Remedies in General; Buyer's Security Interest in Rejected Goods

(1) Where the seller fails to make delivery or repudiates or the buyer rightfully rejects or justifiably revokes acceptance, then with respect to any goods involved, and with respect to the whole if the breach goes to the whole contract (Section 2–612), the buyer may cancel and whether or not he has done so may in addition to recovering so much of the price as has been paid

    (a) "cover" and have damages under the next section as to all the goods affected whether or not they have been identified to the contract; or

    (b) recover damages for nondelivery as provided in this Article (Section 2–713).

(2) Where the seller fails to deliver or repudiates, the buyer may also

    (a) if the goods have been identified recover them as provided in this Article (Section 2–502); or

    (b) in a proper case obtain specific performance or replevy the goods as provided in this Article (Section 2–716).

(3) On rightful rejection or justifiable revocation of acceptance, a buyer has a security interest in goods in his possession or control for any payments made on their price and any expenses reasonably incurred in their inspection, receipt, transportation, care and custody and may hold such goods and resell them in like manner as an aggrieved seller (Section 2–706).

Section 2–712. "Cover"; Buyer's Procurement of Substitute Goods

(1) After a breach within the preceding section, the buyer may "cover" by making in good faith and without unreasonable delay any reasonable purchase of or contract to purchase goods in substitution for those due from the seller.

(2) The buyer may recover from the seller as damages the difference between the cost of cover and the contract price together with any incidental or consequential damages as hereinafter defined (Section 2–715), but less expenses saved in consequence of the seller's breach.

(3) Failure of the buyer to effect cover within this section does not bar him from any other remedy.

Section 2–713. Buyer's Damages for Non-delivery or Repudiation

(1) Subject to the provisions of this Article with respect to proof of market price (Section 2–723), the measure of damages for non-delivery or repudiation by the seller is the difference between the market price at the time when the buyer learned of the breach and the contract price together with any incidental and consequential damages provided in this Article (Section 2–715), but less expenses saved in consequence of the seller's breach.

(2) Market price is to be determined as of the place for tender or, in cases of rejection after arrival or revocation of acceptance, as of the place of arrival.

Section 2–714. Buyer's Damages for Breach in Regard to Accepted Goods

(1) Where the buyer has accepted goods and given notification (subsection (3) of Section 2–607), he may recover as damages for any nonconformity of tender the loss resulting in the ordinary course of events from the seller's breach as determined in any manner which is reasonable.

(2) The measure of damages for breach of warranty is the difference at the time and place of acceptance between the value of the goods accepted and the value they would have had if they had been as warranted, unless special circumstances show proximate damages of a different amount.

(3) In a proper case any incidental and consequential damages under the next section may also be recovered.

Section 2–715. Buyer's Incidental and Consequential Damages

(1) Incidental damages resulting from the seller's breach include expenses reasonably incurred in inspection, receipt, transportation and care and custody of goods rightfully rejected, any commercially reasonable charges, expenses or commissions in connection with effecting cover and any other reasonable expense incident to the delay or other breach.

(2) Consequential damages resulting from the seller's breach include

(a) any loss resulting from general or particular requirements and needs of which the seller at the time of contracting had reason to know and which could not reasonably be prevented by cover or otherwise; and

(b) injury to person or property proximately resulting from any breach of warranty.

Section 2–716. Buyer's Right to Specific Performance or Replevin

(1) Specific performance may be decreed where the goods are unique or in other proper circumstances.

(2) The decree for specific performance may include such terms and conditions as to payment of the price, damages, or other relief as the court may deem just.

(3) The buyer has a right of replevin for goods identified to the contract if after reasonable effort he is unable to effect cover for such goods or the circumstances reasonably indicate that such effort will be unavailing or if the goods have been shipped under reservation and satisfaction of the security interest in them has been made or tendered.

Section 2–717. Deduction of Damages From the Price

The buyer on notifying the seller of his intention to do so may deduct all or any part of the damages resulting from any breach of the contract from any part of the price still due under the same contract.

Section 2–718. Liquidation or Limitation of Damages; Deposits

(1) Damages for breach by either party may be liquidated in the agreement but only at an amount which is reasonable in the light of the anticipated or actual harm caused by the breach, the difficulties of proof of loss, and the inconvenience or nonfeasibility of otherwise obtaining an adequate remedy. A term fixing unreasonably large liquidated damages is void as a penalty.

(2) Where the seller justifiably withholds delivery of goods because of the buyer's breach, the buyer is entitled to restitution of any amount by which the sum of his payments exceeds

    (a) the amount to which the seller is entitled by virtue of terms liquidating the seller's damages in accordance with subsection (1), or

    (b) in the absence of such terms, twenty percent of the value of the total performance for which the buyer is obligated under the contract or $500, whichever is smaller

(3) The buyer's right to restitution under subsection (2) is subject to offset to the extent that the seller establishes

    (a) a right to recover damages under the provisions of this Article other than subsection (1), and

    (b) the amount or value of any benefits received by the buyer directly or indirectly by reason of the contract

(4) Where a seller has received payment in goods, their reasonable value or the proceeds of their resale shall be treated as payments for the purposes of subsection (2); but if the seller has notice of the buyer's breach before reselling goods received in part performance, his resale is subject to the conditions laid down in this Article on resale by an aggrieved seller (Section 2–706).

Section 2–719. Contractual Modification or Limitation of Remedy

(1) Subject to the provisions of subsections (2) and (3) of this section and of the preceding section on liquidation and limitation of damages,

(a) the agreement may provide for remedies in addition to or in substitution for those provided in this Article and may limit or after the measure of damages recoverable under this Article, as by limiting the buyer's remedies to return of the goods and repayment of the price or to repair and replacement of non-conforming goods or parts; and

(b) resort to a remedy as provided is optional unless the remedy is expressly agreed to be exclusive, in which case it is the sole remedy.

(2) Where circumstances cause an exclusive or limited remedy to fail of its essential purpose, remedy may be had as provided in this Act.

(3) Consequential damages may be limited or excluded unless the limitation or exclusion is unconscionable. Limitation of consequential damages for injury to the person in the case of consumer goods is prima facie unconscionable but limitation of damages where the loss is commercial is not.

Section 2–720. Effect of "Cancellation" or "Rescission" on Claims for Antecedent Breach

Unless the contrary intention clearly appears, expressions of "cancellation" or "rescission" of the contract or the like shall not be construed as a renunciation or discharge of any claim in damages for an antecedent breach.

Section 2–721. Remedies for Fraud

Remedies for material mispresentation of fraud include all remedies available under this Article for non-fraudulent breach. Neither rescission or a claim for rescission of the contract for sale nor rejection or return of the goods shall bar or be deemed inconsistent with a claim for damages or other remedy.

Section 2–722. Who Can Sue Third Parties for Injury to Goods

Where a third party so deals with goods which have been identified to a contract for sale as to cause actionable injury to a party to that contract

(a) a right of action against the third party is in either party to the contract for sale who has title to or a security interest or a special property or an insurable interest in the goods; and if the goods have been destroyed or converted, a right of action is also in the party who either bore the risk of loss under the contract for sale or has since the injury assumed that risk as against the other;

(b) if at the time of the injury the party plaintiff did not bear the risk of loss as against the other party to the contract for sale and there is no arrangement between them for disposition of the recovery, his suit or settlement is, subject to his own interest, as a fiduciary for the other party to the contract;

(c) either party may with the consent of the other sue for the benefit of whom it may concern.

Section 2–723. Proof of Market Price: Time and Place

(1) If an action based on anticipatory repudiation comes to trial before the time for performance with respect to some or all of the goods, any damages based on market price (Section 2–708 or Section 2–713) shall be determined according to the price of such goods prevailing at the time when the aggrieved party learned of the repudiation.

(2) If evidence of a price prevailing at the times or places described in this Article is not readily available, the price prevailing within any reasonable time before or after the time described or at any other place which in commercial judgment or under usage of trade would serve as a reasonable substitute for the one described may be used, making any proper allowance for the cost of transporting the goods to or from such other place.

(3) Evidence of a relevant price prevailing at a time or place other than the one described in this Article offered by one party is not admissible unless and until he has given the other party such notice as the court finds sufficient to prevent unfair surprise.

Section 2–724. Admissibility of Market Quotations

Whenever the prevailing price or value of any goods regularly bought and sold in any established commodity market is in issue, reports in official publications or trade journals or in newspapers or periodicals of general circulation published as the reports of such market shall be admissible in evidence. The circumstances of the preparation of such a report may be shown to affect its weight but not its admissibility.

Section 2–725. Statute of Limitations in Contracts for Sale

(1) An action for breach of any contract for sale must be commenced within four years after the cause of action has accrued. By the original agreement, the parties may reduce the period of limitation to not less than one year but may not extend it.

(2) A cause of action accrues when the breach occurs, regardless of the aggrieved party's lack of knowledge of the breach. A breach of warranty occurs when tender of delivery is made, except that where a warranty explicitly extends to future performance of the goods and discovery of the breach must await the time of such performance the cause of action accrues when the breach is or should have been discovered.

(3) Where an action commenced within the time limited by subsection (1) is so terminated as to leave available a remedy by another action for the same breach, such other action may be commenced after the expiration of the time limited and within six months after the termination of the first action unless the termination resulted from voluntary discontinuance or from dismissal for failure or neglect to prosecute.

(4) This section does not alter the law on tolling of the statute of limitations nor does it apply to causes of action which have accrued before this Act becomes effective.

Glossary

Most of the following definitions do not describe products or give product specifications. The list contains primarily words or definitions that are either generally used or encountered by the majority of buyers for business. For words that are more product-oriented, see the glossary in Buying for Manufacturing in *Purchasing for Manufacturing* by Harry E. Hough, published by Industrial Press, Inc. or for many technical and scientific definitions see *McGraw-Hill Dictionary of Scientific and Technical Terms* edited by Sybil P. Parker.

AISI An abbreviation for the American Iron and Steel Institute and for the four or five digit code numbers which describe the chemical composition of each type of steel.

AMA An abbreviation for the American Management Association.

APS An abbreviation for the American Purchasing Society.

ASAP An abbreviation for "as soon as possible" and inappropriately used in place of a specific requested delivery date.

ASCII An abbreviation for American Standard Code for Information Interchange. An ASCII file is a text file that uses codes consisting of a 128 character set. Such a file can be imported into any type of word processing file. Thus for example, text files supplied by the

American Purchasing Society of generic policies and procedures for purchasing may be imported and customized for a company's particular requirements.

A.S.T.M.   The letters stand for the American Society for Testing and Materials, an organization that develops and publishes standard product specifications.

Acknowledgement   The process of notifying the buyer that an offer or purchase order has been received or a form that is used for such notification. If the form is simply a copy of the purchase order submitted to the seller by the buyer, it may be signed by the seller and returned to the buyer indicating acceptance of the order or contract. Alternatively the seller may make changes on the form in effect revising the terms or conditions of the transaction or the seller may use and return his own form with different terms and conditions.

Agency   That portion of the law that spells out the authority and responsibility of the representatives of the owners or company managers, called agents (the buyers or sellers) and the owners and managers, referred to as principals.

Air waybill   A non-negotiable shipping document given as evidence of a contract between the shipper and the carrier for transportation and delivery of goods.

Back-door selling   The practice of salespeople of trying to sell or influence the sale by contacting or dealing with people outside of the purchasing department.

Baldrige Award   The annual Malcolm Baldrige National Quality Awards established by an act of Congress in 1987 to recognize companies that have outstanding quality. Organizations eligible to compete must submit detailed documents and pay a substantial fee to apply for the awards plus pay for any necessary on site reviews.

Benchmarking   A process of comparing business activities with the best other departments or other companies with the object of improving operations.

Bill of lading A written receipt given by a carrier for goods accepted for transportation. When trying to expedite or trace a shipment from a supplier, it is important to obtain the bill of lading number along with other information about the shipment.

Blanket order A purchase order for material or supplies used over an extended period of time often without specifying exact quantities or specific dates for delivery.

Boilerplate Standard company terms and conditions printed on sales or purchase order forms to eliminate the need of composing and retyping usual desired terms for every order. In order to obtain agreement between the parties to the transaction, it may be necessary for one party to the transaction to revise or eliminate one or more of such terms and conditions even though they are the ones approved and desired by an organization.

Brinell hardness tester A device that tests the hardness of metal by pressing a 1 centimeter ball into material and measuring the indentation. The area of the indentation is divided into the load to give a Brinell number and is expressed in kilograms per square millimeter.

CAD An abbreviation for Computer Aided Design referring to the method or software that helps engineers or designers create drawings and product specifications with the use of the computer.

CAM An abbreviation for Computer Aided Manufacturing referring to the method or software that helps managers plan, schedule, and control the manufacturing process.

CIF Letters that stand for cost, insurance, and freight used to indicate who is responsible for payment of marine transportation and insurance to the buyer's country port of entry. The buyer then must bear the costs from the port of entry to the final destination.

C.O.D Letters that mean Cash on Delivery indicating that the buyer must pay for the goods when delivered. This term is seldom used by a professional buyer for business unless the buyer's organization has a bad credit rating, or it is the first purchase from a supplier and the buyer's company is new, small, or unknown. Sometimes sellers request

C.O.D. because they are having financial difficulty and need cash as soon as possible.

CPM Letters that stand for critical path method, a management tool that helps minimize time requirements by scheduling tasks or projects in the proper order. Also refers to Certified Purchasing Manager, formerly used by the American Purchasing Society and replaced by CPP or Certified Purchasing Professional.

CPP Letters that stand for Certified Purchasing Professional, an award given to experienced buyers and purchasing managers who have a high ethical business reputation, have had purchasing experience, and meet certain educational requirements.

Capital equipment Tangible items used in a business and defined by accounting methods. The original purchase value of the item on the accounting records or books is reduced or depreciated over time. Usually capital equipment items have relatively high initial cost and last for a number of years; consequently, purchases of any particular such items are infrequent. Buying techniques differ from those used on MRO items or raw material purchases.

Car load Refers to a full rail car going from one supplier to one buyer. With everything else being equal, carload rates provide the lowest cost of transportation if the buyer can purchase enough to fill the car. If the rail car is owned by the railroad, then it must be unloaded promptly within a specified time period or the buyer will face demurrage charges from the railroad.

Caveat emptor A Latin expression meaning, "let the buyer beware."

Certification A statement or award given by various organizations or companies that indicates an acceptable level of performance. It is given by metal producing companies for a particular shipment of a product. It is given by organizations that evaluate quality levels such as the Underwriters Laboratory. It is given by organizations such as the American Purchasing Society that evaluate ethical reputation of buyers and professional competency.

Commodity exchange   A marketplace for selling certain widely used raw materials called commodities. Typical products include corn, pork bellies, sugar, aluminum, lead, gold, etc.

Common carrier   A company that is licensed and in the business of transporting goods and obligated to accept shipments for any customers willing to pay the published rates.

Common law   That portion of the law that is based on custom or usage. Conflicts between parties are first resolved based on precedent or previous court decisions rather than based on statute or laws enacted by legislatures.

Contract   An agreement reached between capable parties that includes an offer, an acceptance of an offer, and consideration.

Contract carrier   A business that sells its service of transporting goods by motor vehicle to a particular customer or customers and agrees to accept certain terms and conditions.

Cost   Buyers measure cost by considering the length of time the product is needed to the useful life of a product. Price, payment terms, packaging, transportation charges, and all other charges are components of cost as is the suitability and durability of the product. See Price.

Customs   The department of the government that collects fees called duties on imported and sometimes exported goods.

D & B   An abbreviation for Dun & Bradstreet, a credit reporting company. Buyers and sellers can obtain reports, for a fee, that provide the names of principals or officers and indicates the type of facilities, the kind of business, and basic financial data about the company in question. Some of the data may not be available or accurate because it must be obtained from personnel at the company being reviewed, unless it is a public company. Public companies must submit their financial reports to the Securities and Exchange Commission and are available to the public.

D.A.R.   An abbreviation for Defense Acquisition Regulations that are the rules for purchasing for defense by the federal government.

DOS   The letters stand for Disk Operating System and mean a particular software program used for running a personal computer and, to a large extent, replaced by the Windows® system.

Duty   A particular charge applied by customs to various imported products.

EDI   An abbreviation for "Electronic Data Interchange" and referring to the method of transmitting information between one company and another or between the buying and selling company.

EOQ   An abbreviation for "Economic Order Quantity." The EOQ formula considers the holding cost of inventory, the cost of placing an order, and the price. It does not take space limitations, obsolescence, spoilage, pilferage, or quantity price breaks into consideration.

ETA   Estimated time of arrival.

Exchange rate   The amount of the currency of one country that is required to purchase the currency of another country not including any fees charged by the bank or agency that makes the transaction.

F.A.R.   Stands for Federal Acquisition Regulation that governs the policies and procedures for purchasing by federal government buying operations.

F.A.S.   Free Along Side, a term used in international trade whereby the seller agrees to deliver the product to a specified port for ocean shipping. The buyer pays for the cost of loading, marine insurance, and further transportation cost from that point on.

FIFO   First In First Out. See LIFO

F.O.B.   Free On Board, the most commonly-used term indicating the geographical point where ownership (title) passes from the seller to the buyer. The seller is responsible for all costs up to the destination mentioned immediately after the letters F.O.B. The buyer is responsible for all cost after that point.

Forward buying   Making an agreement to buy today for delivery sometime in the future. While most all purchases are delivered later, the term usually refers to a relatively longer time.

Free trade zone   A designated place where imported goods can enter without being charged custom duties if those goods are later exported to another country as the final destination. Re-packaging or other work may be done on such goods in the free trade zone before exporting them.

Future buying or futures   Forward buying, but the term is applied to organized trading of commodities that takes place on exchanges; traders may never actually take delivery of the goods involved because they sell the contracts to other traders or users before the scheduled delivery time arrives.

Guarantee   The word often used by laymen in place of the legally correct and more precise term "warranty."

Hedge buying or hedging   A way of minimizing financial risk by buying or selling for future use. Prices may be established at the time of the agreement or at the time of delivery depending on the objectives of the buyer or seller.

ISO and ISO-9000   International Organization for Standardization and the requirements for certification to meet its standards for quality.

Import duty   A fee charged by a government for certain goods brought into that country. The amount of duty varies by the type of goods and by the exporting country. Some goods have no duty, other goods a small duty, and still other goods a very high duty. A buyer considering importation of goods from a foreign country should investigate the amount of duty that will be imposed before comparing the cost from different suppliers.

Irrevocable letter of credit (see also Letter of credit)   A document used extensively in foreign trade and issued by the bank at the request of a buyer and advised through the seller's bank. Payment is given to the supplier upon delivery of specified goods and specified conditions. The exporting supplier relies on the bank as the source of payment .

J.I.T.   Just In Time; a planning and scheduling system to minimize inventory by having material arrive at the precise time needed.

LCL Less carload, a term referring to the amount of space taken by the shipment in a rail car and being less than a full car. The rate is higher because other goods for other shippers and other customers may be included in the same car.

LIFO Last In First Out, the accounting method that values inventory at current prices. If prices are rising, LIFO shows less income than FIFO, or First In First Out, and thus it tends to postpone outlays for income taxes.

LMM London Metal Market, an exchange for trading in metals such as copper.

LTL Less truckload, a term referring to the amount of space taken by the shipment in a common carrier truck. The rate is higher because other goods for other shippers and other customers may be included in the same truck. See Truckload.

Lead time The amount of time it takes to deliver material after an order has been placed. Different interpretations of the measurement can cause misunderstandings. The buyer should clarify the time for delivery by obtaining a specific date.

Letter of credit L/C, a document requesting a person or company to pay the holder of the letter, or sell a product on credit, and later obtain payment from the writer of the document. It is usually issued and guaranteed by a bank at the request of a buyer and states that the bank will pay for goods if certain specified documents meet the requirements set forth in the letter of credit document. A form letter is usually provided by the bank and there is a fee for the bank service. L/C's are primarily used in foreign trade.

Lot The entire quantity. Sometimes used to give a price based on the total quantity requested or to give a price on the entire shipment of various items without specifying the price of each item separately.

MAPICS Manufacturing Accounting and Production Information Control System.

MBO Management by Objectives, a method of measuring performance compared with goals.

MIL U. S. military specification.

MRO An abbreviation for Maintenance, Repair, and Operating Supplies. Items that are used internally in a business or organization. Most of such items are purchased in low quantities and many have low material value. They include janitorial supplies, office supplies, and items needed for repair. New or inexperienced buyers may be assigned to buy these items because the dollar impact of making a mistake is usually minimal. However, it is a difficult assignment because the volume of work is high and many people in the organization want immediate service.

MRP Materials Requirements Planning, a computer-based system for manufacturing that encompasses the key functions of inventory management, capacity requirements, scheduling, and dispatching.

MTBF Mean Time Before Failure, used to indicate the average time or average production from a piece of equipment or the average time that a machine will work properly before there is a break-down. Buyers should consider this figure.

Make/Buy The analysis of the variable or the decision whether to manufacture internally or buy a particular item from an outside source. Among the factors affecting the decision are financial requirements, evaluation of physical and staffing resources, and the competitiveness of the market for the item.

Manufacturer's agent Usually an independent businessperson who has agreements with one or more manufacturers to sell their products. The agent normally pays most, if not all, expenses connected with selling the product and in return only receives compensation in the form of a commission when products are sold. Buyers should avoid using such agents if the agent does not provide a valuable service since the cost of the product includes the commission. Some manufacturers refuse to deal directly with customers if the agreement with the agent prohibits direct sales. However, if the buyer has sufficient volume most manufacturers will attempt to exclude such potential customers from the agreement.

Materials management The function that includes supervision of various functions relating to material. Typically, they include purchasing, inventory control, warehousing, traffic, shipping, and receiving.

Materials requirement planning   see MRP.

Mean   The most common type of average calculated by the addition of all the numbers of each instance and dividing the total by the number of instances. See Median and Mode.

Median   A type of average, the number that is mid-point of all the instances or half-way between all the numerically listed numbers. See Mean and Mode.

Mill products   Material produced by a manufacturing facility, particularly basic metal items. Prices usually are lower when obtained from a mill, but the mill will only accept orders for large quantities, usually will not hold material in stock, will require a long lead time, and will attempt to ship to their own schedule.

Min-Max   An inventory system that triggers a reorder when stock is at a given level and prohibits ordering stock above a certain given amount.

Mode   A type of average, the most frequently occurring number. See Mean and Median.

Modem (modulator-demodulator)   An electronic device to change computer-generated signals for transmission over telephone lines to communicate with other computers.

Monitor   CRT or cathode ray tube, for viewing computer output on a screen.

Net 10   A typical and frequent payment term that requires payment of invoices within ten days. See Payment terms.

Net 30   The most frequently used payment term used by business buyers and the minimum acceptable payment term by many buyers. Also see Payment terms.

O.E.M.   Original Equipment Manufacturer, the company that makes the product. Prices given to O.E.M. accounts are usually lower because suppliers want to get their component or raw material into or used with the product being manufactured.

OSHA (pronounced O-sha) Occupational Safety and Health Administration, a government agency that helps establish and control rules and regulations regarding health and safety. The buyer must be careful when buying equipment and placing contracts for construction that the purchases meet the required standards. Otherwise, fines can be imposed and the organization will experience the added cost of making required changes to comply with the law.

Open account Established credit allowing purchase of goods or services with payment due at some agreed time after delivery. See Net 10, Net 30, and Payment terms.

PO Purchase order. The purchase order form is used as documentation of most purchasing contracts. It is the most used and most important form used by the purchasing function.

PPI An abbreviation for the Producer Price Index which is calculated by the Bureau of Labor Statistics, Department of Labor, of the federal government. It actually includes many indexes or numbers that show the change of prices of particular product categories from month to month.

Pareto principle Named for Vilfredo Pareto, an Italian economist and sociologist who lived between 1848 and 1923. Sometimes erroneously referred to as the 80-20 rule, the principle is simply that most of the occurrences of any happening are caused by a small percentage of the population. For example, most late shipments are caused by only a few suppliers. Buyers and managers can use time efficiently with this principle by concentrating efforts on the major causes or correcting the problems caused by a few suppliers.

Payment terms The agreed time and method for payment and usually printed on the purchase order by the buyer. The number of days for payment is a subject for negotiation. See C.O.D., Net 10, Net 30.

Pool car A railroad car that is used to collect shipments from many suppliers to send to one customer in order to obtain a low transportation rate. Used by large organizations, such as automobile manufacturers, who have many suppliers in one area or state that need to ship material to a distant location in another state.

Price   The stated charge for a product or service, but only one component of total costs. See Cost.

Pro forma   An invoice sent by a supplier in advance of the actual sale for planning or other purposes. Frequently used in international trade for government licensing or approval.

Procurement card   A type of credit card issued to requestors within a company so they can buy without using the normal purchasing process or going through the purchasing department. The credit card companies may code the cards so that they may be used only with certain suppliers and that only certain products can be obtained. The selling company must pay a percentage of the transaction to the bank or credit card issuer.

Purchase release   A process or form to authorize a supplier to ship material previously contracted for and documented by a purchase order. The release establishes quantities and shipping dates, but all other terms and conditions were previously agreed and documented and need not be repeated. The purpose is to set accurate dates for quantity actually needed at the time of the release. Time is saved and effort is saved because the contract covers a long period without the need to re-negotiate and prepare lengthy documentation for every shipment. The release form simply refers to the purchase order and gives only the information necessary for the shipment.

Purchasing Agent   Words that carry two meanings that are often confused or used inappropriately. They are used as a title for a buyer or they indicate the person legally authorized to buy for the organization. Thus any person who is so authorized may carry any other title and still be a purchasing agent. For example, buyers and purchasing managers are also purchasing agents if they have the authority to buy for the organization.

Quality circles   A method of improving quality by using voluntary employees in small problem-solving groups called circles. The objective is to identify problems that reduce product quality and then recommend solutions to solve them.

RAM or DRAM   Random Access Memory or Dynamic Random Access Memory.

RFQ   Request for Quotation or Request for Bid is a form sent to suppliers asking for product information, delivery time, and the product price. Forms typically give a deadline for the reply. The buyer may include the detailed specification wanted or permit the supplier to submit its own specifications. The buyer may indicate that bids are to be sealed, wherein all bids are opened at the same time and the lowest cost supplier is awarded the business, or the buyer may indicate that all bids are subject to negotiation. In private industry, it is considered poor practice to divulge the names of bidders or the contents of their bids. On the other hand many governments require that, after opening, the information on all bids becomes public knowledge.

Release   see Purchase release

Requisition   A form used by employees to make requests of the purchasing department to buy needed material or services. Companies require requisitions to be properly authorized and the requestor is usually responsible to obtain the authorization for the purchase before the form is submitted to purchasing. The higher the anticipated value of the purchase, the higher the level of authorization that may be required.

Robinson-Patman   Refers to an antitrust law named for the two legislators that drafted the law. The Act prohibits sellers from offering or buyers from asking for a more favorable price, or better terms, or conditions than a competitor receives.

Rockwell hardness tester   A machine to test the hardness of material. See also Brinell hardness.

S.A.E.   Society for Automotive Engineers, an organization that produces material specifications.

S.I.C.   Standard Industrial Classification, a number given to businesses that indicates the industry they are in or the type of products they sell. It is used to gather statistics and used by marketing to produce a list of companies that may need what they sell.

Sales tax   A charge imposed by states on the sale of products. The percentage of tax varies by state. The seller adds the tax to the purchase price for customers in the state(s) where the supplier has facilities and sends the amount of the tax to that state each month. If the buyer is in another state, then it is up to the buyer to pay the appropriate tax to that particular state. However, if the buyer is purchasing the product for resale, then no sales tax is usually due on the purchase price.

Service center   Usually refers to a warehouse or business that keeps inventory of a large selection of a given type of material, particularly basic metal products. Typical products would be various sizes and shapes of steel in a steel service center, or various sizes and shapes of copper and brass in another service center. Although service center prices have traditionally been higher than prices from a mill, they will sell and ship almost any quantity, even one piece. Most service centers will also perform various secondary operations for a charge. These include slitting and cutting to size.

Set-up or Setup   The time or cost spent getting tooling or equipment ready to produce an item. Buyers should attempt to isolate the setup cost because the piece price without setup included should then be the same for all quantities within a given range.

Sight draft   A document used in foreign trade that requires payment by the seller's bank for the shipment when the document is presented and accompanied by any agreed-upon proof of shipment.

Single source   A supplier that furnishes all of the requirements for an item to a buyer. This has the advantage of giving a supplier the highest possible volume and thereby obtaining the economies of scale. It enables the buyer to negotiate a low cost. However, the buyer is at risk if the single source is the only one that has the equipment or tooling necessary to produce the item. Compare with Split source.

Split source   Where any one supplier only has a portion of the business for any one item. This has the advantage of continuous supply if one supplier fails for any reason. Compare with Single source.

Standard cost   An accounting system of assigning an estimated cost to an item to act as a target to build budgets, to gauge manufacturing performance, to obtain a total cost for assigning a selling price, and to minimize record-keeping cost. Sometimes the variances from standard cost are used to measure purchasing performance. This is unfair unless purchasing's estimates or forecasts are used to establish the standard.

Supply chain management   Control of all components that are involved in the delivery of a product and covering each step from the customer's order to the final satisfactory delivery. It involves communicating all plans and activities to engineers, buyers, traffic personnel, carriers, suppliers and any others that help produce or deliver the product.

Systems contract   A special type of agreement made on the basis of competitive bidding and negotiations with a single supplier for each of a number of categories of MRO items such as plumbing supplies, electrical supplies, or office supplies. In return for 100% of the business for a year or more, the supplier agrees to stock all needed items of the particular category. The system improves purchasing efficiency by reducing the number of suppliers and assuring that needed material will be immediately available at a low cost.

TQM   Total Quality Management, a system or philosophy of management that involves the improvement of quality for all aspects of an organization's operation. It assumes that there is a need for continuous improvement and that improving quality also improves productivity. It emphasizes improvements for customers.

Tare weight   The weight of the packaging or wrappings of a product. It is sometimes useful for the buyer to subtract the tare weight from the gross weight to learn how much of the required product was delivered.

Team buying   Using a group of employees to determine needs, develop specifications, find suitable suppliers, and negotiate purchasing transactions. The team may consist of one or more people from the purchasing department plus people from various other departments such as manufacturing, quality control, accounting, and/or engineering.

Text file   A computer file consisting of alpha-numeric characters, punctuation, and symbols that produces text that can be exported to many types of software programs. See ASCII.

Title   Legal ownership.

Truckload   Enough material to fill a truck and thereby obtain a lower freight rate. See LTL.

UCC   Uniform Commercial Code, a standard law for business transactions written and adopted by each state with slight modifications. It is essential that buyers be familiar with the UCC so they can properly execute purchase agreements for their employers.

UL   Underwriters' Laboratories, a testing organization that approves products for safe use, particularly electrical products. The selling company must pay large fees to get its products tested and consequently the cost of those products may be significantly higher than unapproved imported products, even though the products appear to be the same.

Units of measure   The terms used to describe the quantity classification, such as inches, feet, pounds, tons, centimeters, etc. Buyers must be alert to differences in the units of measure between suppliers. They should also make sure that the units of measure for quantities and prices for each item on purchase orders, invoices, receiving documents and containers agree. If not, the differences should be accounted for by converting the numbers so they are in the same units of measure. This is necessary to make certain you are paying the proper price and getting what you are paying for.

Value analysis   A system to reduce cost by using teams to brainstorm for alternative less costly ways to accomplish the same function. For example, costs may be reduced by changing the design of an item, by combining items, or by eliminating items.

Vendor   Synonymous with the word "supplier."

Warehouse   see Service center.

Warranty The legal term referring to the seller's agreement to "stand behind" the product for sale by repairing or replacing an item, or in other ways compensating the buyer for costs incurred or damages experienced as a result of the product's failure. Warranties are of different types and may be limited. See Guarantee and Chapter 4.

Way bill A list of goods sent by a common carrier with shipping directions.

Welcome brochure A booklet or form given to new suppliers that describes the buyer's company, products, and purchasing policies. It helps provide essential information to potential suppliers without having to repeat the same story many times and eliminates the chance that certain important information will not be conveyed. A generic sample "Welcome to Purchasing" brochure is available from the American Purchasing Society.

Windows® A widely-used graphical computer operating system produced by Microsoft Corporation.

Zero defects A specification that permits no errors or rejections of material because of poor quality. This is important for items that may cause serious harm if not made according to specification. For example, it might be a requirement for medical products or certain airplane parts.

Index